Life of Victory

Life of Victory

Alan Redpath

Christian Focus Publications

ISBN 1 85792 582 3

Published in 2000 by
Christian Focus Publications, Geanies House,
Fearn, Ross-shire, IV20 1TW, Great Britain.
Previously published by Marshall Pickering in 1991

Cover design by Owen Daily

Printed and bound in Great Britain by
The Guernsey Press Co. Ltd., Guernsey, Channel Islands

Contents

*To Meryl and Caroline, our daughters,
who have been such a blessing to us,
together with their families,
and as a loving memorial to their Father,
whose living message this book contains.*

PREFACE

2 Kings 13:20-21: 'And Elisha died, and they buried him. And it came to pass, as they were burying a man, … that they cast the man into the sepulchre of Elisha: and when the man was let down, and touched the bones of Elisha, he revived, and stood up on his feet.'

The record has it that Alan Redpath died in 1989. Don't you believe it. For Alan Redpath is a man that, like Elisha, whoever has the opportunity to be let down and touch his bones will be revived and stand up on his feet again.

I first met Alan in 1968. It was at a time when I had been a Christian for about 3 years and very involved in campus ministry. I was also, getting very tired of all the effort it was taking to serve the Lord and all the hypocrisy that was in my own life.

My mother-in-law had been reading Alan's book on the life of Joshua, and gave it to me to read as she knew my struggles and knew that I had to learn to truly put my faith in the finished work of Jesus and discover His resurrection power. His book 'Victorious Christian Living – Studies in the Book of Joshua' opened my heart to a whole new spiritual journey. Soon after that time I was invited to have a meal with Alan after he spoke at my local church. He asked me how I was doing, and I told him of my spiritual struggle and exhaustion. He just smiled and said 'I thought so'. As he said it, his smile also told me that he knew what was missing in my life. The great blessing for me was that he also had the time and desire to see me come into a deeper knowledge of Jesus. You see, what it was that drew me so much to Alan was that what he preached, he preached with an authority that caused the listener to want more of Jesus. He preached in such a way that made the listener want to know Jesus as well as he did.

7

After a few more meetings, Alan invited me and my wife Jean to come to England and go to Bible School there and learn from him. What a blessing for our lives resulted because of his mentoring. Since then Alan and Marjorie have been as family to us.

I invite you to read on and as you do, may you say as those on the road to Damascus.... Did not our heart burn within us, while he talked with us by the way, and while he opened to us the scriptures?

Don McClure

FOREWORD

The original idea of this book was given to me in May 1989 when I was visiting our friends, Don and Jean McClure. Don is Pastor of the Calvary Chapel of Redlands, South California, and this dear couple have been friends for over twenty years. Don said he used many daily devotional books, and would appreciate one with a consecutive theme, and he thought such a book from Alan's sermon material would be of the Lord as a memorial to His servant. I was quite overcome by the whole idea, but I had what was needed by way of books of notes to draw on, so with the encouragement and prayers of my family and many friends, I embarked on the project.

I feel some comments must be made to explain the format. Marshall Pickering agreed to publish the book, and one of the editors visited me, and we worked out the overall pattern to be followed, which is the one on which the book is based. Those remembering Alan's ministry will know his great theme was the Lordship of Christ, which of course is the emphasis of so many of his messages, and is therefore central in the book. Unlike many daily devotional books, this one has turned out to be more of a daily Bible study, and I make no apology for the notes being quite 'meaty', because that was Alan's style. I am sure many readers will recall hearing him preach as they read these notes, and I have certainly been greatly blessed as I delved into the wealth of material I had before me.

Most writers of such books would obviously edit their own material to avoid any quotations which they cannot identify. I have not been able to do that, so if some readers recognize a quote from Campbell Morgan, for instance, I am sure Dr Morgan would not be offended!

The RSV version of the Bible is used, as the NIV was not around during the peak years of Alan's ministry. In earlier years he preached from the AV, but I have not used that unless indicated. It was wonderful to read notes of messages given during the War while we were at Duke Street Baptist Church, Richmond, and then in the 1950s and early 1960s when we were at Moody Church, Chicago, and to find them as up-to-date and relevant for today as they ever were.

I want to thank all those who have encouraged me by their prayers and interest. My thanks, too, to the editors at Marshall Pickering, who have been so helpful, and above all to Pattie Dixie for her typing of the final manuscript. But beyond all these wonderful friends, my heart's thanksgiving is to the Lord for His gracious enabling for a task which at times I thought was beyond me. Twice in one day the verse, 'If any one puts his hand to the plough and looks back, he is not fit for the kingdom' came to me, so I knew this assignment was from the Lord, and I trusted Him all the more for His wisdom in regard to its completion. May it now prove a daily blessing to those who read its pages that they, together with myself, may grow in knowledge and love of the Lord Jesus. To Him be all the praise.

Marjorie Redpath
Birmingham
December 1990

A BIOGRAPHY OF ALAN REDPATH, DD, FCA

Dr Alan Redpath was born on 9th JANUARY 1907, at Gosforth, Newcastle-upon-Tyne, the only child of Presbyterian parents. He was educated at Durham School, and then studied accountancy as an articled clerk in Newcastle. It was during his training that a fellow student led him to the Lord Jesus while on an audit assignment, when they were both staying at the Grey Bull, Haltwhistle. In later years a visit to the outside of that pub was a 'must', in memory of that life-changing experience!

On qualifying, Dr Redpath went to London to take up a good position in ICI under a Mr Dickens, the grandson of the novelist. In 1932 he met Marjorie Barton, and during the months that followed he led her to trust in Christ. In 1934 the wedding took place, and the young couple lived at Amersham, while running a small Mission in Golders Green, N.W. London. However, after about 9 months it was clearly impossible to do a lasting work from such a distance, so the Redpaths moved to the Hampstead Garden Suburb. Increasingly Dr Redpath felt the urge to preach the Gospel, and business life became very meaningless. So at the end of 1935 he left ICI, and on 1st January started an evangelistic ministry under the National Young Life Campaign, founded by Arthur and Frederick Wood. This was a tough training ground, for there was no regular salary, and the staff looked to the Lord for the supply of all their needs. Moreover both sets of parents were dead against such a 'foolish' move, with the stigma of their children living on other people's charity. This early encounter with opposition made an imprint on Dr Redpath's life, and he was always at hand to help young people who felt the call to full-time service but were confronted by family hostility. His involvement with young folk stayed with him almost until his death, and while in his eighties he was

11

receiving invitations to speak at University Christian Unions, for his concern for young lives to be wholly committed to the Lord Jesus was one of his great passions.

An invitation came at the end of 1939 to be Pastor of Duke Street Baptist Church in Richmond, Surrey, and this commenced in May 1940. In October 1939 their first daughter, Meryl, was born, a source of great rejoicing. In later years she married a young American, Don Linquist, and together with their three children they went to the Central African Republic with the Africa Inland Mission, and were there for 19 years until Don was tragically killed in an accident involving a truck.

The church at Richmond was small, with a congregation of about 60, but with the onset of World War II and people with hungry, fearful hearts, numbers increased greatly. As neither of the Redpaths had been brought up in church circles, leading a congregation was something new, and as people, young and old, were converted, pastor and people grew in the Lord together, and many evangelistic enterprises were embarked upon until Dr Redpath became known in the land, and was invited to take 10-day evangelistic missions nationwide. The church, in its wisdom, gave him leave to conduct one in the Spring and one in the Autumn, and this outreach united the fellowship in prayer and vision in a truly wonderful way. When the War was over it soon became apparent that the church was too small to contain everyone, and so started about 10 years of evangelism using Richmond Theatre for the evening service. People came in during the summer with their picnic baskets, having been 'fished' off the streets by the young people of the church. They were exciting days of seeing the Lord work in saving many, and also of seeing a group of missionary-nurses able to leave at last for overseas service, having trained also at Bible Colleges for the day when the end of the War would enable them to sail to their destinations. Others followed over the years, married couples, men and women, and Duke Street became known as a truly missionary-minded fellowship, and still is.

In 1950, while Dr Redpath was speaking for the first time at the Keswick Convention, their second daughter, Caroline, was born. She later married Edward Stott, a Christian businessman, and they live in Birmingham with their three children, very involved in the life of their church and in witness to neighbours and business colleagues.

Later in 1950 Dr Redpath went for his first visit to the U.S.A. for four months, and it was through that visit that an invitation came to the pastorate of Moody Church, Chicago, where the family moved in September 1953. That was a new experience for the church seated over 4000, with a congregation of between 1500 and 2500. It too was a very missionary-minded fellowship, and it was a joy to see during the nine years there, many going overseas in response to the Lord's call. Close links with neighbouring Moody Bible Institute gave oportunities for ministry among hundreds of young people, as well as invitations to many parts of the States for conference and convention ministry.

In 1961 Billy Graham had his first Crusade in Chicago, and Dr Redpath was vice-chairman of the Committee, so there was great involvement in that exciting and fruitful mission. However, an invitation came towards the end of that year from Charlotte Baptist Chapel in Edinburgh, and after much heart-searching and prayer, Dr Redpath felt it right to accept, so in November 1962 they left for Scotland with Caroline, Meryl by this time having married. An exciting two years of ministry in that lovely city, with great opportunities among students, ended suddenly and drastically in 1964 when Dr Redpath suffered a severe stroke. The Lord raised him up in a wonderful way, and he continued at the Chapel for a further two years, but felt he was not physically able to cope with such a large fellowship, with the demands of preaching three times a week. So sadly and reluctantly he resigned at the end of 1966, and on his birthday, 9th January 1967, he started on a 3-month tour of ministry in

Africa, mainly with the Sudan Interior Mission in Ethiopia. Then he went to Kenya where his wife joined him, and they flew into the remote part of Central Africa to spend two weeks with Meryl and Don Linquist. This itinerant ministry overseas was to be Dr Redpath's life for almost 20 years, and in the latter part of that time his wife was able to go with him, as Caroline was by then a trained teacher. It was a time of great privilege and opportunity, and seeing missionary situations world-wide gave a new understanding of the needs of those who proclaimed the Gospel, and the nationals who were brought to faith in Christ.

Soon after leaving Edinburgh the Redpaths, at the invitation of Major and Mrs Ian Thomas, moved to a bungalow built for them in the grounds of Capernwray Hall, Lancashire. This Bible School and Conference Centre had been started by the Thomases after the War, and was a place bursting with activity for the Lord, with hundreds of young people (and older folk) from all over the world coming either for holiday conferences or to Bible School. Dr Redpath taught at the School usually for one week each term, and the bungalow was a home-from-home for many of the students, as there was always a welcome for them. Most of the time the Redpaths were on their travels, and they also visited the States annually, keeping in touch with the work at Moody Church, as the pastors there graciously invited Dr Redpath to preach if he was in or near Chicago.

As the years advanced and so much travel became impossible, the Redpaths moved to Birmingham to be near their daughter Caroline and her family. Dr Redpath still preached around the country, at College Christian Unions and in many churches, but in October 1988 he suffered a further stroke, and after five months in hospital, the Lord called him Home on 16th March, 1989, at the age of 82.

He was truly a Great-heart for the Lord, untiring in fulfilling the ministry to which he was called, active in mind and body, and therefore able to put into action the means of outreach shown him by the Holy Spirit, some of which were very new in their day, such as House Groups which were started in Richmond during the War when people could not get to church for various reasons. Cafe evangelism to reach unchurched young people was very successful in Edinburgh, until·the restaurant being used had to close. However, a similar outreach is still in operation in the city. In Chicago he founded and spearheaded the Mid-America Keswick Convention each October in Moody Church, and this became a regular feature until the family left for Scotland, after which it had to cease. People came from all over the States, and the Chicago Keswick gave birth to many similar conventions in other parts of the country, most of which are going ahead with great blessings to those who attend. Many speakers from the English Keswick Convention were invited, and some are still going over to one or other of the Conventions still continuing.

Dr Redpath had 8 books of sermons published during his life, many of which are still available both in the States and Britain, and this book of devotional readings expresses the sum of his preaching gift, his main burden being the Lordship of Christ in every area of life in every Christian. His life verse was Philippians 4:13, 'I can do all things through Christ who strengthens me', and he particularly liked the Phillips' rendering, 'I am ready for anything by the power of Christ within me', and always called young people to be RFA Christians – Ready for Anything! 'The will of God, nothing less, nothing more, nothing else' epitomizes his commitment to Christ himself, for he was careful to demand nothing from others that he was not prepared to do himself. While by his Homecall he is missed by so many, yet his work lives on through the printed word and also through cassette and video ministry, gathered from many places through many years.

THE CHARACTER OF CHRIST

JANUARY 1

WORSHIP

Matthew 2:1-12

A new year, a reassessment, perhaps a new realization of the greatness of the Saviour leading to a new and deeper commitment. Read in Matthew 2 of the revelation given to three men, and the impact on their lives.

In their own land they saw a star, a unique constellation which pointed the men to Jesus. In fact, its only mission was to point to him, for it was an anonymous star. However, it led seeking kings to the new born Saviour. Bypassing Jerusalem it came to a humble home, and so drew the Magi from the city to a place 'outside' (see Hebrews 13:13). Finally the star stopped where Jesus was; the journey was complete, and the kings were completely satisfied, knowing their quest was fulfilled.

More importantly, the star led to worship, and surely they saw beyond the child to the Saviour of mankind, otherwise they would not have been drawn to worship and the giving of gifts. Note that they were not just star-gazers, but persistent followers. Their response to their arrival where Jesus was is their rejoicing, worship, and giving. This implies that their worship involved their whole being, and as we follow them into the presence of the King of kings, may this be our response, for he alone is worthy.

A Prayer: Lord, like the star, the Christian is the light that belongs to the Master, leading others to him, glad to be at his bidding. May this be true of me throughout the coming year.

JANUARY 2

SALVATION IN CHRIST ALONE

Luke 2:29-32

Simeon lived in a momentous hour, at the very beginning of Christ's coming into the world, taking that great step from glory to poverty. Simeon merges the Old and New Testaments, for he was a Jew; righteous, devout, waiting for the Messiah. And it was he who was privileged to hold Jesus in his arms, and to recognize the moment when the great promise of a Redeemer was fulfilled.

Then and there Simeon entered into a new relationship. Although he held but a baby in his arms, yet he knew that Jesus is Lord with absolute authority, while Simeon himself is his servant, his slave, willingly and devotedly offering Israel the Redeemer of the world – and he rejoiced in a new hope. The eyes of his soul were opened, and he was now ready and anxious to depart in peace, his life's search over, his joy complete.

That is the glorious goal of all who truly seek, for it is written that those who seek shall find (Matthew 7:7-8) and it is to those who have true heart hunger that the Lord reveals himself. So many these days, who have been seeking for satisfaction in the many empty systems of the world, including various sects and cults, have found that salvation is in Christ alone, and now rejoice in him. Let us praise him that he is the same yesterday, and today, and forever!

JANUARY 3

GROWING TALL

Luke 2:40

Here is the brief record of the first twelve years of the life of Jesus, and it should be the growth rate of every boy, girl, man and woman.

Jesus **'grew and became strong'**. Physically he matured during a brief period of no responsibility except that of obedience to authority (v. 51). Living in a small town in a humble, working-class home, he was removed from the public eye, but all the time he was learning the qualities that were to fit him for Messiahship.

Jesus was **'filled with wisdom'**. He grew mentally, no doubt by asking questions and receiving instruction. Never short-cut the questions of children, but always seek to lead them into the truth of the Word of God.

'The grace (favour) of God was upon him'. Spiritually he was increasing in the knowledge of his heavenly Father, which was publicly affirmed at his baptism (Luke 3:22). The Master is the role model of a rounded childhood upbringing in which the reality of God makes a lasting impact upon life, behaviour, and future career and service.

A Prayer: May the qualities given in Luke 2:40 be true in my life, and in the lives of those whom I seek to bring to Jesus.

JANUARY 4

WHO IS JESUS?

Luke 2:41-52

The boy Jesus (v. 43) is now twelve and with his parents went to Jerusalem for Passover and his Bar Mitzvah, according to the Jewish law. He went to the scribes and doctors of the Law for instruction, and was now prepared to take responsibility and act for himself – so engrossed that he failed to return home with his parents.

The story is well known, and when his earthly parents found him after three anxious days, his reply to their concerned query was 'I must...' showing his knowledge of who he was: 'My Father', Almighty God. He realized his responsibility to God in a dedication to the purpose of his Father as a priority claim. In the same way our priority has to be seen in exactly the same way, that the claims of God himself to our lives, because of the giving of his Son at Calvary, demand the whole-hearted commitment of our lives to his service.

As Jesus returned with his parents (v. 51) and was obedient to them, he showed his responsibility was, in the third instance, to be in the home. Under the mastery of the will of God, Jesus submitted his life in obedience to his parents. So he advanced into maturity (v. 52) mentally, physically, and spiritually filled with the Spirit and power of God. What lessons are here for all of us, at every age, to follow?

JANUARY 5

THE OBEDIENCE OF CHRIST

John 1:14

Here is a further glimpse into the mighty impact of the coming of Jesus into the world, majoring on the glory of God which he radiated, and which was recognized as something which could only come from God himself in heaven.

The prologue to John's Gospel, chapter 1:1-18, shows in a remarkable way not only the glory of Jesus, but the obedience of the Son to the Father. Jesus was sent from God to earth, and came down to those who refused to receive him. Yet to those with eyes to see, he was the Word (the Logos, the very thought and mind of Almighty God) made flesh, full of grace, truth, and glory.

His eternal character is shown by his demonstration here on earth that:
(a) he is eternal life (vv. 1-5);
(b) he is eternal light (vv. 6-13);
(c) he is eternal love (vv. 14-18).

In stepping down from heaven to earth, Jesus became truly man, but through him continued to shine the light of heaven with all the glory that enshrines. If his light has shone in our hearts, we too demonstrate his grace and glory, and become reflectors of his love to a desperate world. Selah – think on that.

JANUARY 6

THE LAMB OF GOD

John 1:29

The baptism of Jesus by John the Baptist was a momentous occasion and is recorded in all four Gospels. For Jesus it was identification with mankind; for John it was the sublime fulfilment of his life's work.

John had a ministry in calling for repentance acknowledged by baptism. He was a 'voice' (v. 23), and his voice was heard by multitudes, including the religious leaders of the day. He was a signpost pointing to Jesus (vv. 29, 30) whom he knew to be God's true sacrificial Lamb. This takes us back to the Passover when a lamb was sacrificed and its blood sprinkled on the doorposts to save the family within the home from death (see Exodus 12). This is the great Old Testament event which foreshadowed redemption through the blood of the Lamb of God, the Lord Jesus himself. Hence the significance of John's announcement, 'Behold the Lamb of God!'

This led to a drastic change in John's later ministry. He was content to decrease as Jesus was now to be the focal figure (John 3:30), and in this he was a true witness. No wonder Jesus said later of him, 'Among those born of women there has arisen no one greater than John the Baptist' (Matthew 11:11).

A Prayer: Lord, use my voice to speak of your love, and my life as a witness of your saving grace. Accept my worship as I surrender myself to your complete authority and lordship.

JANUARY 7

PREPARATION FOR SERVICE – AVAILABILITY

Mark 1:9-11

Much could be said about Christ's preparation for service in the thirty years of obscurity for only three years of ministry. The verses on which these thoughts are based tell of three things that took place on the eve of the Lord's public ministry which were vital and essential for all that followed.

a) First was his availability. What was John's baptism? The answer is in Mark 1:4, where he is seen exercising a ministry which produced repentance in order to prepare for Christ's ministry which secured forgiveness. Seeing that Jesus had no need for repentance, why should he be baptized? John himself asked that question in Matthew 3:14. Jesus made himself available to his Father in obedience by identifying himself with the sins and repentance of mankind. He was not repenting or confessing for himself, but for them. If he had never identified himself with our sin, we would never be identified with his holiness. Because he stooped we may rise; because he humbled himself we may be exalted.

b) In making himself open and available for God's good and perfect will in his life, Jesus demonstrated that the way 'up' is 'down'. He descended to the depths of human experience not only in the waters of baptism, but in his passion and suffering on the Cross. Calvary was the furthest 'down' he could go, but it was followed by his resurrection and ascension, and as we share in his humbling and shame, so one day we share in his glory and exaltation.

JANUARY 8

PREPARATION FOR SERVICE – IDENTIFICATION

Matthew 3:13-17; Mark 1:10, 11

c) In his baptism Jesus took upon himself the burden of human sin, counting it as his own. Here is the whole principle of his service as proclaimed in Isaiah 53:6: 'All we like sheep have gone astray; we have turned every one to his own way; and the Lord has laid on him the iniquity of us all.'

Jesus had no more need of baptism for himself than he had of the Cross. But he accepted both for us – one at the beginning, the other at the end of his earthly ministry. Indeed Calvary was his second baptism (Luke 12:50).

How can we prepare for Christ's service in a similar way? By putting to death our rights to ourselves as his concern for others is expressed in and through us, 'I have been crucified with Christ; it is no longer I who live, but Christ who lives in me' (Galatians 2:20).

We must not be willing only to die to ourselves, but also to live unto him: 'Present your bodies as a living sacrifice to God...' (Romans 12:1, 2). Every power and gift we claim to have must be brought to the Cross to be cleansed and sanctified for his use. The Lord cannot use unclean vessels, and only the blood of Calvary is adequate 'to make a sinner clean'.

How completely are you identified with Christ in your preparation to be used in his service daily? Remember, he is more concerned with your daily dying than your right to live.

PREPARATION FOR SERVICE – ANOINTING

Luke 3:21, 22; John 1:29-34

Following Jesus' act of identification in submitting to John's baptism came the Father's attestation of approval, given in all four Gospels. The heavens opened as the Holy Spirit came down in the form of a dove. However, this was not an initial anointing, for there was never a time when Jesus was not filled with the Spirit. But now on the eve of his public ministry he received a special visitation and enduement. These were needed for service as well as character in order that the authority of Heaven rested on both.

The Holy Spirit came as a dove, the symbol of gentleness. Jesus said his disciples were to be wise as serpents and harmless as doves (Matthew 10:16). Gentleness is part of the fruit of the Spirit (Galatians 5:23), and as it characterized the Lord's ministry and teaching, so it must be seen in our lives and testimony. It is not a characteristic that is weak and emasculated, for David himself said, 'Thy gentleness has made me great' (Psalm 18:35). It takes a strong person to exhibit this fruit of the Spirit.

A dove also expresses lowliness, for the Law stated that those who cannot afford to sacrifice a lamb may offer 'two turtledoves or two young pigeons' (Leviticus 5:7), and that is what Joseph and Mary offered when they presented Jesus for his circumcision (Luke 2:24). Just as there was no revelation of the fact that Jesus was the Son of God when he was born in an outhouse in Bethlehem, so the poverty of his human parents in their thanksgiving offering to God belied the fact that Jesus is Lord of lords. Never let us be tempted to elevate ourselves higher in our own estimation (and in that of others) than the Lord Jesus, who said of himself that he was gentle and lowly in heart (Matthew 11:29).

PREPARATION FOR SERVICE – APPROVAL

Mark 1:11

The enduement of the Holy Spirit was accompanied by the authority of Heaven. These words are the Father's approval on the blamelessness of thirty years of obscurity, 'Thou art my beloved Son in whom I have ever been well-pleased.'

This statement refers us to John 1:1, 2 speaking of the eternal existence of the Son with the Father, that he is truly God and truly man. It is essential that his followers know just who he is, and are well acquainted with every facet of his character in order that they can submit to the authority of his lordship in their own lives. A long, meditative look at the person of Jesus will save us from falling for a 'Jesus-plus-something-else' teaching so prevalent today.

What are the essentials needed for vital Christian service? We need his baptism for our life in him; his fullness for our holiness; his anointing for our service. Do we have what we need? Do we have God's approval on our lives, his attestation of his love for us? If he is pleased with us, as he was with his Son, what else matters? But can he ever accept us like that? Yes, for if he sees Jesus living in us, then we are those in whom he is well pleased.

JANUARY 11

PREPARATION FOR SERVICE – CONFRONTATION

Mark 1:12

'Immediately!' After the testimony the test; after the dove, the devil. Heaven's approval is followed by Hell's attack.

'The Spirit drove him' – does the dove drive? The word is the same as that used in verses 34 and 39 for the casting out of demons, and is a severe word.

Think long and hard on Mark 1:12. Jesus faced the onslaught of the enemy alone, therefore Peter can write, 'Do not be surprised at the fiery ordeal which comes upon you to prove you' (1 Peter 4:12). If the Son of God was attacked after the experiences of his baptism, we will not escape the attentions of the enemy, particularly after times of spiritual uplift and blessing. There is no place where temptation cannot reach us, but there is no place where the Holy Spirit cannot strengthen us. If he 'drives' us into such a situation, he will be with us in it to triumph.

Failure in our daily living comes when we are so overwhelmed by circumstances and our inability to meet them that we lose sight of our ever-present Saviour. This was Peter's problem when he got out of the boat to walk to Jesus. The moment he became aware of wind and wave and took his eye off his Master, he began to sink (Matthew 14:30).

A Prayer: Lord, help me in every testing situation to remember that Jesus is greater than Satan and sin; Satan to Jesus must bow.

THE SCOPE OF TEMPTATION (1)

James 1:2, 3

Temptation comes to every person every day in some form or other. How it is tackled produces various effects in that person's life. If he falls to temptation there may be guilt and disaster. If he overcomes there is strength added to character, and a sense of victory and achievement. Therefore to consider the unique experience of Christ's temptation is to answer many questions regarding this very important aspect of daily living.

There is no sin in being tempted. It is only when we yield to it that we experience guilt, so do not be discouraged if you are being sorely tried.

Temptation does not necessitate sinning. That which was possible for the Lord Jesus can be made possible for each of us by his power. You can be kept through the power of God and come through unscathed. If you fall it is always your fault. As we study the reason for Christ's conflict with the devil, and the way he overcame, we will see clearly the path of deliverance.

A Prayer: Loving Father, you know what this day will bring across my path. Keep me from the evil one that I may not fall into temptation, and grant me a special awareness of the presence of my Saviour, Jesus.

THE SCOPE OF TEMPTATION (2)

Matthew 4:1

It may be hard to believe, but it is necessary for us to be put to the test. It was for Jesus as the Spirit led him into the wilderness, but, we may ask, why?

Temptation is necessary for usefulness, for he who has never been tempted can never help those who are. If Jesus had not overcome Satan in the wilderness Hebrews 4:15, 16 could never have been written: '... one who in every respect has been tempted as we are, yet without sin. Let us then with confidence draw near to the throne of grace...'. Yes, we can see Jesus in a different light because he was victorious in the deadly battle about to be unfolded in Matthew 4. Jesus is the mighty Conqueror, and in our daily contests with the enemy we can reckon on the fact that he is really a defeated foe, for in the wilderness, on the Cross, by his resurrection, the Lord has abolished Satan's power and authority.

Without temptation there is no battle, and therefore no crown. If there is no conflict there is no conquest. So without question spiritual battle is part of Christian living, and Jesus shows the way to rout the enemy.

THE SCOPE OF TEMPTATION (3)

Matthew 4:1-4

As we look – maybe on our knees – at the titanic battle about to take place, note that the arena of attack is the question of the will of God. In the verses given above the first temptation concerned the will of God for the body. When Jesus was physically weak and hungry the devil came with the temptation to work a private miracle. Hunger is a legitimate desire, but Satan's ploy was to make Jesus satisfy his need in a manner outside the will of God. In the wilderness, at that hour, Jesus was as secure in his Father's will and kept by his love as ever he was, despite the circumstances. Satan used that moment to try to cause Jesus to doubt his Father's love and ability to help him in a tight corner. 'If (since) you are the son of God, *command...*'

The swift rebuttal from Jesus revealed his reliance on the power of the Word of God. He draws a circle around himself, and standing within it declares, 'What God's will permits I will do. What it makes no provision for I will do without, for God's will only permits what his word declares.'

How subtle is Satan's voice, for after 40 days and nights without food and water, Jesus was at the ultimate of physical weakness. How easy to exert his power to work a miracle, for later he provided food for over five thousand people from a boy's snack. But the Lord was firm in his reliance on the fact that he was where he was, and in those extreme circumstances, in the centre of his Father's will.

A Prayer: Lord, I will face temptation this day in one form or another. Grant that I too may be found standing firm within the circle of God's love and will for me at this very hour.

JANUARY 15

THE SCOPE OF TEMPTATION (4)

Matthew 4:5-7

Having failed in his assault on the Lord's weakness, Satan now attacks his strength in an onslaught on the will of God for the spirit, the very centre of human personality.

Jesus is taken to the pinnacle of the Temple where he could see the whole city, over which later he wept as he saw the rejection and disobedience of the people. Satan seemed to suggest a spectacular way to get the attention of the people. 'I can quote scripture too, so throw yourself down, and God will send his angels to protect you from falling.'

This is an all too common temptation that, in a hopeless situation, we go out and do the spectacular in our own strength. Failure in any area of our lives is something to be avoided at all costs, we think. And no doubt Satan imagined Jesus would think along those lines. But in reply the Lord give a terse retort. To submit to Satan's suggestion would prove Jesus' trust was not in God's will but in his own fear of failure. So he tells the enemy his faith is utterly in his Father in whose will he stands. To choose the commonplace is not easy, but when the will of God is involved, it is the way of victory. When you are faced with the choice of an easy way out of a tight corner, or the temptation to resign from a different assignment, rebuke the tempter by refusing to move from the circle of God's will for you in that situation.

THE SCOPE OF TEMPTATION (5)

Matthew 4:8-11

The final attack was on the Lord's obedience to the will of God for his service. Satan insolently and blatantly demanded his worship, which implies both obedience and service.

What was the temptation? To accept instant possession of 'the kingdoms of the world' and so bypass Calvary, through which Jesus would inherit them when they became the kingdom of God and of his Christ (Revelation 11:15). Bow the knee to Satan now, and reject God's plan for the salvation and redemption of mankind? Never! for Jesus knew that one day every knee will bow before HIM, and acknowledge him to be Lord of all (Philippians 2:10, 11). It was a challenge to achievement without redemption; to a crown without a cross.

Jesus' response was an utter rejection of the sinister suggestion, without any compromise. Better to suffer hunger and thirst, a crown of thorns and the Cross, than bypass the will of God for his life's work. How many lives have been wrecked by compromise with an evil suggestion, from which there can be no recovery? Learn from the Master, the authority of whose dismissal of the enemy was such that Satan retreated, completely routed.

A Prayer: Lord, give me wisdom to follow the way you took that I may stand firm in the centre of your will in every area of my life.

JANUARY 17

VICTOR AND VANQUISHED

Luke 4:13

Satan had exhausted himself, and had no other line of approach to the inner life of the Spirit by which Jesus overcame all his fiery darts. The Lord stood complete and unscathed in his hour of victory as the enemy beat a humiliating retreat. Matthew 4:11 says, 'then the devil left him, and behold, angels came and ministered to him.' Jesus had never been outside the loving concern of his Father, and now the battle had ended, the Victor received all he needed in sustenance and caring. It had been a lonely battle, but he was not alone, and never had been. The Spirit was within him, and the angels around him, though out of sight. How wonderful to think that the same provision from the Father is ours too!

We share the same daily battleground, and the purpose in God's heart of love is that we may 'stand mature and fully assured in all the will of God' (Colossians 4:12). Many lessons and experiences have to pass our way before we submit totally to the will of God in our lives, for temptation comes in the same way it came to the Saviour, to cause him to resist the will of God for body, spirit and service. He endured complete exhaustion while the enemy was alert and on the attack; but it was at the end, when Satan had launched his most violent temptations, he in turn was exhausted and had to retreat.

As we meditate again on that wilderness battlefield, we can say with all the conviction of our hearts, 'Hallelujah, what a Saviour!'

JANUARY 18

GLAD TIDINGS

Isaiah 61:1-2; Luke 4:18, 19; Matthew 11:2-6

The ministry of Jesus did not suddenly and unexpectedly take place during his three years of public life. Every detail had been made known in Isaiah 61, and that very passage was read by Christ himself in the synagogue (Luke 4). In Matthew 11 the Lord repeats the words to the friends of the imprisoned John the Baptist.

No doubt John wondered deeply at the seeming inactivity of Jesus. There was no sign of the kingdom being restored, no move to liberate John – what was the Master doing?

The reply Jesus sent to John was to make him go back to the scriptures, and to Isaiah 61 in particular. What was to be the activity of the Messiah? Healing to the blind, the lame, the deaf, the lepers, and even life to the dead. And above all, good news would be preached to those in desperate need. 'John, do not despair. I am the Messiah, I fulfil prophecy, so even if you do not understand, trust me' (Matthew 11:6).

In days of pressure from so many new theologies and the resurgence of old faiths, it is a battle with the enemy to maintain the uniqueness of the Christian truths as one seeks to present the Saviour to an unbelieving society. 'God is dead' is the tenet of the majority, and by life and lip it is the duty of the believer to show that Jesus is very much alive, and is still fulfilling the promise made by Isaiah so long ago. God give us grace not to sink into the quagmire of humanism, but to remain firm and alive in him, for Jesus says, 'Today, this scripture has been fulfilled in your hearing.'

JANUARY 19

OVERFLOW OF BLESSING

Luke 5:1-11

This early encounter of the fishermen with Jesus is remarkable for being like a parable. In verse 3 a boat is empty of fish; in verse 7 it is filled to danger point. What is the secret?

In verse 5 Simon confessed the failure of the night's fishing, and that was a hard thing for him to do. 'We toiled all night and took nothing.' Night was the time to fish, not daylight, so when Jesus said, 'Let down your nets,' Simon was about to argue. However the authority of Christ made him say, 'At your word I will...' The Lord's presence in the boat made Simon see who was really in charge now, so in obedience he did what he thought was foolish and reaped a harvest.

In life we are told to launch out, but so often we are dogged by past failure and are fearful. If we act in obedience to Christ and at his command, then the overflow of his blessing is our experience, though we may not always sense it at the moment. Notice again that Jesus does not call for our effort but for recognition of his Lordship in our lives and service. 'Without me,' he said later, 'you can do nothing' (John 15:5), and that is a hard lesson for the flesh to learn.

JANUARY 20

THE AUTHORITY OF CHRIST'S PREACHING

Matthew 7:28,29

These verses are at the close of the Sermon on the Mount, and tell the effect on those who heard. We should ask if in any way the teaching in Matthew chapters 5 to 7 has the same effect on us today.

The immediate hearers realized the authority of the Teacher. Many knew him as the son of Joseph, the carpenter from Nazareth. His teaching was so fresh that it expressed reality in a way the scribes never did in their dead interpretations of the Law. Jesus' repetition of 'but I say to you' gripped his audience so they listened with both ears.

Because of this the crowds gave him full attention, and at the end expressed their astonishment at his learning and all he had taught them. The reality and impact of the preaching of God's word is immediately felt by the hearers because they sense the Spirit speaking into their hearts and souls, demanding a response to the truth they have heard. No doubt many who heard Jesus that day followed him as he went about preaching, and became his true disciples.

It is essential that those who come to church and have a concern for the world in general, and their own neighbourhood in particular, pray for the men in the pulpits that the effect of preaching the Gospel and of pointing to Jesus as Saviour and Lord should produce disciples today.

JANUARY 21

DID JESUS SAY 'SELL ALL'?

Mark 10:17-22

The well-known story of the Rich Young Ruler needs to be read and studied constantly to keep before us the offering of our lives and use of our money from God's viewpoint.

Look first at the young man, a wealthy, highly respected member of the Sanhedrin (Luke 18:18). He was very much in earnest and respectful, for he ran up to Christ and knelt before him. But the quality that drew out the Saviour's love was the sincerity and frankness with which he admitted his sense of lack in his life. Yet his question in verse 18 was naïve: one does nothing to inherit. Inheritance is received as a gift, a birthright.

Jesus did not answer directly except through another question, 'Why do you call me good?' Because only God is good, Jesus is either not good or he is God. What a claim to deity!

Seeing the man was devout, Jesus pointed to the second section of the Law relating to life on the horizontal plane, relationship with others, but in this his character was flawless (v. 20). No wonder Jesus loved him. Alas, there was a vital aspect missing, the one thing that hindered – his wealth. To have treasure in heaven, that on earth must no longer be the guiding principle of life. Jesus' test, 'sell all and follow me' is to achieve abiding riches, but at that point the young man faded away. The cost of true discipleship was too great for him. What a sad story, but a salutary warning to us all in the light of Matthew 6:21.

FORGIVENESS

Luke 7:36-50

Two people from the extremes of society meet in the presence of Jesus. The one is a Pharisee who, while hostile to Jesus, invited him to a meal but ignored all eastern hospitality: no water, no kiss, no oil. He was obviously hoping to trap the Master, putting him in an embarrassing situation. Then to his horror, there was the woman. At least, he thought he saw her as a prostitute giving to Jesus all the tokens he, the host, had refused to give.

The other person, the woman, is 'a sinner', with the urgency and temerity to enter a house in order to show the Lord the love and gratitude she had for him because at some point he had forgiven her. Now she is mastered by her love for him, quite oblivious to the feelings of others towards her.

The Lord loved both equally, but how to reach the man was a problem! Hence the story of the two debtors and the conclusion in verse 47: 'Her sins, which are many, are forgiven; for she loved much; but he who is forgiven little, loves little.' How did that man feel to hear these words spoken in front of all his guests, and no doubt onlookers at the doors? The need for forgiveness could not be shown more clearly to that proud man, but did he respond? Do we respond?

A Prayer: Dear Lord Jesus, give me today such a sense of forgiveness and cleansing that my life will reflect your life in me and my love for you.

JANUARY 23

DELIVERANCE

Luke 9:37-43a

The root of world chaos is the fact of universal sin seen in the urge, the power, which impels the wrong choice, the selfish and sinful living that is seen everywhere today. Man's system refuses to admit it, but the Bible declares it, so God begins with an impossibility: to bring recalcitrant, rebellious humanity to listen to him and accept the deliverance from the tyranny of sin he alone can give.

The Gospel alone has the answer, and the power of the living Lord Jesus alone can turn sin out of a life and bring holiness (wholeness) in, as a person cries out for cleansing and purity in the place of sin and guilt in his life.

In the passage given above is a picture of a lad gripped by the power of evil, and in fact had been so for years. What a picture of the multitudes around us who are right now in that state. Not all the religion or learning of his time could deliver that boy; only the Son of God had power to drive out the enemy, and he is the same today. After a final literal fling by the devil, the Lord in all his authority rebuked him, and healed and delivered the lad. The power of evil was broken, and the captive was set free. The authority of Jesus is without limit, and we can experience it at any time in our place of need, if we cry out to him for his releasing power. Praise him that 'he sets the captives free'!

JANUARY 24

COMMITMENT

Luke 9:57-62; Key verse 62

There is a time for everything, and if we miss God's timetable we have missed our opportunity. How often in our ignorant impetuosity we urge God to act, and we get bitterly disappointed when he does not answer that prayer. Then in his perfect timing the answer comes, and we know that it was perfectly planned.

In the Middle East the farmer takes advantage of the rainy season to plough. After that time the ground is hard and incapable of receiving the seed. The Christian cannot claim a harvest for God unless his own heart has known the softening power of the Holy Spirit. God must take the initiative by pouring out his Spirit upon us, for only in that way can we experience a harvest that will speak of his power, and also be made fit for his kingdom. We cannot serve him unless we are cleansed and filled, until his rains have fallen upon us to wash out all of self-effort. Immediately that happens, the hand is on the plough and the eye is on the harvest. God has no place for those who shirk and daydream.

Once the hand is on the plough there is no going back and no looking back. How often when storms come and the way is hard Christian service is abandoned, and the Lord is denied and forsaken. It is the perseverance shown by Jesus en route to Calvary that should spur us, his disciples, to have that iron in our souls which keeps us on track for him, making us fit for his kingdom.

JANUARY 25

PRAYER

Luke 11:5-8

So little is known by most Christians of believing prayer. So much blessing is missed because we quit praying too soon. Yet often the trouble is not our unwillingness to pray but our inability, and this story in Luke 11 gives us the 'how to' of believing prayer.

First there is a need (v. 6), an unexpected visitor lost at midnight and in desperate need. How do we react to those around us, lost in the darkness of sin?

The man takes the traveller into his home, though he knows his own cupboard is bare. But love and concern prompt him to receive the guest, who becomes his friend (v. 6), and to seek help from a neighbour. The man openly confesses his inability to help, 'I have nothing to set before him', and that is the way we come into the Lord's presence. Of ourselves we are nothing and have nothing, and can in no way help needy people around us. At first the rich neighbour seems reluctant, but the man convinces him of the desperate need and his own bankruptcy so that ultimately he is given all he needs.

What a lesson! When we tell our Father our abysmal need, that we have nothing, in his love and mercy he gives us all we need. Like the man in the story, it is essential that we are not just seeking to make ourselves richer by claiming all God can give us, but that our desire is to share his goodness and grace with those who are in desperate plight around us.

A Prayer: Dear Lord, make me aware of my weakness and inadequacy as I face the demands of a needy world around me, that in my inability I may prove your sufficiency to supply all my needs, for your name's sake.

JANUARY 26

A LESSON IN TRUE SERVICE

Luke 10:38-42

Martha and Mary of Bethany occupied a large place in the latter years of Jesus' life. Theirs was perhaps one of the few places he could call 'home'. There are three references to this household in the New Testament, and this is the first, and is a well-known story.

Martha is the older sister, the hostess, and is often thought of as the busy housewife while Mary is a dreamer. In her desire to serve the Lord, Martha became 'distracted' – hot and bothered – and she accused Mary of not doing her fair share, and even became angry with Jesus. Mary, meanwhile, realized the guest was so special he needed attention that was more than a meal, and that he had more to give than small talk. To sit at his feet meant for Mary both worship and instruction, fellowship without distraction. She gave love and worship and received teaching. Martha, while prompted also by love, sought to fill the opportunity with busy service, and became distracted.

Jesus summed up the situation by saying that only one thing is needful and that is to give him his proper place and recognize his Lordship in every area of daily living. We may object and say, 'But that is impossible! I have a job to do and I cannot always be praying and reading my Bible!' What a shallow concept this is of moment by moment fellowship with Jesus! Our heart's attitude should be 'at his feet', and that can be true in the busy humdrum of daily life and work. If Nehemiah had not possessed that rest of heart and soul in the power and presence of God, he could never have accomplished his work, and the walls of Jerusalem might never have been built. It should be our first priority to learn from Jesus the secret of true and acceptable service and devotion.

A LESSON IN ACCEPTANCE

John 11:17-32

The death of Lazarus is the means of teaching us all the power of Jesus over that 'last enemy, death' (1 Corinthians 15:26). When the Lord came to Bethany he found Martha ready to meet him, breaking with convention that mourning women stay in the house, as Mary did.

The two sisters must have been discussing their situation: a sick brother, but no help from their friend and master Jesus, so the brother died. Now we see the difference in their approach to the Lord when he arrived. They both used the same words (vv. 21 and 32), but Martha stood to meet Jesus while Mary fell at his feet. Martha challenged his friendship while Mary lamented his absence. Martha said in effect, 'Why didn't you come?' while Mary said, 'I wish you could have come.'

In times of deep personal grief and distress we show one or other of these attitudes as we seek to accept the trial we are facing. The revelation of John 11 that Jesus is both Resurrection and Life and has power to raise the dead gives to the child of God the glorious assurance that the Lord is in charge of every situation, of the distress we are encountering, and the love with which he stands to meet us in our place and time of need.

A Prayer: Lord, give me grace in difficult times to be found where Mary was, at the Master's feet, looking to him for the comfort and love he alone can give.

A LESSON IN DEVOTION

John 12:1-8

The same house in Bethany, the same hostess, Martha, with Mary and the host Simon the leper (Matthew 26:6), Lazarus raised from the dead, and the disciples – a large number for a supper to honour Jesus. To the amazement of everyone, the quiet Mary brought in a box of very costly ointment, which she broke over the Master's feet so that the perfume filled the whole house.

How astonished the guests must have been! In fact Judas saw it only as 'waste'. Mary, however, saw her Lord that day as no other did, for she sensed his coming death and was sensitive to his sorrow and suffering. Jesus understood everything and rebuked his disciples by pointing out Mary's perception and pure devotion: 'She has done a beautiful thing to me' (Matthew 26:10).

We are faced with the challenge of how much our devotion to Christ costs, not only in money, but in love poured out to him which has no measure. To be prepared to go the extra mile for his sake; to speak a word of encouragement to a sad and depressed person, even if we feel much the same ourselves at the time; to care for and love the unlovely and unlovable for Jesus' sake – in so many ways we can show our devotion and obedience to the Master who went all the way to Calvary for us. The result of Mary's action is that it is known worldwide (Matthew 26:13). May our devotion to our risen Lord be so lacking in self-glory and so full of his presence that our actions spread a perfume in the place where we live and work.

JANUARY 29

THE MOST IMPORTANT QUESTION

Mark 8:27-30

The time the Lord Jesus had for teaching his disciples was becoming short, and it was necessary for him to call for a verdict. The crowds would gladly have crowned him king of a material kingdom. The rulers were increasingly hostile and angry, and were bent on his murder. The disciples, caught between two lines of opinion, were confused and uncertain of themselves. Jesus must receive from the people, and above all his disciples, their verdict concerning himself. So suddenly he asks his friends, 'Who do *men* say that I am?' and receives a confused answer. It is the same today. To so many Jesus is just a teacher, a good man, and so on, but not the central figure of the Christian faith, whereas he is the very centre and heart, for without him there would be no Christianity. So people today need to be challenged by this question.

Jesus does not stop there, however, but asks, 'Who do *you* say that I am?' He is not asking what they think about his teaching or his actions. The question is not a What but a Who. Each one of us, in the day and age in which we live, has to answer that question.

Jesus asked a similar question of the Pharisees, 'What do you think of the Christ? Whose son is he?' and they could scarcely answer (Matthew 22:42). Do you know him as the Son of God, the Saviour of the world? If so, Jesus says you are blessed, because this knowledge comes to your heart from the heart of God (Matthew 16:17).

JANUARY 30

MAJESTY

John 8:48-59

The battle with the Jewish leaders, that John describes from chapter 5, draws to one of its climaxes in today's meditation. Three statements of the Jews elicit Jesus's claim of his divine majesty.

In verses 48-51 he is insulted by being called a Samaritan (when the Jews know he is Galilean) and demon-possessed. His quiet answer in verse 49 makes us ask how we react when insulted.

The Jews take up the argument that Jesus is demon-possessed (vv. 52-56), but prove they have misunderstood his statement about death. His claims are astounding, especially to Jewish ears, especially his assertion that he is greater than Abraham, knowing him intimately. Such sayings are only credible if the speaker is truly God.

Finally in verses 57-59 the Jews have not only misunderstood Christ's words but misquote him. Their rage draws him to a further mighty claim, which sealed his death: 'Before Abraham was, I AM.' The Greek reads, 'Before Abraham was born [created], I am [implying eternal existence]'. For Jesus to claim the title of Jehovah, I AM, was blasphemy to the Jews. Their response was to cast stones at the Sovereign of the Universe. May our response be to fall at his feet and worship him with all our hearts, and yield to him our lives.

CHRIST THE SUSTAINER OF LIFE

John 6:47-58

It is significant that in John's Gospel some of the miracles wrought by Christ were followed by a discourse that seems to interpret the miracle. Here the revelation of Jesus as the Bread of Life follows the feeding of the five thousand (6:1-14). The two essentials for life are bread and water, and Jesus categorically claimed to be both for the nourishment and growth of spiritual life.

In verses 47 and 48 he declares that to believe in him is to possess life, and thereafter he is the only one who can sustain that life. In contrast with manna, which could not prevent death, those who maintain spiritual life by a close walk and relationship with Jesus will never die. His divine nature imparted to us at our new birth by the Holy Spirit is to be our real food, and the shedding of his blood at Calvary is for our souls what water is to a man dying of thirst.

These symbols, of course, point to the inauguration of the Lord's Supper, as given in all the Gospels and in 1 Corinthians 11:23-36. This is the most sacred sharing of the life and death of the Saviour, and our daily prayer should be that we will be drawn into an increasingly close relationship with him as we experience his indwelling life. The disciples said to him, 'Lord, give us this bread always' (v. 34). May this be our prayer, as we realize increasingly that the hunger of our hearts is only met by his sustaining life, and the thirst of our souls is only quenched by his lifegiving water (v. 35), the indwelling Holy Spirit.

FEBRUARY 1

CHRIST THE LIGHT

John 8:12; 9:5

The majestic statement in John 8:12 is illustrated by the healing in John 9. Pause a moment in chapter 8 to note the repetition of the words that assert his claim to be the Son of the Father, the Messiah – I AM (vv. 23,28). No wonder there was the response of verse 30.

The incident in chapter 9 begins with four significant words, 'he saw a man'. That man, blind from birth, was a wellknown beggar, but Jesus *saw* him, from head to toe, inside and out. The healing of that man was followed by the command 'Go, wash'. It was a specific order to prove the man's faith in his healing *and* in the one who had healed. It was simple, for anyone can wash, and it was personal, for no one else could go for him.

That is the Gospel message: Christ alone can heal and forgive, but the recipient must show his personal faith and trust in complete obedience.

From the night of blindness the man received the light of Christ (v. 5). This is conversion. But the Pharisees persisted in their unbelief (vv. 39-41). They thought it incredible that they should be included among the blind. Jesus met them on their own ground: they could be excused being in the darkness of ignorance, but never the blind self-satisfaction which prevented them from seeing the truth and coming into the light of the knowledge of Jesus Christ; their condemnation would be all the greater because of their privileges.

A Prayer: Lord Jesus, save me from the blindness of pride. Lead me into the light of your truth that I too can say, once I was blind, but now I see (v. 25).

CHRIST THE DOOR

John 10:1-10

To understand this passage one has to refer to the healing of the blind man and the reaction of the Jewish leaders as given in chapter 9. The statements of Jesus in John 10:1-10 announce his Messiahship, as he stresses the words 'I AM', reminding the Jews of the name Jehovah, 'I AM WHO I AM' (Exodus 3:14).

What did Jesus mean when he said, 'I am the door of the sheepfold'? The eastern shepherd, having put his flock into the fold for the night, would often lie down at the entrance, so becoming the door, or gate. No enemy, human or animal, could get at the sheep without first encountering the shepherd. The fold was a place of security because of the watchful care of the master.

What does this mean to us? It tells us that Jesus is the way into eternal life, and that entrance is exclusive, only by way of the door (see Matthew 7:13, 14). The shepherd knows wolves in sheep's clothing who are debarred from admission (v. 8). But the blessings of entrance are overwhelming, for Jesus promises firstly that it is an in and out life (v. 9): in for fellowship with the Shepherd and out for service in his strength. Secondly it is abundant life (v. 10), nothing weak or anaemic, but victorious. It is life which is *given* by Jesus himself to those who trust him and follow him; it is nothing that we can work up ourselves, though it is possible to try to imitate. However, because it is life in the Spirit, the sham is quickly shown up. May we know not only life from the deadness sin brings, but that quality of living that Jesus calls 'life more abundant'.

FEBRUARY 3

CHRIST THE GOOD SHEPHERD

John 10:11-18

This is a magnificent, regal passage, and needs to be read slowly, word for word, to gain the full impact.

A shepherd will go to great lengths to protect his flock, but only the Good Shepherd voluntarily gives his life for the unworthy sheep. The hired shepherd (false teacher) flees when danger comes and leaves the flock unprotected and stranded (v. 12). What a picture of the false cults, who leave such a trail of heartbreak and disillusionment.

The Good Shepherd states the price he paid for our redemption (v. 15), and throughout verses 1-18 it is shown there is a mutual understanding between sheep and shepherd, as there is between the Father and the Son. What a wonderful thing it is to be in the family and to be part of his flock!

Further, the Good Shepherd is neither nationalistic nor racist, but his redemption reaches worldwide, until every tribe and nation is gathered into his kingdom of glory. There may be many sheepfolds (churches, etc.), but only one flock. The Shepherd died that the sheep may live, but Jesus here foretells his resurrection in the most wonderful and authoritative words. As you read them, let them soak not only into your mind but into your heart, as you see the omniscience of Jesus, and the majesty with which he faced the Cross, because he knew resurrection was inevitable.

A Prayer: Thank you, Lord Jesus, that you are both Door and Shepherd, and for your love and authority as Redeemer of the world. May I today be an obedient member of your flock as I take time to hear your voice, and then follow you with all my being.

FEBRUARY 4

DO YOU BELIEVE?

John 11:23-27

The great pronouncement Jesus made in verse 25, '1 am the resurrection and the life', is perhaps the climax to the challenge of this chapter to the true basis of faith in the lives of many people. The incident concerns the death of Lazarus, and the attitude of Martha and Mary toward the Lord Jesus because he delayed his coming to them in spite of their urgent request in verse 3. As the story unfolds, Jesus explains the reasons for his delay, the main one being he was about to do for the family something far more wonderful than healing sickness.

In verse 15 he explained to the disciples why he delayed his departure, 'that you may believe.' To Martha he gave the revelation that he was the source of life now and after death, and challenged her faith in him: 'Do you believe this?' In verse 40 he had to remind her of this, because the family and the crowd were about to see 'the glory of God' − a man raised from the dead.

In his prayer in verse 42 Jesus again stressed that this miracle was not a spectacle, but in order that people may believe he is the one sent from God, and that the signs accompanying his words were the proof, fulfilling some of the passages concerning Messiah in the Old Testament.

It is not the miracle we need, it is faith in the living Lord who himself was raised from the dead so that those who believe in him may never see death. Can you answer his question, 'Do you believe this?'

FEBRUARY 5

CHRIST THE WAY, TRUTH AND LIFE

John 14:6

Jesus said, 'I am the way, the truth, and the life'. These three statements are one. What is 'a way'? It is a road that has a starting point and leads to a terminus.

'I am the Way to my Father's house (the terminus) because I am the Truth.' Jesus was not one teacher of a truth among others. He was truth personified. Truth is not just something we *know,* but something to *be,* for it is not a dogma but a life. Therefore we need have no fear to follow, for his way is open, just, and transparent.

Jesus is the Way because he is the Life. The starting point of his way is the place where we are all dead in trespasses and sin, and he gives us life. He quickens, empowers and delivers us; he is the Way from the kingdom of darkness to the presence of the Father.

Moreover Jesus states categorically that he is the *only* way: no one comes to the Father except through him. The way into the Father's presence is by Calvary, where Jesus, the only true Son of God, gave his life for the redemption of the world. We must not be confused by the babel of noises that announce 'all faiths come to the common end', for that is grossly untrue. The home of God is only reached by one path, and that is the way Jesus trod. Let us bow in his presence and acknowledge our utter unworthiness of such love, and our commitment to follow him in the way.

FEBRUARY 6

CHRIST THE TRUE VINE

John 15:1-5

To the Jews, Jesus' statement 'I am the true vine' had special significance. Israel was symbolized by the vine, as in Isaiah 5:1-7. The vine was embossed upon the door of the Temple, recalling the grapes brought back by the spies to prove the fruitfulness of the land in Numbers 13:23. The Lord chose his illustrations carefully, but the analogy of the vine goes further than history.

The branch depends on the life of the vine-stock. When the fruitbearing period is ended the plant is pruned ruthlessly so that a mere stump remains. The next season, as each new branch appears it is carefully trained so that the fruit will be of the very best quality and quantity.

As the branch is part of the vine, drawing life-giving sap from the stock, so the Christian through the new birth is brought into a relationship with God through faith in Christ. This is not a friendship which can be broken, but a permanent relationship. As the life of the vine flows to its uttermost branches, so the sustaining power of the life of the Lord Jesus, by his indwelling Spirit, is the very sustenance of every believer. Indeed, without his life within we achieve *nothing* (v. 5). This is a hard but necessary lesson to learn, for in our pride we imagine there is much we can do that is good, which may be true in many instances, but will count for little in God's summing-up of our life and service, as Paul points out graphically in 1 Corinthians 3:10-15. May we be saved from such devastation, and learn daily to know we are a branch in the vine who is Christ himself.

FEBRUARY 7

FRUITFULNESS IN THE VINE

John 15:5-8

The fruit Jesus speaks of is not our service for him. It is primarily character, as Paul explains the fruit of the Spirit in Galatians 5:22, 23. There are degrees of fruitfulness: fruit, more fruit (v. 2), much fruit (v. 5). How much fruit do we bear? In other words, how like Christ are we becoming?

It is important to remember that grapes do not grow on the vine stock but on the branches. The grape is the proof of life in the vine, and is the very purpose of the vine. As Jesus fulfilled the purpose of God in his life, so the believer fulfils God's purpose in his life (John 15:16). As the Father depended on his Son for that, so he depends on us.

Fruit reflects the nature of the plant on which it grows. If we by our new birth are part of the vine which is Christ, we are to reflect his very nature, and this can only be accomplished as we learn the secret and discipline of abiding in him (v. 5). Just as a branch does not struggle to be part of the vine, no more do we as we live in fellowship with Jesus. A branch is vitally related to the vine and draws up nourishment from the root-stock, and therefore bears fruit effortlessly. May this be our experience as we learn daily the secret of abiding in Christ.

AUTHORITY OVER SATAN –
A POWERFUL DELIVERANCE
Mark 5:1-20

The amazing story of the man called Legion is perhaps the supreme example of Jesus' authority over demonic powers. See the misery of this man, vividly told in verses 2-5. Day and night he was tormented by the mysterious powers that gripped him more strongly than the chains which he broke as if they were of wool. He terrorized the neighbourhood with his plaintive cries and shrieks day and night, and the eerie rattling of the chains among the tombs. How long this had been happening we are not told.

We must not be deceived. Satan has his chained victims today, and brings misery to so many in the grip of drugs, alcohol, the lust for power, the slavery of money, and so on. People are unchecked by any moral standard of decency, knowing no law but those of their own creating. Such is the misery of bondage to Satan, unchanged through the centuries.

Deliverance is at hand, however, as we see the mighty Saviour coming to meet the pressing need. How wonderful that the man saw Jesus, and then besought him to deliver him from his dreadful condition (vv. 6-8). The glorious outcome is in verse 15, a sense of calm after the raging storm: complete deliverance, sanity restored, a normal man now begging to follow Jesus, but told to remain as a testimony in his own area. This he did with great success as he gave all the glory to Jesus.

A Prayer: Lord Jesus, once I was in bondage to sin and Satan, but you have cleansed and redeemed me, just as you did to Legion. May I be true and faithful to you, and witness to your saving grace, as that man did.

FEBRUARY 9

AUTHORITY OVER SIN

Matthew 8:1-4

The leper must have been among those listening to Christ's teaching on the mountain, and sensed here was the only person who could help an outcast such as he was. Leprosy has always been a picture of sin because of its ravaging of a human body, causing the person to become a social outcast. In Bible times there was no cure; today there is. In O.T. times there was no permanent remedy for cleansing sin, only the blood of bulls, goats, sheep, etc. Today there is, because of Calvary. But why are so few coming to Jesus for his forgiveness and salvation? Why do so many look to a multitude of experiences and cults which can never bring the peace and joy they seek so diligently?

The leper knew his desperate need, and he was aware of the power of Jesus. So he came to him and said, 'Lord, if you will...' He never doubted Christ's ability, only his willingness. As Jesus responded to that man's insight and faith he said, 'I will', and that love touched the man, and through that contact was communicated all the Saviour's powers. Note that Jesus did not obtain defilement, but he imparted purity.

He is against sin, and his will is cleansing from sin because of the work of redemption and the shedding of blood at Calvary. We have to come to him in humility and penitence as this leper did.

A Prayer: Cleanse me from my sin, Lord;
Put thy power within, Lord,
Take me as I am, Lord,
and make me all Thine own.

FEBRUARY 10

AUTHORITY OVER PREJUDICE –
NEVER ON SUNDAY?

Mark 2:23-28

The Sabbath was, and is, a most important day in the Jewish calendar, and rightly so, for it commemorates the rest God took after   creation. Over the centuries the prime cause for the Sabbath became encrusted with rules and regulations, and was no longer a day for man's enjoyment, commanded by God for man's good. The Christian Sunday – the first day of the week – became the day of worship to celebrate the resurrection of Jesus Christ.

Mark records the authority of Jesus over prejudice on the matter of Sabbath observance, and so often he performed miracles of healing on that day, even in the synagogue (Mark 3:1).

The rules the Pharisees produced covering the Sabbath became absurd, as illustrated in their accusation that Jesus and his disciples were 'harvesting grain' as they walked through the cornfield. He brought them face to face with the principle of Sabbath-keeping, that it was for man's benefit and rest from toil so that he is free to worship God.

Prejudice and conformity say, 'Thou shalt not.'

The principle of God's command is, 'Thou shalt worship him', and he graciously gives a day when we can rest in body, mind and heart, and spend it in his presence. The best rest of all is in Christian service, and the worship of God together with those who delight in his presence.

FEBRUARY 11

AUTHORITY OVER NATURE – PEACE, BE STILL

Mark 4:35-41

After a day of preaching and the demands of the crowds, Jesus, being a man, was tired, so he worked a mini-miracle by escaping from the ever-present people and getting into a boat, and immediately he fell asleep. This speaks to us of the inner peace he enjoyed, the sense of relaxation into his Father's arms. He was in fact so soundly asleep that the sudden violent storm did not awaken him, but the cry of his disciples did! Note the panicky words that burst from them, 'Do you not care that *we* perish?' How quickly the 'me first' attitude surfaces in danger!

In contrast to the men's panic is the calmness of the Master, and in the minimum of words Mark sketches the Lord's instant action and reaction. He awoke, he spoke, and there was a great calm.

The calming of the sea did not at first calm the fears of the men, who were so awestruck they scarcely knew what to do next. It would seem that nature responds to the authority of Jesus more quickly and more easily than the storm-tossed hearts and minds of men. In times of upheaval and distress we must learn to listen to the majestic voice of Jesus saying, 'Peace, be still', for he alone has the power and ability to calm our fears. Whatever may be distressing you today, never *doubt* his love by saying, 'Don't you care?', but *trust* his love to deliver you from fear and bring his peace flooding into your heart.

FEBRUARY 12

MADE STRAIGHT

Luke 13:10-17

Here is a graphic encounter with Jesus that took place in the synagogue, illustrating what should be the result of meeting in God's presence and hearing his word, provided we are honest and confess our deepest needs to him.

The woman had been a sad sight for eighteen years. No doubt when young she had been lively and upright, but over the years disease attacked her until she was so bent she could not straighten herself. Eyes made to look Godward were now earthbound. How wonderful to know the Lord can heal long-term complaints, for his love is unceasing and his power unlimited.

Three wonderful things happened when this poor woman came into contact with Jesus. He saw her, though probably to everyone else she was just 'the cripple'. He called her to him, for as the Good Shepherd he comes to seek and save those who are lost. He spoke and then touched her. How wonderful that touch and that word must have been to that sad soul, who probably came to the sabbath service out of custom, and never expected anything unusual to happen. Behind every word of Jesus is the authority of Calvary: 'you are free!' (v. 12).

The result was immediate, for at once she was made straight, and – glorious thought – after all those years the first face she saw was that of the Saviour. Think of that!

A Prayer: Lord Jesus, make me straight, honest and upright, so that I too can look into your face as a sinner saved by grace, and made clean by your sacrifice on Calvary. If Satan tempts me to doubt these facts today, may I too hear your voice say, 'you are free!'.

FEBRUARY 13

A SMALL MAN WITH BIG POTENTIAL

Luke 19:1-10

The well-known story of Zacchaeus is far more than a small, unpopular but curious man who wanted to see Jesus. Look at him as he is sketched in Luke's account.

Zacchaeus was a chief tax collector and rich. He was employed by the Romans, but kept back money for himself, otherwise he could never have become wealthy. It is said 'once a crook, always a crook', but crooked lives can be made straight, not by effort, but by Jesus.

Zacchaeus was hated by the Jews, which was natural, but how pitiful. He must have been a lonely man with only his money to comfort him. Yet he had heard of Jesus, and knowing he was coming through Jericho, Zacchaeus determined to see him without being seen himself. Being short of stature he left his dignity behind and climbed a tree, peering through the leaves to see Jesus. Had the Saviour considered public opinion he would have looked straight ahead and continued walking. Instead he looked up, saw the man, spoke his name, and commanded him to come down and stand by him. Imagine the shock Zacchaeus must have felt at this outcome! Imagine the surprise of the crowd as he and Jesus walked away together to his home!

Jesus is the master of the personal approach, and to this lonely man he demonstrated love, interest, friendship and, best of all, redemption. Zacchaeus was a lost man, a sheep gone astray, and the Son of man has come into the world to seek and to save all who acknowledge their need of salvation from the sin that has dragged them into the plight they now find themselves in. May the Lord use each one of us today to be such a friend and bringer of good news as Jesus proved to be to Zacchaeus.

FEBRUARY 14

THE JOYS OF OBEDIENCE

Luke 19:1-10

See the story now from the Master's viewpoint, as he sought to bring his love and life to this unhappy man.

The call of Christ is personal (v. 5). As Zacchaeus was peering down from the tree, Jesus looked up and saw him, then called him by name. Yes, the Lord knew all about him and was yearning over him in order to make his crooked life straight. To us today the call of Christ is personal, for he knows the deepest needs of our lives and seeks entry in order to make us clean and straight.

The call of Christ is urgent, for he told Zacchaeus to make haste. No one can play with God, for eternity is at stake and so is the salvation of each individual soul.

The call of Christ is humbling, for everyone has to come down to the ground that is level at the side of Jesus, at the foot of his Cross. Zacchaeus obeyed instantly, and found the Lord's response too was immediate, 'today', and abiding (vv. 5, 6). The little, scared man now became bold, for he testified to all the change of heart he experienced through contact with Jesus, and publicly distributed his ill-gotten money. Someone has written of this story,

Jesus looked up   Zacchaeus said, He SEES me
Jesus said, 'Zacchaeus'   Zacchaeus said, He KNOWS me
Jesus said, 'Make haste'   Zacchaeus said, He WANTS me
Jesus said, 'today I must'   Zacchaeus said, He NEEDS me
Zacchaeus said, 'Lord, I give...' He was saying, He HAS me

May that be our response too to the call of Christ, that we may this day experience the joys of obedience.

FEBRUARY 15

STIRRED INTO ACTION

Mark 3:1-6

This passage follows closely on the clash between Jesus and the Pharisees over the use and misuse of the Sabbath. Very naturally, as was his custom, Jesus was in the synagogue and there too was a man with a useless, withered hand. Look at him, with all power gone, the hand and arm stiff and shrunken, no doubt unable to work. Sense the tenseness in the synagogue as the Pharisees wait to see what happens 'so that they might accuse him' (v. 2). They had no sympathy for the handicapped man because they were so full of prejudice and animosity toward Jesus.

In complete control, Jesus asks a question: what *is* lawful to do on the Sabbath? to do good or evil? to save life or to kill? No wonder all were silent, and he was angry at their cold-heartedness. Then came his command to the man, 'Stretch out your hand', and as he did so it was healed.

Look at your hand. Is it being used for the Lord, or is it withered and useless, for disuse destroys power. Listless, idle hands are prevalent in the Church today, and such hands soon wither. The Lord says, 'stretch forth your hand!' Stir it into action for him! He will take that which is yielded to him and make it fit and usable in his service, but he can only use that which is committed into his own hand to experience his healing and life-giving touch.

FEBRUARY 16

BEGINNING TO SINK

Matthew 14:22-33

A businessman said to the minister, 'All you have said today made sense to me once, but not now. I have a large business and am a multi-millionaire, but I am rarely at home, and my family have grown up not knowing their father.' Then with tears in his eyes he said, 'It's been a huge success financially, but, O God, at what a cost!' and he wept uncontrollably. That man was a successful failure.

When did the slide start? Watch Peter as in great faith he climbed out of the boat to go to Jesus, which was a good thing to do. Then he looked at his circumstances – wind, waves, water – and began to sink. This is always the start of backsliding, when a person gets so involved with the immediate, be it church work or making a living, that tensions come in, and prayer and a close walk with Jesus go out of the daily routine. It is all so easy, so disastrously simple, that one can be unaware when or where the first downward step was taken.

Peter's reaction was immediate, the briefest arrow prayer, 'Lord, save me!' But what more was there to say? He knew the person who alone could give help, and that no long plea was needed to secure it.

How did Jesus respond? By pointing out the root of the failure: doubt and unbelief. He had to show Peter where he had gone wrong before rescuing him, when he took Peter by the hand, and *together* they rejoined the boat. What a wonderful picture that brings to mind! Complete restoration physically for Peter, but beyond that, the knowledge that his failure had not alienated him from his Lord, but rather gave him further insight into the love and care that would follow him all the days of his life.

Confess your need as Peter did, and show the Lord your thanksgiving by learning the lessons he seeks to teach you.

BEARING AND SHARING

Matthew 3:11

Christians are called into a unique relationship with Jesus. To be a child of God is not just the joy of knowing one's sins are forgiven, but to live a life so linked with the Lord that we share the experiences he went through and bear the same joys and sorrows (see Hebrews 4:15, 16). There are some things we are told to carry for him, and as we consider them we shall see something of his plan for each one in his family.

We are to bear his shoes. In Matthew 3:11 John the Baptist says he is not even worthy to do that, despite this being the task of a bondslave, the lowest of the low.

The Christian life starts when we recognize we are his servants, slaves, and are prepared for the most menial and humble of tasks. The thought of servanthood can bewilder us: surely as I mature I will be promoted. Never! It is often thought that a person may accept Jesus as Saviour without yielding to him as Lord. Christ as Saviour *and* Sovereign Lord is the object of saving faith, and no one else. It is impossible for someone to be saved who comes to Jesus for his help, but with no intention of obeying him. His Saviourhood is forever linked to his Lordship, and we must learn daily to submit and 'bear his shoes', in the role of his devoted slave, for 'if Christ is not Lord of all, he is not Lord at all.'

FEBRUARY 18

BEARING HIS NAME

Acts 9:15

Read this verse carefully to understand the special commission given to Paul. He was to bear (carry) the name of Jesus to the world, and that would involve suffering. This implies representing Christ faithfully, not successfully, and to be the guardian of his reputation. This is also the role of an ambassador who in a foreign land represents his country and those who govern it. Paul states this is what a Christian is, and commands us all to recognize the privilege and honour (2 Corinthians 5:20).

A person's name is his character. This is especially true in Old Testament times when children's names were very carefully chosen for their meaning. As family members we can either enhance or bring shame to the family name. How much more important for those in God's family to bear his name with loving pride, great humility, and constant care, fully cognizant of the responsibility that is ours.

The name of Jesus Christ is like no other name, for there is no other name under heaven given among men by which we can be saved (Acts 4:12). Does it cause you pain when you hear his precious name used as a swear word or expletive? Sometimes it is necessary to point out to a person speaking like that just who Jesus is, and that so far as you are concerned, he is your Lord and Saviour, the most important person in your life.

Are we fulfilling our commission as ambassadors in this alien world, to lift high the name of Jesus? Meditate on John Newton's wonderful hymn, 'How sweet the name of Jesus sounds in a believer's ear', and make it a prayer of commitment.

FEBRUARY 19

BEARING HIS CROSS

Luke 14:27

These are strong words: 'whoever does not ... cannot be ...' In understanding true discipleship, in order to follow Christ in obedience and full commitment, it is vital to let these words sink in. Crossbearing is sharing with Jesus. Think of his shame, his persecution, his loneliness, his death. Are we fully prepared for all that involves in our daily lives?

Paul, the supreme example of one who fully understood the cost of discipleship, shares his experience in I Corinthians 9. He outlines what he suffered for Christ, but it was worth it all for the knowledge of God's approval on his life (v. 1). In verse 4 he says he was entitled to normal rations, romance (v. 5), remuneration (vv. 6, 7), but he willingly gave them up for Christ's sake (vv. 15-18). Meditate on how far you have travelled along this road, and whether any of these things we take for granted come between yourself and full devotion to Jesus himself.

In this day and age of soft living and self-centred outlook, how much do we as God's people know of bearing the Cross with Jesus and sharing in his suffering and rejection? It can be comparatively easy to nod the head and have heroic thoughts about cross-bearing, but actually fulfilling the conditions and meeting the challenge daily can be an entirely different matter. God grant us iron in our souls and the power of the Holy Spirit in our hearts so that we are his disciples indeed.

FEBRUARY 20

BEARING HIS MARKS

Galatians 6:17

'I bear in my body the marks of the Lord Jesus', Paul writes. The word is 'stigma', a red-hot iron or very sharp point used for the branding of slaves or cattle. In verse 14 Paul wrote about the glory of knowing the crucified Lord Jesus. Glory and branding – what a contrast!

It is possible Paul was talking of physical scars, such as his thorn in the flesh (2 Corinthians 12:7), which some think was an eye problem. He was above all talking of marks which proved him to be a follower of Christ. Do you covet those marks which would betray you as a Christian? This is not done by a false piety, but by daily discipline in seeking the mind and will of God in the things we do and don't do, what we say and when we keep silent, the friends we make and the places we go. We need to build up a secret history with God, and that cannot be done unless we forsake frivolity and time-wasting, and take our commitment to Christ as seriously as is his commitment to us. Amy Carmichael put it thus: 'Hast thou no wound, no scar?... He has not followed far who has no wound, no scar.'

As followers of Jesus Christ we cannot avoid the scars, and should bear them proudly, just as the Hindu is proud of his marks, the Muslim is unashamed of his praying five times a day.

As a slave I am to carry his shoes (see Isaiah 52:7; Ephesians 6:15).

As an ambassador I am to carry his name.

As a fellow-sufferer I am to carry his Cross.

As his partner I am to carry his marks.

Dear Lord Jesus, make me strong in your strength, and worthy by the cleansing of your blood at Calvary, to become a true disciple.

FEBRUARY 21

SPIRITUAL PERCEPTION

Matthew 9:35-10:1

It is imperative that every Christian studies the relationship between Jesus and people, both en masse and individually. In the above verses we will see three responses he gave in a normal situation. He was travelling the country – by foot, probably – visiting large towns and out of the way hamlets, teaching and preaching 'the gospel of the kingdom'.

The first reaction of Jesus to the crowds was compassion, a combination of pity, deep feeling, and love. He saw the people bereft, hopeless, helpless, sheep without a shepherd, and he yearned over them with the love of his shepherd's heart (John 10). How do we regard a crowd? As a nuisance, in our way, unsavoury? Or do we have Calvary love in our hearts, and eyes open to see people as Jesus did, not merely a mass but a collection of individuals with great needs?

The second reaction was to do something, and Jesus turned to his disciples and said, 'Pray'. The Lord would work no instant miracle of redemption; that came at Calvary. But the people needed the help and teaching the disciples could give as they were pointed to the Saviour.

So the third reaction was the commissioning of the disciples to this task. May the Lord call each one of us to our part of his harvest, and give us hearts to love and understand the urgent needs of those around us.

FEBRUARY 22

COMMISSIONED

Matthew 10:1-5

From those told in 9:38 to pray, Jesus commissioned 12 to go (10:5). Sometimes it can be dangerous to pray, for God might use you as the one to answer your own prayers!

Jesus saw the crowds and felt the almost physical pain of compassion, and then called 12 men to go into the battle for the souls of men. Did he sense that these disciples were filled with the same divine urge that he himself had? Maybe not at first, but he gave them authority over the evils of demons and disease.

In Mark 3:13-15 the commission is three-fold: 'to be with him', a walk of fellowship with the Master; 'to preach', to witness to the one they knew to be God's anointed one; 'to have authority to cast out demons', to war with the devil.

This is our commission today, to be *in* for communion and fellowship with Jesus himself, and then strengthened by his power to be *out* in his service of witness and warfare. To be *in* with him day after day leads to spiritual indigestion, but to be *out* for him constantly leads to spiritual barrenness. We must keep the balance of devotion to Christ in the secret place with service for him in the public arena. He will never fail us; God grant we never fail him.

A Prayer:
> Lord crucified, give me a heart like thine,
> And give me love, pure Calvary love
>> To lead the lost to Thee.

FEBRUARY 23

A STORMY ADVENTURE

Matthew 14:22-33

The disciples had been in a storm before, but Jesus had been with them in the boat (Matthew 8:23-27). Now he was nowhere to be seen. This storm was a test of faith and courage, and for those reasons God sends storms into our lives, otherwise we would be spineless and supine.

When the storm arose, as it does so suddenly on Lake Galilee, the men in the boat saw something so fearful they supposed it to be a phantom. It was Jesus walking on the water making the very element, so terrifying to the fishermen, a pathway for his feet. To quell their fears he first identified himself, then gave them courage (v. 27). It is in the darkest hours in our spiritual experience, when we can be tempted to doubt, that Jesus comes alongside to say those same words.

Peter responded in typical fashion, out of the boat to imitate the Master; but that, alas, did not last long as he focused his eyes on wind and waves. Many lives are run on impetuous emotions. Enthusiasm may have the right motive, but must have permanence that is not the result of emotion, but on the call of God.

The moment Peter ceased looking to Jesus he shut out Christ's power to help him, and later he wrote that believers are kept by the power of God through faith (see I Peter 1:5). Was he thinking of this experience when, in answer to his cry of desperation, Jesus caught his hand and they returned together to the boat?

A Prayer: Father in heaven, by the power of your Holy Spirit may I be saved from looking at circumstances and not at your Son, and so falling into the sin of disbelief and failure in my testimony to your love and power. I long to be together with Jesus, safe in the boat of your will for my life today.

THE GUEST BECOMES HOST

John 2:1-11

This is a lovely glimpse of Christ in a home as guest at a wedding. This was to be the venue for the first of his 'signs', miracles, and doubtless the other guests and his disciples never suspected the event that was to come. Here was Jesus enjoying the happiness of a wedding, and his very presence sanctified one of the most precious occasions in life. A Christless wedding is a tragedy, for he is the one who brings true love and unity into a home.

Suddenly there is a commotion: 'They have no wine', Jesus' mother told him. Life often ends sadly with the joy and thrill of early years turned to disillusionment. The world gives the best wine first; Christ supplies the best wine last. How important it is for our daily lives that we take the cup he offers, and not the second-rate pleasures of the world which have no substance or lasting satisfaction.

Mary's important statement in verse 5 shows a dawning recognition of who her Son was. She had lived for thirty years observing, and somehow she knew he could help in this situation. Although he told her his time was not fully ripe, nevertheless he responded to the need of the hour. And he has been doing that ever since! That which he offers brings no sorrow or distress, but complete satisfaction to the deepest needs of the human heart.

A Prayer: Lord Jesus, you are in my life as Lord of all, not as guest (Rev. 2:20). Today please lead me into the fulfilment of your will so that I experience the wonder of your gracious supply of all my deepest needs.

AN EVENING INTERVIEW

John 3:1-15

Nicodemus, a member of the Sanhedrin, came to Jesus secretly. He was a ruler of the Jews, but he needed a Redeemer. He thought well of Jesus (v. 2), but not well enough (vv. 12,13). The Lord went immediately to the heart of this man's need, as well as the need of every single person: entrance into God's kingdom is only by new birth (v. 3). This he explained in verses 5-8 as the work of the Spirit in the heart through the confession of personal need and recognition of the inability to save oneself.

The illustration Jesus used is found in Numbers 21:8, 9, and brings out two important points. In verse 7 Jesus said, 'You *must* be born anew.' In verse 14 he said, 'so *must* the Son of man be lifted up.' In order to accomplish a way for men to be born from above, Jesus himself paid the price by his death and resurrection. There was no other way, and Nicodemus three years later saw that happen at Calvary, and understood.

To be in the presence of Jesus quickly reveals the sin and inadequacy of our lives, so it is easy to realize we need a change of heart, a cleansing, a new goal in life. That is what Jesus is talking about, to which Nicodemus responded, as he went out to become a disciple of the Son of God (John 7:45-52, his defence of Christ; John 19:38-42, his devotion to Christ). May we too be challenged by this once proud man to stand for Christ today and let others see that he has first place in every area of our lives.

FEBRUARY 26

A MIDDAY INTERVIEW

John 4:1-15

Jesus dealt with many individuals, each with specific needs, and therefore his approach varied. To the proud Pharisee Jesus showed the need of a new birth. To the sinful woman he pointed to himself as living water, the only one capable of satisfying life's deepest needs.

On this occasion he took the first step to get the woman's attention by asking a favour, a drink of water, and this led to the glorious revelation of verses 13 and 14. While the woman first thought only in material terms, she soon realized Jesus was offering more than satisfaction for bodily thirst, but something that would quench her unfilled and dissatisfied thirst for quality living.

They were talking by a well. Jesus promised a fountain springing up in a person's soul that would never run dry. Later Jesus explained that the Holy Spirit within was this source (John 7:38, 39). It is no wonder the woman begged for this supply, but Jesus first had to confront her with a need that was the source of all the unhappiness of her life. Before the cure there must be diagnosis and perhaps surgery. In his deep love and compassion Jesus knew this radical method was the only way to make this woman understand that he alone had the answer to the problems in her life. And he succeeded.

A Prayer: Heavenly Father, help me to understand fully the truth that Jesus is the water of life that alone can satisfy my deepest need. May I know the infilling of the Holy Spirit life which can make this experience of your abundance real to me this day. I ask this for your glory alone.

REVELATION LEADS TO WITNESS

John 4:16-42

The woman heard, to her amazement, her tragic life story from the lips of Jesus, and immediately thought of him as a prophet (v. 19), not merely as a Jew who deigned to speak to a Samaritan woman (v. 9). So many times people want what Jesus offers without confessing their desperate plight and overwhelming sense of sin and failure. The blessing of his supply is withheld until confession is made and forgiveness asked and given.

In her confusion the woman started a debate on religion until Jesus cut her short by pointing out worship from God's point of view (vv. 23, 24) – it must be in spirit (oneness with God) and in truth. At this point Jesus revealed himself to her as Messiah, and she immediately left her useless waterpot to run to the village and tell the story to everyone, calling this amazing stranger the Christ (v. 29). She came back to the well with the whole town following her, and after Jesus had stayed with them two days, the people testified that while some had believed the words of the woman (v. 39) now many more believed because of the mighty words of Jesus himself, and all testified that he was the Saviour of the world. This is significant, because as Samaritans they thought themselves excluded from the special blessings given to the Jews. Now they saw Jesus as he truly was, Redeemer of mankind. May our testimony today by life and lip glorify Jesus as Saviour and Lord.

A MEETING BY A POOL

John 5:1-9

The story in these verses is a graphic illustration in minuscule of the world in which we live, and Jesus' response to its need in his dealing with one man. He always deals with the individual, not the crowd, for while God loved the whole world and gave his Son, it is the 'whosoever' believing in Christ who receives life (John 3:16).

Here at Bethesda is a multitude with differing ailments, all waiting for a miracle. Jesus sees them all, but focuses on one man who had been there for 38 years, with an illness related to his sin (v. 14). This is not always the case, but with this man Jesus looked beyond the symptoms to the cause. He knew all about the man, and then asked him if he wanted to be made 'whole'. There has only been one such person in all the world who can be termed truly 'whole', right in body, mind, soul and spirit. That is Jesus himself, so the challenge to the sick man, and to ourselves, is to become complete and perfect like the Master.

Needless to say the man knew this was impossible (v. 7), but Jesus told him to *get up,* to do the thing he couldn't do, in the power that Christ gives; to *remove the bed* for which he would have no further use at Bethesda; to *walk,* taking one step at a time. And the man did just that! What a display of Christ's love, grace and power!

His demand upon each redeemed person is just the same: leave the place of defeat by his strength; remove all elements which would call for a relapse, for in Christ's healing there is no need for convalescence; and walk daily in the power of his might, step by step, growing in grace and in the knowledge of the Lord Jesus.

THE MIRACLE OF SUPPLY

John 6:1-14

The feeding of the five thousand is the only miracle recorded in all four Gospels. Let us meditate on John's remembrance of it, for the incident commenced the Lord's public Galilean ministry. In John 5:39, 40 he claimed to be the Source of life, while now he claims to be the Sustainer of life (John 6:48).

Jesus and his disciples were actually seeking a respite from the crowds, but they followed him, and after teaching them he realized they were without food and unable to purchase any (Mark 6:30-36). The disciples proposed sending them away, but Jesus said, 'You give them something to eat' – what a challenge!

Andrew came up with the small boy's lunch of five loaves and two fish, and an apologetic, 'But what are they among so many?' and that opened the gateway of God's supply.

How often in Christian work we lose the compassion because we do not yet love as Jesus did, and we say, 'Send the people away.' Jesus says, 'Sit them down and I will feed them,' and he set to work using what he had – five loaves and two small fish. He took them in his hands, he prayed, he broke, he gave – and the people were fully satisfied. This is the blueprint for Christian service, and the line of supply can be made from the throne of God through us to a desperately needy world if we are prepared to put ourselves into the almighty hands of Jesus.

A Prayer: Lord Jesus, take me, break me, mould me and fill me, so that I can be your channel of Holy Spirit life to those I meet every day.

THE CROSS OF CHRIST

MARCH 1

HOW IT ALL STARTED

Genesis 3:15

This section of daily meditations includes the Easter period and will concentrate on the Cross, the death, burial, resurrection and ascension of the Lord Jesus Christ. So we need to start at the beginning and ask, 'Why the Cross?'

Genesis 3 relates the story of the fall of man, an account that is sneered at today, but the only explanation for the mess the world is in, and the dilemma of every human being.

God had done everything to give Adam and Eve the love and security he designed for them – then enter the enemy. After he had done his dastardly work (vv. 1-7), God the Creator came into the Garden and began the questions.

It is important to note that it was Eve who fell to Satan's temptations and sinned (see 2 Corinthians 11:3; 1 Timothy 2:14). Adam had no contact with the serpent, but followed his wife when he should have been leading. Thus he transgressed and deliberately disobeyed God. There is no hope of redemption through man, so the promise is to the woman in verse 15 of a Saviour. While Satan would be mortally wounded, he was only allowed to 'bruise the heel' of the woman's seed, Jesus.

Yes, a Saviour was promised to save from the power and guilt of sin; the first animals were slain to provide protection for sinners (v. 21); and the way was cleared by expulsion from the Garden lest the couple eat of the fruit of the tree of life. If ever man is to come back to a life of fellowship with God, it could only be procured by the physical death of one who, as God, could bear the guilt and sin of all humanity. At Calvary, Jesus – child of Mary and Son of God – died physically, bearing 'our sins in his body on the tree' (1 Peter 2:24), and opened the way into God's presence to all who repent and believe, and follow him.

MARCH 2

PAUL'S SUPREME MESSAGE

Galatians 6:14

This is an outstanding statement, and each word needs to be fully understood so that the full impact is felt. The Galatian church to whom Paul was writing was bound by Jewish tradition, and circumcision, for example, was a big thing in their theology (see 5:2-6; 6:12). They were shirking the central message of the Christian faith – the death and resurrection of Jesus – and trying to produce a religion without offence. That is the emaciated condition of much preaching today, Christianity without the Cross. Paul warns of this in Galatians 5:11 where he calls the Cross a stumbling block, an offence, to so many to keep them from faith. Talk of the blood of Jesus is especially offensive to those with no sense of sin, and therefore they feel there is no need for salvation.

Paul talks of three crucifixions: of Christ, of the world, and of himself. The Cross of Christ means even more than his *death,* for it was the *form* death took that is so horrible. It was the Romans' way of killing felons, and was the most barbarous method. Yet because Jesus endured that death the Cross now has a very special significance. How do we 'glory' in such a death? Because we acknowledge that the Lord Jesus Christ (note Paul's use of his full title) became SIN for us, and we have not just a creed but an inward revelation of the Spirit in our hearts as we each acknowledge that 'he loved *me,* and gave himself for *me'.* Never be ashamed of naming the one who endured so much for us. Let us make the Cross our only glory too, understanding all the implications which surround that word.

MARCH 3

AN UNPROMISING BEGINNING

Isaiah 52:13-53:2

For a few days we will look at the Passion of the Lord Jesus through the insights given to the prophet Isaiah. This is holy ground, so approach with prayer.

In the passage for consideration, the Messiah is shown in a manner seemingly incredible. No wonder the Jews never understood this section; do we?

See first the background of the word-picture: the servant of God with nothing outward to commend him (52:13-15), a root out of dry soil. The situation into which Jesus was born offered nothing that could of itself nurture the Messiah – it was dry, unproductive ground. Jesus derived nothing from his humble origin, but he put everything into it. He did not live because of his surroundings, but he made everything around him to live. The soil may point to barrenness, but the root within it had life. Out of the lowly home came one who was to fulfil the hopes of all Israel and the world, if they have eyes to see, ears to hear, and responsive hearts. For the one planted in dry soil, reared in obscurity, was the Glory of Israel, the Saviour of the world.

May our hearts respond afresh to every aspect of the life, love and sacrifice of the Lord Jesus that is revealed in God's holy word.

MARCH 4

A MAN OF SORROWS

Isaiah 53:3,4

How different everything was from what the Jews expected! The Messiah was to be the Son of David, and he was, though his immediate family was poor. He was expected to take the country by storm, but he grew up quietly before God. All along he was being prepared for the great climax of his life, which was his death – the only person born to die.

So he humbled himself. He who was radiant with all the glory of Heaven stooped to the depths of humiliation that he might lift fallen humanity into the very presence of God. Further, he became obedient to death and to suffer at the hands of men.

Because the Good News is also Solemn News it is often thought necessary to dress up its presentation to avoid offending, and to give Jesus a 'pop' image. No, never. The heart of the message is the sorrow and suffering he bore on our behalf as he stooped to save my soul and to redeem me. He stooped so low to accomplish this that none can ever be lower than he was.

Jesus is called here a man of sorrows – what a name! It is easy to remember his holiness, his love, and he is all that and much more, but his sorrow is caused because those he loves shun and reject him, and the message of redemption he came to bring is flung back at him by an unrepentant world.

May we never trifle with the love that took Jesus to Calvary on our behalf, to add to the sorrow and grief he bore during his life on earth.

MARCH 5

THE HEART OF THE GOSPEL

Isaiah 53:4,5

Why did Jesus have to die? The answer is in these verses. The Father was prepared to smite his Son for the redemption of mankind (vv. 4, 6c). Then comes an attention catching BUT, and we are led to the heart of his sufferings.

Transgression is disobedience, flouting laws.

Iniquity is defilement, the downward drag of human nature.

Jesus dealt with the consequences of sin in his own body, wounded, bruised, chastised. Then we read 'with his stripes we are *healed*'. Through the suffering of our Saviour our sin is pardoned; here it is regarded as the healing of a deadly disease. God deals with us as suffering from a disease for which he has the cure. One day those who have not claimed his cure will be treated as rebels.

Disease usually incites pity, but not in this case because we sin wilfully, with our eyes open. We choose evil and transgress in heart. Yet God in his mercy looks not so much on the wickedness of sin as its sickness, and deals with it as a spiritual complaint of the worst possible kind. It is so dreadful it has driven man completely away from the centre of God's purpose. The only cure and deliverance is found in these verses which must be accepted by each individually, and in place of 'us', 'our', 'we', we put our own name and take our stand at the Cross saying with deep love and thankfulness, 'Lord Jesus, you did all this for ME, as if I were the only sick and sinful person in the world: I thank you and praise your name.'

MARCH 6

GOD'S REMEDY FOR SIN

Isaiah 53:6

The picture changes, but the truth is the same. Like stupid, stubborn sheep each one of us has gone astray into – note this – our own way. That is the mark against us. We follow the herd, but it is the way we choose, which is the road that leads away from God, and can end by being the broad road leading to destruction.

If we are the wilful sheep, Jesus is the willing Lamb, who bears away the sin of the world. God was in Christ reconciling the world to himself (2 Corinthians 5:19), for he is not a God of vengeance. The sacrifice of Jesus was vicarious, and the dreadful concentration of the sin of the world – past, present and future – is caused to meet upon him.

A preacher was about to board a train and a young man rushed up to him, 'Sir, what must I do to be saved?' Shouting from the carriage window the preacher said, 'Read Isaiah 53:6. Go in at the first 'all' and come out at the last 'all'.' And that sums it up. If we recognize our lost and sinful condition, realize the price for our redemption has been paid by the offering up of Jesus himself in our stead and accept as a freed soul the new life opened up, then we know personally God's remedy for our sin problem.

Make the words of Mrs Booth-Clibborn your prayer of thanksgiving and renewed surrender:

> At Thy feet I fall, yield Thee up my all
> To suffer, live or die, for my Lord crucified.

MARCH 7

WHEN SILENCE IS GOLDEN

Isaiah 53:7

Look at the attitude of the Lord Jesus in the face of suffering. Silence.

Before Caiaphas the High Priest he was accused of blasphemy (Matthew 26:62-64). He said not a word, except when to remain silent would have been to deny his claim to deity.

Before Pilate the Roman Governor he was accused of treason (Matthew 27:11-14). Again he said not a word except when to remain silent would have been to deny his claim to kingship.

Before the whole band of soldiers (Matthew 27:28-30) not a single word crossed his lips as they tortured and tormented him. This was a direct fulfilment of Isaiah's vision, the silent Lamb.

Before Herod he was questioned regarding many things, but he said nothing to the man who had sinned away his opportunity when John the Baptist faced him with his evil ways (Luke 23:8, 9).

At Calvary there was darkness and silence for three hours (Matthew 27:45, 46). Then came the cry, 'My God, why have YOU forsaken me?' as he took the role of the sacrificial Lamb. Then the final triumphant shout, 'It is finished!' and voluntarily he surrendered his soul and life to his Father. The majestic silence of the Lord.

It is said that true humility is the silence of the soul before God, when a person ceases to argue or debate but rests in his Word. May we too know when silence is golden, for though at many times most of us can be unnecessarily verbose, it is also said we are not heard for our much speaking.

MARCH 8

HOW TO SATISFY GOD

Isaiah 53:10,11

The word 'satisfy' has many meanings, but it seems a strange
one to use concerning God. To concentrate our thoughts on
this, I quote something someone has said, which is relevant:

There is no satisfaction without love.
There is no love without travail.
There is no travail without joy.
The measure of the travail governs the depth of joy.

There must be a cause for the satisfaction of God, and Isaiah
relates it to the poignancy of suffering, bruising, being put to
grief, an offering for sin. A self-centred life never experiences
true satisfaction, and even God found that the outpouring of his
love for lost humanity through the death of his Son gave him
satisfaction – everything had been done by which mankind could
be reconciled to God.

His satisfaction is continued as one after another, generation
after generation, men, women, children, come to faith in Jesus.
'He shall see his seed (offspring) ... he shall see the fruit ... '

God's satisfaction is complete when one day the redeemed
stand before him in glory from every tribe and nation. Many
will be accounted righteous (v. 11). How many? Only God
knows that, and the millions upon millions will one day be singing praises in his presence, and then the Almighty will be fully
satisfied.

THE SATISFACTION OF THE REDEEMED

Psalm 17:15

This verse is the other side of the coin of Isaiah 53:10, 11. In what way does our satisfaction in God measure up to what we have learned about the reasons for him being satisfied?

The cause of our rest of faith is in what Jesus Christ has done for us. Read verse 10 thus: 'When I make Jesus an offering for my sin (what does the Lord see?), he shall see his offspring, his seed.' The moment a person accepts by faith the death of Jesus as atonement for sin, at that moment he or she is one of God's family. Oh joy! Oh mystery!

Satisfaction continues as we grow in the knowledge of the Lord Jesus. So many Christians stay in the hallway of salvation and never enter into the full riches there are in Christ. So few are totally committed to him, and maintain just a nominal relationship that never sees them involved in service or testimony for Christ.

Continued satisfaction means living at the Cross, and as Jesus gave his lifeblood there, that must be the measure of personal commitment for his followers – maybe not literally, but in dedication. For the completion of satisfaction is expressed in Psalm 17:15, when we see him face to face. May that be a time of reward and rejoicing for each of us.

A Prayer: Lord Jesus, you know there are times of difficulty and sadness on this earth, of frustration and opposition, for you have experienced it all. May that mind which was yours be in me, so that I am a true follower and faithful witness of your love and grace in my life, demonstrated at Calvary and the empty tomb.

MARCH 10

THE PRINCIPLE OF SACRIFICE

Matthew 16:24-26

In verse 16 of this chapter Peter had confessed the deity of Christ, and immediately the Lord revealed the Cross as the centre of his programme for the salvation of mankind. Thus he declared that the principle of sacrifice lies at the very heart of the Godhead. That same sacrifice is demanded of his followers: 'If any man will come after me...' is the invitation, the challenge, that is given to everyone, and each has the choice to accept or reject. What does it imply?

Deny himself: not a period of self-denial but a deliberate turning from all self-interests and giving first place to the Lord and to the will of God.

Take up his Cross: This is not carrying some burden or trial, but recognizing the Cross as a means of death. For us it is the daily dying to all that is of the flesh in us to give room to the living Lord Jesus.

Follow him: even to the place of death to everything that is outside his will for daily life.

A tough calling? Yes, but it is the way the Master went, and if we yearn to follow him it is the way we too must tread. But it is the way of joy, satisfaction and fulfilment (Hebrews 12:2). Is this your aim?

MARCH 11

THE PRACTICE OF THE CROSS

Matthew 16:24, 25

To talk of a 'crucified life' is sadly strange to many Christians today. Not many delight to echo Paul's words, 'I have been crucified with Christ; it is no longer I who live, but Christ who lives in me' (Galatians 2:20). Yet it is what the Master taught and demanded.

What does it mean? It is trusting Christ to do within us what we cannot possibly do ourselves. It is maintained by faith, and by faith alone. Every activity of Christian life is performed by the Holy Spirit's indwelling while we trust him. The moment effort comes in at the door, faith flies out of the window, and so does power. Faith and effort cannot co-exist in this area of Christian experience.

We learn to 'die' to ourselves, our pride, touchiness, sensitivity, and become alive to the glorious fact of a living Saviour whose power is now within us in the person of the Holy Spirit. He died to everything apart from his obedience to his Father's will, which was our salvation – never forget that. He Himself said that the servant is not above the Master, therefore our delight must be to follow him wherever he leads.

The Christian life is hard – no it is impossible! It is a supernatural life, and only the Son of God can live it, and faith is the channel for him to work in our lives.

MARCH 12

THE EFFECT OF THE MESSAGE

Galatians 6: 14b

Paul talks of 'the world crucified to me'. What does he mean? He saw the whole concept of 'the world' as condemned because the system was responsible for the actual crucifixion of Christ. Truth was rejected and a lie preferred, so Paul condemns its character and despises its judgement, ignoring its opinion about himself. Paul cared nothing for its pleasures, honours, dignity, or wealth. All the things that could allure had no attraction for him because the Cross of Christ was the magnet that drew him every moment of every day. Is that true of us in our hectic modern age? Or does the world have such a strong pull that often the things of Christ seem dim and distant, and give little real joy and fulfilment? If that is so, we need to reassess the reality of our salvation and the depth of our commitment to the Lord.

Paul says further that he was crucified to the world: if Paul had no use for the world, neither had it for him. Once he was an up-and-coming scholar. Now he was a nobody, all because he preached Christ crucified. Old friends became foes almost overnight. Run with the world, and you are O.K. Glory in Christ, and you are a fool. If that is your present experience, in a humble way you are sharing in the rejection and despising suffered by Jesus himself. Therefore look up! See him not only on the Cross, but on the throne, for he alone is the way to a life of joy and victory.

A Prayer: Lord Jesus, in the stress and testing of modern life's advertising and materialism, help keep my eyes on you, alone, so that my living may mark me out as one who is controlled by your love and power, utterly content with the complete satisfaction obedience to you can bring.

MARCH 13

A LADDER OF BLESSING

Philippians 2:5-11

This amazing passage, one of the loftiest of Paul's writings, gives the six rungs by which Jesus descended from the throne in Heaven to earth, and the three great leaps that took him back to glory.

The emptying of the Lord Jesus of all his glory and deity was complete; not a shred remained. He became a bondslave; a man, all man and human who became tired and hungry, and was tempted. He did not just act as a man, but was in our likeness, our representative, and as such he humbled himself to an obscure life in poor surroundings. Further he became obedient even to death on a cross. What a death! Three crosses were erected that day, two for thieves and the central one for a murderer, Barabbas. At the last moment there was a change. Barabbas was set free and Jesus our Saviour took his place. What a vast distance he came down the ladder until he touched the lowest limit!

Verse 9 begins with a majestic 'therefore' – God saw the complete obedience of his Son who was willing to 'humble *himself*' (v. 8), but it was the Father who exalted the Son in three dramatic leaps back to his rightful place at the right hand of God. What a glorious day it will be when we see Jesus, no longer a lonely figure on a cross, but risen, victorious, the one before whom every knee shall bow, and every tongue confess he is Lord of all!

A Prayer:
As I look at this picture of Christ,
Two wonders I confess:
The wonder of his glorious love,
And my own worthlessness.

MARCH 14

THE SUPREMACY OF CHRIST

Colossians 1:15-23

Let us admit it: sometimes our God is too small, and we think of him as being unable to cope with this runaway world and the great problems each one of us faces. Read anew Colossians 1 and focus on the greatness of the Saviour.

In the verses for this meditation Christ is seen in relation to God, being of the same essence; in relation to creation he was before all things for he is the architect, owner and controller (vv. 16, 17). In relation to the Church he is the head, the first-born of the new creation through his triumphant resurrection and ascension. He is the preeminent one in whom all the fullness of the Godhead dwells. That is what the Father thinks of his Son. What do we think of him?

The great work of Jesus was reconciliation (vv. 20, 21), 'all things . . . and you'. This has been accomplished by the blood of his Cross. Here is the offended one – God – making reconciliation with the offending one by giving his own life. That is almost beyond our grasp, because we turned our backs on him and have no right to expect a welcome, but he himself has prepared the way back from the dark paths of sin. The purpose of his reconciliation is that we might become like himself, holy, faultless, irreproachable before him (v. 22). Amazing grace!

A Prayer: Father, may your purpose in saving me from hell and reconciling me to yourself be fulfilled this day and every day as by your grace I continue steadfast in the faith.

THE CROSS – GOD'S BRIDGE

Ephesians 2:13-18

It will take all eternity to discover the far-reaching meaning and effectiveness of the Cross. With our finite minds we can only dabble in the shallows of understanding our so great redemption, and in the verses to be considered we are introduced to God's bridge building.

This is twofold. Paul is dealing here with the animosity between Jew and Gentile into which Jesus came to bring his peace and reconciliation, for he is the Good Shepherd with sheep other than the Jews to be brought into his fold.

The passage also deals with the state of each person born into this world who is 'far off' (v. 13), without hope and without God. The tragedy of those words! Let us think of them to see the depths from which we have been delivered, if we are believers in Christ.

Now we have been brought near through Calvary. Peace with God is not a treaty but a person, Christ who is our peace (vv. 13, 14). Not only can Jew and Gentile be reconciled to one another, but so can men and women with God himself, brought into one body through his Cross, and the Holy Spirit gives access into the very presence of God.

We have been brought near by God's gracious act of making the death of his Son the pathway into his presence. But where are we living? Near to God and to fellow believers, or far away in disobedience? As we have been reconciled to God through the Lord Jesus, pray that each one of us may exercise a life of witness to his saving grace that will make us bridges over which people may also find life hope, peace and salvation.

UNWELCOME NEWS

Mark 8:31-33

The incident prior to the above verses tells of Peter's recognition that Jesus was no ordinary prophet or teacher but the Christ, Messiah. It was to gain such a confession that Jesus had asked his two questions: Who do *men* say that I am?.. . But who do *you* say that I am?

Having received their verdict about his person he 'began to teach them' his plan of redemption. Contrary to the disciples' great expectations, it was not to be a kingdom brought in through military power, but by pain and suffering, the Cross and resurrection. This they could or would not understand. They were right about his person, but wrong about his plan, and it is impossible to have one without the other.

Impetuous Peter immediately rebuked the Lord – imagine that! – and in turn was severely rebuked for siding with Satan against the will and plan of God. There are times no doubt when each one of us is guilty of such behaviour. Yes, we know and love Jesus Christ with a whole heart, but when the revelation of his plan for our lives comes as unwelcome news, we start to argue and lose our peace. Sometimes it is necessary to recall the warning in Proverbs 14:12, 'There is a way that seems right to a man, but its end is the way of death'. We need to pray before the Lord, 'I know, O Lord, that the way of man is not in himself, that it is not in man to direct his steps' (Jeremiah 10:23). Teach me THY way, O Lord.

JESUS REVEALS HIS GLORY

Mark 9:2-8

This epic event is recorded in three Gospels with exactly the same timing – about six days after that recorded in yesterday's meditation. No doubt the disciples needed the time to digest the awesome revelation they had received, as they all travelled south from Caesarea Philippi.

How thankful Peter must have been to be included among the favoured three after the rebuke of only a week ago! But see the patience and love of the Lord, who saw the potential and future ministry of this headstrong man. How eager Jesus was to give them all a new vision of himself. The grace of the Lord is limitless as he restores those who repent of their sin and disobedience, and in doing so he reveals fresh facets of his power and glory.

Heaven touched earth on this occasion as Jesus was transfigured before them. Mark speaks of his dazzling garments; Matthew 17:2 and Luke 9:29 comment first on his face, shining as the sun. Whether or not this radiance came from within or without we are not told, but Luke says it happened as Jesus prayed. No doubt he prayed about the events of the previous week, the problem of how to relate the Cross to the crown in the minds of his disciples. The dark shadow of Calvary was across his path, something from which he shrank as well as they, though for a different reason. The answer to his prayer was not a removal of the Cross, but a revelation of the crown which must surely follow the obedience to the will of God, and fulfilment of his plan of redemption. The mystery of the Cross was misunderstood on earth but known and identified in Heaven, and so the glory shone in him and through him.

MARCH 18

A SIGNIFICANT GATHERING

Luke 9:30,31

The three privileged disciples are joined by two strategic Old Testament figures, Moses representing the Law and Elijah the Prophets, while the disciples were the first of those in the new covenant of the Gospel. They all arrived on the mountain by different ways. Moses had died but was miraculously revived (Jude v. 9); Elijah had gone to heaven in the chariot of fire; the others were led there by Christ himself.

He is central to all, and this is a picture of the coming kingdom: Father, Son and the saints of all ages. In Revelation chapters 4 and 5 God is on the throne, the Lamb is in the midst, and the elders surround them, representing the twelve tribes of the Old Testament and the twelve apostles of the New Testament.

What, on this occasion, was the object of the meeting? 'They spoke of his departure' (Luke 9:31), his exodus, his death which (note carefully) he was to accomplish at Jerusalem. The coming of the two prophets reveal that Calvary was the ever-present topic in Heaven, and that it was not a disaster but a victory. How different it must have been for Christ to listen to them talk about it after hearing the confusion, doubt and unbelief of the disciples!

Look on to verses 51-53: Jesus was set on fulfilling the purpose of his coming to earth, undeterred and unflinching, and the secret of his strength is found in part in Isaiah 50:7, 8a.

A Prayer: O Lord, may I be steadfast in my commitment to you as you were as you trod the lonely road to Calvary in obedience to the plan of the Father, which brought my salvation. Grant that, even today, I may not be sidetracked or vacillating in my desire that 'Thy will be done'.

MARCH 19

ASLEEP OR AWAKE?

Mark 9:5,6; Luke 9:32,33

What an awesome experience this was for the three disciples, something so far beyond their knowledge that they must have wondered if they were dreaming.

People sleep in strange places, and the fact that these men could do so in such a situation, and again in Gethsemane, can be incomprehensible to us. Yet the Lord did not chide them, for when they awoke they saw his glory – think on that. How much of his glory do we see, or do we miss his revelations because we are too inert?

Peter once again rushes into speech, because he did not know what to say (Luke 9:33)! There are times to remain silent in awe and wonder in the presence of the risen Lord. So often nervous tension clouds any discernment we might have, as it was with Peter. He wanted the mountain without the valley, the prize without the cost. If Peter had slept less he would have seen more, and then he would have spoken differently. At least it is to his credit that he, through Mark, so frankly tells us the story!

A Prayer: Father, keep me awake and alert in these days when the world is falling apart, that I may look up and see your glory, then look out to see the need around me, and speak your words to those you bring across my path. I ask this for the glory of your dear Son, my Saviour.

MARCH 20

JESUS ONLY

Mark 9:7, 8

After the rash words of the spokesman of the privileged three, and the significant conversation with the strategic Old Testament figures, God's chosen One is the focus of the voice of the Father (Luke 9:35). The full text is in Matthew 17:5, and is taken from three Old Testament scriptures:

Psalm 2:7; Deuteronomy 18:15; Isaiah 42:1. Heaven is bearing witness to the authority of the Psalms, Prophets and Law, and to Christ as the subject and fulfilment of them all.

Hear him! This is for us as well as the disciples, for they had challenged the way of the Cross, and are now taken up into this intimate fellowship, given a glimpse of what God the Father has to say about it, and receive this command, 'Hear him!' How much time do you spend doing just that? Thinking about the life and ministry of the Saviour and how it concerns your life; asking him to cleanse you from all sin, and commission you to his service.

The final scene in this drama is in verse 8, 'suddenly' things returned to their norm – but did they? Matthew 17:6-8 gives the reaction of the three men after the withdrawal of Moses and Elijah. The awe they felt perhaps never left them (see 2 Peter 1:16-18). The touch of Jesus revived and reassured them, and when finally they had the courage to raise their eyes, they 'saw no one but Jesus'. Yes, the same Master, yet somehow never to be the same again for they had seen his glory, heard God's voice, and for the first time realized – albeit perhaps hazily – who Jesus really was.

God grant that our eyes may be open to see afresh the full wonder of the person of Jesus, so that it can never be said of us that our grasp of the Godhead brings them down to our finite understanding, rather than our knowledge of them being lifted up by the working of the Holy Spirit in our hearts.

MARCH 21

THE CORN OF WHEAT

John 12:24

Here is one of the great statements of Jesus which we may hear with our ears but fail to understand in our hearts. He has previously foretold his death, now he gives the deeper meaning to it.

In its context it is spoken to some Greeks who had come to Jerusalem for the Passover. There was a Greek settlement at Bethsaida, where Philip originated, so maybe they were acquainted. How wise of those Gentiles to seek the Saviour! They may have been telling him that they were ready to receive him, even though his own people rejected him.

A seed has to have contact with soil and water before it germinates, otherwise it just rots. The life of Jesus is as seed that goes into the ground, a dead thing, but in contact with the necessary elements it springs into life. He came to give his life not only for the Jews but also for Gentiles, but first he had to die, physically. Then in resurrection life there is a harvest.

Jesus then brings this truth home in verses 25 and 26, which are given in every Gospel. We follow the Master into death to self in order to be of use to him and his kingdom. Strong words here – hate, loss, love, gain, serve, follow, and finally the promise of acceptance by the Father.

Are we prepared to follow the Master by way of the Cross?

MARCH 22

PALM SUNDAY

John 12:12-19

The symbolic entry of Jesus is recorded in all the Gospels (Matthew 21, Mark 11, Luke 19). John does not mention how the Lord came into the city but the reaction of the people.

Luke tells in detail of the Lord's command regarding the donkey and the disciples' obedience. They went where he told them to go, they said what he told them to say, and they did what he told them to do. They neither added nor subtracted from his implicit orders, and this underlines the importance of obedience. Can we be trusted to do his bidding in just that way, and be willing to remain anonymous (Luke 19:29)?

As John describes the welcome given to Jesus as he rode into Jerusalem there is something sad about it, because all too soon he would be crowned with thorns and led away as a criminal to die. It is always easier to shout for him in a crowd than to stand alone for him at the Cross.

It was a bad day for the Pharisees. Lazarus, once dead, was very much alive, and in verse 19 the jubilation of the people convinced them of their weakness in the face of such an irresistible power. Would that it were true that 'the world has gone after him'! It would be more likely to be true if Christians were more like Jesus, and more faithful in witness and simple declaration of the Gospel.

A Prayer: Dear Father, may I never be found just one of the crowd, led along by emotion, rather than making a bold stand for Jesus even in hostile surroundings. This is impossible without the enabling of the Holy Spirit, and I ask for his power to be mine for this day.

THE MAGNETISM OF THE CROSS

John 12:27-36

The shadow of Calvary is growing longer, and Jesus expresses his humanity in his heart-cry of verse 27. Then he says, as if rebuffing Satan, 'NO! for this purpose I have come to this hour. Father, glorify your name.' That is victory. His rescue would have been our ruin, but his death brought about our deliverance.

For the third time the Father bore testimony to his Son (Mark 1:11, 9:7). And Jesus was enabled to stand and look the future in the face, as it were, by the repetition of the word NOW. This is it, the time had come, and he was prepared for action whatever it might cost.

Verse 32 is another of the Lord's great statements. It signalled the mode of his death, but also pointed the Jews back to the story of the brazen serpent in Numbers 21:9, to which he had already referred when talking to Nicodemus in John 3:14. Jesus already had his arms open wide to receive all who will come to him – 'all' without distinction, not without exception.

Jesus draws and then sends: first we must yield to his love and then walk in his light (v. 35). There is, in verse 36a, a spiritual opportunity, personal response, and the transformation worked in us by the Holy Spirit. Check your own life and witness by these words.

ONCE FOR ALL

Hebrews 10:1-14

Here the transition from Old to New Testament is clearly shown. See the weakness of the one compared with the power of the other:

v. 1 No perfection	v. 14 Perfected for ever
v. 2 No silencing of conscience	v. 14 Forgiven and sanctified
v. 3 No forgetting of sins	v. 17 Remembered no more
v. 4 No taking away of sins	v. 12 One sacrifice for sins for ever

The comparison too is in the actual sacrifice for sin. Once a continual animal sacrifice which could never take away sins had to be made, day in and year in. Then Jesus came, a body prepared (v. 5), an obedient will (v. 7), a perfect sacrifice once for all – for all time and for all people.

The contrast of the priestly work is amazing. In verse 11 the Old Testament priest stood, for in the Tabernacle there was a table, a candlestick, an altar, but no seat. The work was unending, and the priest was continually standing. Such monotony and weariness!

From that to sheer wonder in verse 12; 'BUT when Christ had offered for all time a single sacrifice for sins, he sat down...' The work of redemption was finished, never to be repeated. The stream of animal blood is now ended, for the one sacrifice for ever has been made, and nothing can be added to its finality or perfection. All has been *done,* and there is nothing we can ever *do* to achieve salvation. The death of Christ once for all is the secret forever of the power of his sacrifice (v. 14). Let us bow before him in renewed wonder and praise for such love, that he may see in us the result of the travail of his soul, and be satisfied.

MARCH 25

THE HOUR HAS COME

John 13:1

In meditating upon the events of Holy Week it is necessary to refer to all four Gospels. Luke 21:37 gives a brief glimpse of Jesus' habit each night of going to the Mount of Olives —did he ever sleep? Then come accounts of the preparation of the Passover feast, but John gives a special incident of great importance.

The key words now are in verse 1: 'Jesus knew that his hour had come to depart.., to the Father.' He was led through his life by God's timetable, so to speak, and his progress was majestic and unhurried. John points this out as he records the Master's journey, and the first reference is at Cana during the marriage, the place of his first miracle (Ch. 2:4). In 7:30 and 8:20 it was impossible for him to be arrested by his enemies, for the hands of God's clock were not at the hour. In chapter 12 the scene changes, and in verses 23 and 27 Jesus knows his time on earth is rapidly drawing to a close, and in 13:1 it is imminent. Now turn to 17:1, and the clock is striking: 'The hour has come', and there is no turning back.

It is impossible to imagine the thoughts in the Lord's mind on these occasions, but the steadfastness of his obedience to the will of God is supremely evident, and we marvel that he walked a lonely road for our sake, not his. In this connection read and pray over Paul's words in Romans 5:6-8: 'At the right time . . . Christ died for us while we were yet sinners.' Oh, matchless love!

MARCH 26

THE SERVANT KING

John 13:1-5

John must be thanked for including this incident in his record. Isaiah had proclaimed Messiah to be God's servant in 52:13, and now Jesus was demonstrating his servanthood.

First note his knowledge of himself in four areas: that the hour for which he was born had come; that the Father had given all things to him; that he came from God; that he was returning to God. How great he is, yet how humble! Knowing all that, what did he then do? He took a towel and girded himself with it. In the beginning of creation (Genesis 3) man wanted to become as God. Now God, in the person of Jesus, became a servant.

Why was this act of Jesus' necessary? Prior to this (Luke 22:24) contention had arisen among the disciples as to who was to be the greatest, and this must have concerned the Lord greatly. Of what use were all his teaching and praying, his love and example, if these men were no different? They were about to be entrusted with a world task in which the Holy Spirit is indispensable, yet it was impossible for him to be given unless they were cleansed and delivered from pride. What an important moment this was in the Lord's life, for how was this lesson to be learned? Only by a visual demonstration of true servanthood.

As tomorrow we meditate on just what happened in that upper room, let us have open minds and hearts as we too learn from Jesus the all important lesson of humility.

MARCH 27

WIPE YOUR FEET!

John 13:3-10

The important thing was not only that these men should know the way of cleansing, but that they should be willing for it, so the Lord's focus was first on Peter. No doubt we shall find the Holy Spirit focusing on us.

Peter was a man with defiled feet, and the dust of the road is a picture of a defiled heart, picking up all the dross of life's journey. Peter had always been the spokesman, for he was a leader, impetuous, hot-tempered, but in great need. So are all God's servants. The world does not respond to the Gospel because so often those who proclaim it are unattractive, lacking in grace and love, full of pride and self importance. These are shocking words, but let's face it – we all serve the Lord with defiled feet and hearts.

In the east a guest would bathe before going to a feast, so only the feet needed to be washed by a slave on arrival – the equivalent of a doormat. So imagine Peter's reaction when Jesus knelt before him with basin and towel to wash his feet. He might have thought for an instant that he should have been doing that to his Lord. So his emotional cry in verse 6 is very understandable, as no doubt he emphasized 'you', 'my'. Then of course Peter wanted to be wholly cleansed, which was not necessary physically, nor spiritually, because within hours the blood of Jesus, which cleanses from all sin, would be shed for rebels, for sinners, for you and me – and for Peter.

LEARN THE LESSON

John 13:12-30

Imagine the stunned silence as Jesus completed his lowly task, removed the towel, and replaced his robe. What thoughts and emotions must have been going through the men's minds! Was it possible they had really experienced the scene, or were they dreaming?

When Jesus sat down he roused them from their thoughts, and asked them a question. How much of his action-picture had they understood? How much do we? In his words Jesus told them plainly what he, their Lord and Teacher, had done, that he had set an example of true humility and the role of being a servant, and that they should do as he had done. Finally he placed the onus on them – and on us – in verse 17, 'blessed are you if you do them.'

Jesus, the light of the world, has expressed his love for his own; how do we show our love to him, to fellow Christians, to the world? The disciples were looking for prestige and greatness. Christ showed them their eyes were in the wrong place, for they were to learn the meaning of service. This involves being travelworn, soiled and weary, and receiving similar rough treatment to that which Jesus met. Are we learning the lessons he teaches here?

A Thought: Clean hands and pure hearts are for heaven. Dirty hands and warm hearts are for earth. May we be prepared to get dug into the tasks the Lord sets before us without counting the cost to our reputations so that we may be his true representatives upon earth.

MARCH 29

BEHIND THE SCENES

Luke 22:1-13

The Lord's final day on earth was packed with incident, but everything was moving to a climax and the atmosphere was tense. Behind the everyday actions, preparations of cosmic importance were in progress.

On earth (v. 2) the hostility of the rulers was reaching a head. They were set upon the Lord's death, but the sympathy of the people was still with him. Finally they would clamour for his death, but in these last hours the rulers feared them.

Satan (vv. 3-6) was having his final fling as he used Judas as his vehicle. After the battle in the wilderness Satan was routed, and departed until an opportune time (Luke 4:13). Here he is back, but not to make a direct attack on Jesus, but on Judas who made a pact not only with the priests, but with the evil one himself.

Heaven was very close at this time as the Passover feast was prepared (vv. 7-13). This was a family occasion and Jesus was sharing it with the representatives of his new family, his called-out ones, those who do the will of God (see Mark 3:31-35). Here for Jesus was the time of final intimacy with his chief disciples on whom rested the evangelization of the world.

Christians today are part of that family line, but how alive are we to the responsibility and privilege of the charge given us by the Master? There is a similarity in the world today in the rejection of God, the ridicule cast on the name of Jesus, the ignorance of the majority of people to the message of the Word of God. Pray that you may be emboldened by the power of the indwelling Holy Spirit to witness a good confession to the name and the power of Jesus Christ.

MARCH 30

A FEAST TO BE REMEMBERED

Matthew 26:26-30

As soon as Judas had left the company (vv. 20-25) Jesus began the meal which was to be known as the Lord's Supper, the most precious and intimate time of fellowship a Christian can experience. It was tremendously important to Jesus himself: 'I have earnestly desired to eat this Passover with you before I suffer' (Luke 22:15). Why?

It was a feast of life; we remember his death, but we share his life. 'This is my body . . . this is my blood.' The life is in the blood, and shed blood secures atonement. Jesus surrendered his life, and as I share the bread and wine so I partake of that gift of life. Thank you, Jesus, that you live, and you live in me.

It was a feast of the *new* covenant, with the new heart and new spirit promised centuries before (e.g. Jeremiah 31:31-33). By that covenant Jesus is pledged to secure the fulfilling of his law in our lives. Therefore I dare not betray him nor count the blood of the covenant an unholy thing. Thank you, Jesus, for all you did for *me* on the Cross.

It was a feast of forgiveness. We come as sinners to the table to rejoice in his outpouring of love in forgiveness, for therein lies the entrance to all the treasures of his grace and power.

It was a feast of fellowship, for Calvary's sacrifice is for *many*. His blood was shed for all people everywhere, for all of time. Thank you, Jesus, that the 'many' includes me. I give you afresh my love and worship as I kneel before you to ask that you accept the willing offering of myself, body, soul and spirit, to be under your authority and lordship.

MARCH 31

GETHSEMANE

Luke 22:39-46

The walk from the upper room to the Garden was accompanied with singing (Matthew 26:30), probably Psalms 113-118, the Hallel, praise songs sung by pilgrims going up to Jerusalem. Strengthened by praise, Jesus led his friends to a place dear to him on the Mount of Olives, and the mood changed to one charged with uncertainty and impending doom. Jesus went to meet with his Father. The disciples met with sleep. In spite of previous boasting, the events of the day caught up with them, and they were overcome with exhaustion. Who are we to censure? How often, and for how long, have we kept watch with the Master?

The Lord was looking Calvary in the face, and as man he was overcome with the horror of it. He prayed so earnestly that the sweat – an evidence of fear and tension – fell down as blood. Would God answer and remove the bitter cup of suffering, of being made sin, of being forsaken by the Father? This was a battle that is quite beyond our comprehension as we watch from the sidelines. He prayed three times 'not my will but thine be done.' Satan must have slunk away then for victory was won, Jesus was fully in command of the situation, and he was strengthened by a messenger from Heaven (v. 43).

Never let us forget that the great battle for the souls of men was won during that time in Gethsemane. It was a conflict between Heaven and Hell, and Jesus was the one in the middle. Although cast down in anguish of spirit, knowing the physical suffering that was to follow, he arose from his knees triumphant, with clear eyes, resolute step, the Saviour of the world. May this fill your heart with praise and adoration.

APRIL 1

BETRAYAL!

Matthew 26:46-50

The actions of Judas are hard to understand – or are they? They can be a mirror reflecting the inmost conflicts of many Christians, but which in Judas' life grew to utter treachery. Look at Matthew's account. Jesus knew exactly what was about to happen, and whose hand had turned against him:

'My betrayer,' he said. And the most treacherous act of all:

'Judas came up to Jesus at once and said, 'Hail Master!' and kissed him.' Luke states Jesus said, 'Judas, would you betray the Son of man with a kiss?' (22:48). Matthew records the response of Jesus was also, 'Friend, why are you here?'

Although the Lord knew the end from the beginning, the grief of this betrayal must have been overwhelming. If we read all the references to Judas we can see how the Lord sought to win his love and loyalty, and save him from self-destruction. The man must ever remain a mystery. He had been with Jesus for at least two years, heard his wonderful words, seen his mighty deeds, beheld his blameless life – and now he betrayed him. He had already made his bargain (Matthew 26:14-16), and sold his Master for the price of a slave (see Exodus 21:32). His repentance (or was it just remorse?) came too late, and he ended his own tragic life (Matthew 27:3-10).

How can this dreadful story affect our lives? How do we betray our Lord? By keeping silent when we should bear witness to him; by insidious love of the things of the world and thereby denying his lordship over our lives in every area; by neglecting his Word and prayer. In so many ways moral kinship with Judas can be seen. May the Lord open our eyes to see where we are slipping and failing, bring us to our knees in repentance, and in earnestness claim the renewing of the Holy Spirit in our lives so we can truthfully say, 'If ever I loved Thee, Lord Jesus, 'tis now.'

APRIL 2

LOVE ON TRIAL

John 18:12-14, 19-24

Christ was led away by his captors, not because he was helpless, but because he was willing. It was not their fetters that bound him, but his love.

The so-called trial before the religious leaders, headed by Annas, was a farce. They questioned him about his doctrine and disciples (v. 19), not in order to believe, but in order to incriminate. Jesus pointed out that he had taught publicly, he was not a schemer behind locked doors, but a preacher out in the open. But these religious humbugs found it easier to strike Christ than to convict him (v. 22). Never was justice so grossly perverted as in these 'trials' of Jesus.

While Annas was conducting that initial 'enquiry' he was not himself any longer high priest, his son-in-law Caiaphas having that position at that time. Hence the meaning behind verses 22, 23, which led to Jesus being taken to Caiaphas. Yet what the Lord had said was irrefutable – he was either right or wrong, and it was for his accusers to decide which.

The Lord spoke very rarely throughout the various trials, but every word he said was significant. When we face challenging situations how do we respond? Often by anger and bluster, maybe, or do we allow the love of the Lord Jesus to shine through with the dignity, power and grace he manifested at the time of his total degradation?

APRIL 3

TRUTH ON TRIAL

John 18:28-38a

Pilate was in a dilemma for he knew the Jews wanted nothing less than the death sentence for Jesus, which they themselves were unable to pronounce. Here men's evil design and God's mercy dovetail, for while Jesus was put to death by men, he also died voluntarily.

So Pilate took Jesus aside for a private interview. Here Jesus stood before the Governor; one day Pilate will stand before Jesus Christ. The Roman was obviously perplexed, for he had heard the word 'king' applied to the prisoner, and questioned him about the truth of it. The Lord's answer must have seemed very enigmatic. To Pilate a king ruled on earth, so what and where was the kingdom being referred to? Jesus told him it is a spiritual kingdom based on *truth*. He himself is the Truth, born to bear witness to it, and all who respond to his message and his authority recognize that glorious fact. But Pilate couldn't – 'What is truth?' he asked. In the world of political intrigue in which he lived, he could well have doubted the meaning and existence of such a quality. Or was he wistfully expressing his inmost desire? It will never be fully known.

Do we know why we were born, and for what cause we are in the world? God has a plan for each one, and we can either frustrate or fulfil that plan. May we be found as those who hear the Word of the Lord, and thereby show we acknowledge Jesus Christ to be God's Way, Truth and Life, and the only entry into his Kingdom, here on earth as well as in the eternity of Heaven.

APRIL 4

THE PLOT THICKENS

John 18:38b-19:7

Pilate's justice was a mockery: 'I find no fault in him. But ...'
So he used a custom as a sop to his conscience and gave the
Jews a choice between a robber and a redeemer, and the people
did not hesitate. Those who a few days previously had been
shouting 'Hosanna' were now shrieking 'crucify'.

Are you ever presented with a choice between wholehearted
allegiance to Jesus and some lesser way of life? Any alternative
to him is always fatal. The disciples faced this in John 6:68, and
came up with the only life-giving response.

Pilate feebly sought to avoid a death sentence by scourging
Jesus, which act was followed by complete humiliation by the
soldiers. Perhaps this would satisfy the Jews, but no. Pilate had
observed their custom, now they insisted on their law for
blasphemy being observed – death, which they had no power to
carry out.

It appears that the Governor suddenly felt himself in the grip
of a web from which he could not extricate himself. This quiet,
dignified prisoner was accused not only of kingship but also of
deity. What could it all mean? In spite of having all the power of
Rome behind him, he was a feeble man, and powerless to cope
with such an immense and intricate problem.

As you read the records of the trial of Christ, meditate anew
on his bearing before his accusers, his silence and refusal to
defend himself, because he was fulfilling the prophecy
concerning him in Isaiah 53:7,8; remember it was 'in my place,
condemned, he stood', and thank him in adoration.

APRIL 5

THE SOURCE OF POWER

John 19:8-11

John records two incidents where Pilate took Jesus aside to question him privately. The first time was with regard to the Lord's claim to a kingdom, now it is in panic at the accusation made by the Jews. Three times Pilate declared he found no fault in Jesus, and his duty then was obvious: he should have pronounced him 'not guilty' and released him. But the judge was fast becoming the criminal, and the final accusation of the Jews, the sin of blasphemy, was the final nail in Jesus' coffin.

So he talked again to Jesus, and in his fear he chattered on about 'power'. It was a pathetic bluster, because everyone – the prisoner, the Jews, the people, Pilate himself – knew he was devoid of power. The only way left open to him was to yield to the clamour of people-power.

The frantic questions gave Jesus the opening for his final words. Read them carefully in verse 11. The power for his death sentence was in the hands of God. Pilate had no power over him or what was to happen to him, for Jesus was delivered up by the definite plan and foreknowledge of God (Acts 2:23). This was a mystery to Pilate, and it is to us, but we accept the glorious truth by faith and rejoice in its outcome, our eternal salvation.

APRIL 6

AN ALL-IMPORTANT QUESTION

Matthew 27:19-22

The heart of Christian experience is a question of relationship to God. Because that relationship is established through a person, and the answer to the question Pilate asked decides eternity, and is therefore more important than any other – than career, marriage, anything. It is not a question settled once for all at conversion, but one to be faced daily and hourly, and it must be remembered the direction faced by the answer to this question decides the destiny of the speaker. **The question? 'What shall I do with Jesus?'**

It was Pilate who first asked it in extraordinary circumstances. In the midst of the trial a servant came with a message from his wife. He was already at his wits' end at the complicated machinations of the accusers and, though judge, was himself being judged because of his inadequacies. Then his wife's warning in verse 19 after a terrifying but revealing dream, was almost the last straw. 'This righteous man', she called Jesus, and Pilate knew she was right, for he asked 'What evil has he done?' and no one gave concrete evidence, for there was none.

Under extreme pressure Pilate was in such a dilemma he knew not where to turn. He released Barabbas, but was left with Jesus, whom he knew to be innocent. So, ironically, the judge asked the prosecutors the all-important question, and he asked it in the first person, 'What shall I do with Jesus?' He knew what he ought to do, but fear chained him, and he completed the farce by trying to wash his hands of his part in the verdict. Poor Pilate, a wrong decision has made his name a byword throughout history. But have we sometimes done the same by our inconsistency when we claim to be disciples of Christ? The opposite of acceptance is rejection, and like Pilate, it is impossible to be inactive and sit on the fence.

APRIL 7

SENTENCE PASSED

John 19:12-16

The hour of which Jesus spoke is now sounding out. He stands alone, with regal dignity and divine calm, while accusers and judge wrangle over the final sentence. What a tragic farce!

Pilate had utter contempt for the Jews. He did not understand their outlook, their religion or history, or anything about them. But when they shouted the words that clinched the whole horrible procedure, he was shaking with terror and anger. Hear the low, menacing threat of verse 12, and Pilate's precipitous action. Showing Jesus to them as 'your King', they cry out 'away with him!' and finally disown the rule of God's Messiah, as Jesus himself predicted in the parable of Luke 19:14, where the citizens rejected the rule of the rightful landowner. See also John 1:11-13.

The sentence is passed in the terse words of verse 16: THEN he handed him over to them to be crucified. He, Pilate the Gentile; him, Jesus the Son of God and Saviour of the world; them, the Jews who were baying for his blood. The whole of mankind was involved in Calvary, and they are equally involved in being told the reason for the death of the sinless Son of God. Are we today sharing in that responsibility of proclaiming his saving grace? If not, what does Calvary mean deep down in our hearts? May the Lord give us a fresh view of his love and sacrifice for our redemption and total commitment.

APRIL 8

THE LONELINESS OF THE CROSS

John 19:17

The poignancy of these words! The soldiers took Jesus, he went out, *bearing his own Cross.* Yes, that was true at that moment in time, but it must always be remembered it is in fact *our* Cross, for he was to die for sins not his own.

In the early years of his life and of his ministry Christ was surrounded by crowds, some seeking healing, many to hear his words, people pressing to touch and see him. During the final months he became increasingly alone. Once he started talking about his death the crowds departed, the ranks of the disciples thinned (John 6:66-69), and finally they forsook him and fled (Matthew 26:56).

The soldiers and Jesus came to the place called Calvary He was about to solve the great problem of reconciliation between a holy God and sinful men. Now nobody could help, or sympathize, or understand. He alone, he only could bear the horror of the Cross. If sin is ever to be put away, if men are to be cleared from every trace of guilt and to be justified before God, Jesus must do this mighty work ALONE.

Loneliness is one of the main modern ailments. There are so many people today experiencing that, elderly folk housebound in high rise blocks with no one to talk to day after day. The tragic results of broken homes with the loneliness resulting from lost love and companionship. If any of us are in a lonely situation today, remember that Jesus has tasted it all too, and he knows just what it involves, though we can never share the depths he had to go, for he was rejected and despised on our account.

'There was no other good enough to pay the price of sin; HE ONLY...' Let that fact be always borne in mind as we gaze upon the Cross, and the lonely walk up Calvary's hill.

THE CENTRALITY OF THE CROSS

John 19:18

'There they crucified him.' Nothing more is said in the Gospel records of the actual act of crucifixion – the pain, the agony, the horror of it. Just four stark words to mark God's greatest act.

All highways of biblical truth lead to the Cross. The whole emphasis of the Gospel records is upon his death and not upon his life – the latter was ever leading to the former. All through Scripture God is pointing to Calvary: the Passover, the Temple worship, the Old Testament offerings and sacrifices. The Cross was no afterthought in God's mind, as 1 Peter 1:18-20 makes clear. From before the foundation of the world Calvary was planned. As Jesus walked and taught for three years, he was on a steady march to the great climax where every sin of man would be healed and forgiven, and the last enemy, death, overcome.

Jesus was the great and final Passover Lamb. Since the destruction of the Temple and the scattering of the Jews, while Passover is observed there is no sacrificial Lamb. When we look at Calvary, can we ever make light of sin? Nothing so reveals the depths of our lostness and the dreadful disease of sin which ravages all mankind, and shows there is no hope for anyone until we can say,

Nothing in my hand I bring,
simply to thy cross I cling.

That is the whole emphasis of the Gospel. Get on your knees in thankfulness, adoration and praise.

APRIL 10

FATHER, FORGIVE

Luke 23:32-38

Only Luke records this first 'word' of Jesus from the Cross, and it is a very revealing, all-embracing plea. There are people who listen anxiously and eagerly for the last words spoken by a dying loved one. In Scripture only three men spoke at their death: Jacob, the first of the nation Israel; Moses, the first under the Law; Stephen, the first martyr.

Seven times Jesus spoke from the Cross, and here is the first, almost immediately the Cross had been thrust into the socket. Note carefully, he prayed for those who murdered him, not only the soldiers but the crowds who milled around a place of execution, filled with blood-lust, yelling and shrieking. Included with the rabble were the priests, elders, scribes, all adding their mockery and derision. What horror, what tumult!

'Father, forgive them, for they know not what they do.' No doubt he prayed that also for Pilate and for those who had said, 'His blood be on our heads and on our children' (Matthew 27:25). They did not understand fully what they were doing, and as Jesus prayed at a time of excruciating agony, so weeks later God would answer that prayer, for Peter confronted the people after Pentecost saying, 'I know you acted in ignorance, as did your rulers... Repent', and many, including priests, turned to Christ as Lord (Acts 3:17; 4:4; 6:7).

Jesus is also praying for us today, as we sometimes act unthinkingly, in ignorance and disobedience. As we repent so his forgiveness flows into our hearts, in restoring and energizing power. If we are forgiven by him, so ought we to forgive one another so that the flowing of the Lord's love goes unhindered.

APRIL 11

TODAY... WITH ME

Luke 23:39-43

It is no doubt Luke's medical training that gave him eyes to note details. Matthew and Mark only note that the two criminals joined in reviling Jesus, whereas Luke records a man's conversion to Christ, in fact the first person to put faith for eternity in a crucified Lord.

Apart from four friends (John 19:25, 26), all the disciples had fled, while around the Cross the hostile, howling mob of priests, elders, scribes and ordinary people mocked and railed. But one man, and he a criminal, was given Holy Spirit insight to see who Jesus was and what he was accomplishing. Nothing is known of the man except that he was an evildoer. Now he hangs alongside Christ, in his own eyes justly condemned.

Suddenly something happened, and he spoke to the other criminal, 'Do you not fear God?' Amazing, for no doubt he had scarcely thought of God all his life. More amazing, he confessed his sinfulness and that of his fellow, but knew instinctively Christ had done nothing wrong.

All that man saw was a body bruised and broken, a crown of thorns, a title over the Cross, blood streaming from the wounds, all speaking of failure. Yet that man had seen the glory of God in the face of Jesus Christ, and knew he was who he claimed to be. 'Lord, remember me when you come in your kingly power.' Though the two figures were immovable, that man flung himself on Jesus and pleaded for mercy. And the Lord replied, 'Today *you* will be with *me* in Paradise.'

Picture Jesus returning to heaven with the first repentant sinner to be cleansed from his sin by the blood of the Cross! Today there will be those going that same route, from darkness to light, from death to life. Pray anew for those whom you are seeking to lead along that path to Jesus.

THEY STOOD AT THE CROSS

John 19:25b-27

There were four women and one disciple who are mentioned as those whose love enabled them to bear the horror of seeing the death of Jesus. One of the women was his own mother, Mary.

Picture her, maybe on John's arm, threading her way through the crowd to the very front of that awful Cross. Where now were those who wanted to make Jesus King? Where were all those whom he had healed? Where were the crowds who listened enthralled to his teaching? Above all, where were the other disciples? Fear kept them from Calvary; love drew Mary and John.

Yet what anguish must have been in her heart. Maybe she thought back to the words of Simeon (Luke 2:35), but nevertheless she showed great strength as she stood by the Cross. Surely this was supernatural strength given to her at such a time, both physically and spiritually, for there she was, making such a wonderful public confession of her love for, and faith in, her son, Jesus Christ.

Then Jesus spoke, commending her to the care of the beloved disciple, John. He was not one of the human family of Mary and Joseph, but was part of the family of God, redeemed by the merit of the death he was observing, no doubt with a mixture of great love and horror. Immediately he responded to the dying request of the Saviour, and Mary was part of his family from that day.

To experience the joy of service for Christ, like Mary and John we must be out in the open, standing by the Cross, for that is where he gives his blessing and strength to obey.

APRIL 13

FORSAKEN BY GOD?

Matthew 27:45-46

The crucifixion of Jesus took place at 9 a.m. and for three hours he endured the great uproar and clamour of the crowd which increased in intensity as the morning drew on (vv. 39-44). Then at midday for three hours darkness covered the land, and an awesome silence covered the people.

Jesus was fighting the powers of darkness with Satan at the helm: Genesis 3:15 was being fulfilled, and the conflict was at its height. Suddenly out of the darkness came the cry of verse 46. For six hours he had hung on that cross (what have you been doing during the last six hours, half a day?), and here is the crowning point of all his suffering, something that cannot be fully expressed in human thought or word.

That he was at that moment forsaken was real. Jesus called upon the Almighty not as his Father (as in Luke 23:46), but as MY GOD. Yet this cry shows his faith never faltered, for he knew that although forsaken, God was still there and was in control. Jesus knew God never wholly forsook his people. Yet it was a terrible experience for at that moment the sinless Son of God was bearing the sin of the whole world. He was the sacrificial Lamb, and God, who cannot look on evil, turned his face away from his Son. This is a fearful mystery, and we must approach it on our knees, literally and metaphorically.

We may feel at times that God is against us, but the truth is that we are pulling against his will, and we can immediately renew fellowship by confessing our sin and claiming the cleansing of the blood of Jesus (1 John 1:9). But Jesus had no sin to confess; he was bearing the punishment for our sins, and experiencing estrangement from the Father so that we can for ever know his acceptance and blessing. Thank you, Lord Jesus.

APRIL 14

THE REASON FOR HIS SUFFERING

Matthew 27:46; 1 Peter 2:24, 25

The cry from the Cross is a quotation from Psalm 22, which should be read at this time. It is not a cry against God, but to him. There can be no doubt Jesus knew why he was forsaken, yet it seemed that, being crushed and pounded, he must enquire the reason for so great a grief.

The Man of sorrows was overcome by sorrow, and the finite soul of Jesus the man came into awful contact with the infinite justice of God. In that sense he tasted death for us (Hebrews 2:9). What a strange word to use – taste – yet surely it implies that Jesus, who is eternal life, became the one – even the last one – who need ever feel or fear death. He tasted it so that we need never experience it, for death is eternal separation from God, and that was precisely what Jesus was experiencing at that moment of time. As Peter puts it, he was bearing in his own body our sins on the tree.

Perhaps the full implication of Calvary has not come to our spiritual knowledge so clearly before, therefore our prayer should be,

> The dearest idol I have known,
> whate'er that idol be,
> Lord, help me tear it from its throne
> and worship only thee.

CHRIST'S GREAT DESIRE

John 19:28,29

'I lay down my life that I may take it again. No one takes it from me. . . I have power to lay it down, and I have power to take it again' John 10:17, 18). That moment of laying down his life had come, for he knew that all was now finished in the great work of redemption, but there were yet two events still to take place.

The great Messianic Psalm 22 – which should be read – spoke so clearly of a crucifixion and the physical, mental and spiritual agony borne by the sufferer, of which thirst is part (v. 15). So after hours of suffering Jesus said, 'I thirst', and vinegar was given him (see Psalm 69:21).

The thirst of God is never quenched, and will not be until the final soul redeemed by the blood of Jesus is brought into his family. He thirsts for his people to be holy and perfect even as he is (Matthew 5:48), for he knows that is the way of fulfilment, joy and peace. He thirsts for our love and witness, that we are obedient to his call for service in his name whatever that might involve: is he being satisfied?

The thirst of the believer is quenched by the inflow of his Holy Spirit, the living water of which Jesus spoke. That is the satisfaction given until we gather in his presence, where the promise is, 'they shall hunger no more, neither thirst any more' (Revelation 7:16). In the meantime, how great is your thirst for God, and are you allowing him to satisfy it in his own perfect way?

A Prayer:
 I hunger and I thirst; Jesus my manna be:
 Ye living waters burst out of the rock for me!
J.S.B. Monsell

APRIL 16

CHRIST'S FINAL COMMITTAL

Luke 23:46

There is something so majestic in these final words of Jesus, also something miraculous. After the hours of agony, of thirst, of intense suffering, he cried out with a *loud* voice. This was no stammering, whispered committal, but a shout of triumph for all to hear.

'Father,' he said, no longer sensing isolation from God, but the work of atonement being accomplished, he was communing with his Father. He had completed God's plan for his life, and his work on earth was done. Jesus has shown all men in all time that God the Creator is our heavenly Father too, a relationship that is everlasting, that distance cannot sever, suffering cannot alter, and death can only secure: are you enjoying that privilege?

'My spirit', said Jesus – the real person, Jesus, went out of the flesh in which he had dwelt for thirty-three years, and heaven celebrated the victory. He came from the Father, and he returned to the Father. Death henceforth has no terror.

'Into thy hands,' said Jesus. This is a fulfilment of Psalm 31:5, and no doubt the Scriptures were stored up in his mind and heart, for he constantly drew on the promises and prophecies. From the hands of sinful men who had done what they would with the Lord (see Matthew 17:22; Acts 2:23), he yielded himself to his Father's hand.

The reputation of Jesus is in the hands of his followers today. The life of every believer is in the Lord's hands. Think on these things, and pray that at any moment when God's call comes to you, you may be ready to commit your spirit into his hands for all eternity.

THE FINAL ACT

John 19:28-30

The final commitment, linked to Luke 23:46, ended the sufferings of the Son of God. The work of redemption is finished, completed. He did what he came to do, for it cannot be stressed enough that his death was not a surprise to him, for he came to die. He was sinless, therefore deathless, but 'in my place condemned he stood, sealed my pardon with his blood'. It was his will to die, for he said, 'I lay down my life.' He assumed it when he pleased, he retained it while he chose, he dismissed it when he would. Here is absolute power linked with divine love.

Finished! Death is conquered and Satan defeated.

Finished! In Hebrews 12:2 it is written that Jesus is the pioneer and perfecter (finisher, AV) of our faith, who for the joy that was set before him endured the Cross, despising the shame, and is seated at the right hand of God. Note the significant words: joy, endured, despised, shame, seated. This statement sums up all that Calvary means, and our precious Lord went through all the experiences of shame and suffering that he might return as victor to heaven, and bring with him multitudes whom no man can number, redeemed by his precious blood. He is the perfecter, the finisher, of our faith, the one who went all the way to Calvary.

Get on your knees in worship as you say to him, Hallelujah, what a Saviour – and he is mine!

APRIL 18

STRANGE SCENES

Matthew 27:51

If Jesus was only a man, then his death is inexplicable, for it was accompanied by some startling evidences of the fact that this was the death of none other than the Son of God who, in his dying, had accomplished a mighty deliverance for humanity.

Here is one significant sign, the rending of the veil in the Temple. The Jewish Tabernacle in the wilderness, and later the Temple in Jerusalem were both in three parts: the Outer Court, open to all; the Holy Place where the priests offered the daily sacrifices; the Holy of Holies where the High Priest entered only once a year on the Day of Atonement. Between these last two sections hung the veil, a beautiful curtain, shutting sinful man out of God's holy presence, wrapping him in mystery and inaccessibility.

The moment Jesus died, when the great cry rang out, 'It is finished!' that veil was taken by mighty hands and torn asunder from the top to the bottom. Note the direction, for by human hands it would have been torn from the bottom upwards.

Praise him, this means that the barrier between man and God is no more. No longer is the Almighty hidden in mystery, but is now revealed through his Son who, with wide open arms, welcomes us into his very presence. Jesus plainly said he is the way into the Father's presence, and that those who have seen Jesus have seen God (John 14:6-9). Forgive the repetition, but it is only sin which excludes us, but when we fully understand that Jesus has carried our individual sins, then we come with boldness before the Father (Hebrews 4:15, 16). Thank him for this with a full heart, and claim your access to the throne in Heaven because the veil is rent now that sin has been dealt with on Calvary.

APRIL 19

LOW IN THE GRAVE HE LAY

John 19:31-42

The last act of a crucifixion was to bring hasty death to the sufferers usually by breaking their legs, which was done to the two thieves. At the request of the Jews this occurred on the same day, because the Sabbath was approaching. When the soldiers came to Jesus they found him *already dead*. Note those words, for they categorically refute any suggestion that he merely swooned. His legs were therefore not broken (see Exodus 12:46), but the soldiers pierced his side, from which came blood and water. How minutely God fulfils prophecy! In Zechariah 12:10 and Revelation 1:7 it is definitely stated that the Jews would look on him who was *pierced*. The blood is a cleansing power, water a quickening power, the symbol of the Holy Spirit.

A second request was made by a secret disciple, Joseph of Arimathea who, together with Nicodemus, begged Pilate for the body of Jesus. They now lavish upon him the love which he could have done with while he was alive, but better late than not at all. May God forbid that I should be a secret disciple.

The two men, both wealthy rulers of the people, bore the body to a tomb already prepared within a rock, and lovingly laid it to rest, with no other thought than that would be their Master's final resting-place. But Jesus is now alive! Give him the love and devotion due, and show your thankfulness to him that you are now part of his body, the Church, his called-out ones.

THE FINALITY OF THE STONE

Mark 15: 42-47

While Joseph of Arimathea lovingly prepared the body of Jesus for the grave, two women watched anxiously, for they longed to show their love by embalming the body as soon as the Sabbath ended. To their dismay they saw the huge stone rolled across the mouth of the grave. What a symbol of the end of all their hopes and dreams! Suddenly there was no Jesus, no beloved Master and Teacher, and their grief knew no bounds.

If the stone for the disciples meant they could not reach Jesus for they could not get *into* the tomb, the authorities wanted to make sure the body of Jesus would never get *out*. The priests went to Pilate with an extraordinary request. The words 'three days' burned in their hearts, though seemingly were never understood by the disciples. So a seal on the stone and a guard to protect the tomb from body-snatchers were granted (Matthew 27:62-66).

Not only was the body of Jesus dead inside the grave, hidden by the great stone, but all his preaching, his revelation of the Fatherhood of God, all his teaching of love and grace, mercy and justice, peace and truth and righteousness, shown in his very person – all were now dead. The past three years were like a dream, and now they were living a nightmare.

In these days too it is possible for a believer to feel cut off from the presence of the Saviour, when the joys of close fellowship with him seem to have departed. Whose fault is that? A husband and wife were driving together in the car, and the wife recalled the days of courtship when they had been so close that her boyfriend was able to have only one hand on the wheel. So she said to her husband, 'Why is this space between us now?' To which he replied with a smile, 'I haven't moved!' And neither has God.

THE MESSAGE OF THE STONE

Mark 16:4

Early in the morning the two Marys returned with their spices and oil thinking fearfully of the stone when, looking up, they saw it was rolled back. The delivering angel had terrified the guards, who rushed to H.Q. to tell the news (Matt 28: 11-15). To the women he gave the message of the now risen Lord Jesus, and they too hastened back to base to pass on the good news and reassure the disciples.

Yes, the 'very large' stone was rolled back, not that Jesus might pass out of the tomb, but to show he had gone. The grave was empty! There were undisturbed grave clothes, lying just as they had been around his dead body, and the napkin that bound his head was by itself where his head had lain. There is no doubt that his rising was miraculous, for he disregarded shroud, rock, and every material thing that could have hindered him.

The message of the stone is HE IS RISEN! Death could not keep its prey, Satan's power was incapable of killing Jesus and destroying him forever. The power of God is absolute, and his sign of approval on the obedience of his Son, even to death on the Cross, was his glorious resurrection. He was not just revived, but now lives for evermore in the glory of Heaven and the presence of his Father.

A Prayer: Dear Lord Jesus, thank you for showing to all that your return to life was truly from death itself, and is made clear by many infallible proofs. One of these proofs is that you now live in my heart, and I thank you for your presence with me, and the power of the Holy Spirit to enable me to live by your resurrection might.

APRIL 22

LOVE REWARDED

John 20:1-18

The interview between Mary and her Master is recorded by John, who was there also with Peter, viewing the empty tomb. When Mary reported to the disciples her amazing discovery, Peter and John were off like a shot, and seeing, believed. Yet how ignorant they were! In verse 2 they did not know *where* he was; in verse 9 they did not know the Scriptures; in verse 14 Mary did not know *who* he was. Are we also lacking in understanding the fundamentals of the faith?

The two men returned to their homes, but Mary stayed on. She was deeply disturbed, not knowing where her Lord could be if he was not in the tomb. Who had taken his body, and where was it now? Her love was rewarded in a special way, because she was the first to see the risen Lord and to be commissioned by him.

At first she failed to recognize Jesus until he spoke her name. She fell at his feet to hold him, but he forbade her, 'cease touching me', he said. She was no longer to cling to him, but prepare herself for the time when he was ascended to his Father, and she would henceforth live by faith and not by sight and touch.

Jesus is seen and known today in the hearts of his followers because the Holy Spirit has been given for that very reason. He is the seal, the earnest of our inheritance as children of God, and he imparts to us the knowledge of Jesus as Saviour and Lord, as by his inspiration the Scriptures are opened up to us. For us, that is the reward of our love for and devotion to the Lord, and what more do we need?

APRIL 23

PEACE REPLACES FEAR

John 20:19-31

Though they knew Jesus had risen from the dead, the bewildered disciples were huddling in fear behind locked doors in Jerusalem. Suddenly he was in their midst, with words of peace on his lips. He was no phantom, but a spiritual body (see 1 Corinthians 15:44).

This meeting was a fulfilment of the promises made by the Lord in his final discourses. He imparts his peace, and their joy is fulfilled. It is not hard to imagine the great release of spirit the men experienced as they were freed from their fear. Then came the Lord's commissioning of them as he breathed power into them in anticipation of the Holy Spirit's indwelling at Pentecost.

One man, however, was missing, Thomas, who just could not believe what had happened to the others. 'Except I see ... I will not believe', he said. Then the Lord was with them again, challenging Thomas to place his finger in the nailprints, and replace doubt with certainty. Did Thomas ever touch Jesus? We don't know, but are told he worshipped and recognized Jesus as Lord and God. The final word is for all those who come to faith in the Saviour without having seen or touched him. True faith rises above the necessity of being shown tangible proofs of the passion. If you are trusting in Jesus because his truth has been revealed to you by faith, you are truly blessed.

APRIL 24

LIFE AFTER DEATH

1 Corinthians 15:12-22

The title could end in a question mark, to be answered True or False. No one could avoid the fact of death, so why bother to think about it? Eat, drink and be merry while there is opportunity. So says the hedonist, and against that is the word of Jesus, 'I am the Resurrection and the Life.' This claim has an implication upon everyone: 'Do you believe this?' The concept of resurrection challenges modern thought, and gives the lie to atheism. If Christ rose again and is alive, why say there is no life after death?

The Risen Christ is a fact (vv. 12, 20). Men have repeatedly tried to prove the resurrection to be a fallacy, but cannot. It is the greatest attested fact in history, and some who sought to disprove it ended by being so convinced they committed their lives by faith to the living Saviour. The fact of his resurrection is proved by Christians who can say, 'He lives in me'. There is no answer to those who claim to walk and talk with Jesus, who know the reality of his presence and power, and who take the Bible as the living Word of God.

Nothing can deal with human defeat except the power of Christ, who lives and reigns forever. No militant unbeliever or atheist can ever testify to a power that can change human lives, enable people to turn from despair, ruin, degradation, to a life of radiant joy and peace, with an urge to share this with others. Only the resurrection power of Christ can do this. Read carefully Romans 8:11 and rejoice in the liberating and enabling power of God's Holy Spirit.

RESURRECTION AND ME

1 Corinthians 15:50-57

Consider now the significance of the Risen Christ. Jesus had power which took him right through death. Because there was no sin *in* him, only the weight of sin he bore *for us* made it possible for him to die in the first place. The sentence given by God on the disobedience and sin of Adam was death – separation from God (see Genesis 3:16). All through subsequent history sin was atoned for by the shedding of blood. Now Calvary has purchased redemption for all who believe, and more than that, through Christ's resurrection, when a believer dies, he or she goes directly into God's presence.

Think too of the challenge of the Risen Christ. At death, taken into God's presence – are we ready for that? No wonder Paul concludes this chapter with the exhortation of verse 58. Salvation is not through works, however good they may be, but our behaviour and mode of living should be the outcome of faith, a life lived for the glory of God by the power of the living Christ, and not for selfish ends.

Fear of death comes through unbelief or unconfessed sin. The risen Lord Jesus is the way of victory, right through the dark portals of death straight into the glory of Heaven. Well might we ask where now is the sting of death or its victory, for that has been gained and given to us by the raising of Jesus from the dead.

Again and again we proclaim Hallelujah, what a Saviour!

APRIL 26

A LIFE-CHANGING ENCOUNTER

Luke 24:13-53

The wonderful story of the encounter on the road to Emmaus between the risen Lord and two downcast disciples is so very well-known one must rely on the Holy Spirit to bring out new thoughts and lessons.

When the Lord joined himself to them, he asked what they were talking about, for they were so sad. Amazed at the question, they thought he must be a stranger in the area, so they told him of all that had happened 'concerning Jesus of Nazareth'. They knew all the facts and they knew all about him, but they did not know him. How true this can be of some present-day followers of a person they know about historically, but not personally.

The Lord saw their distress and sensed their heart-hunger, and three things happened: he opened up the Scriptures (v.27); he opened their eyes to see him (v. 31); he opened their hearts to receive the truth (v. 32).

At last they knew him, their risen Lord and Saviour, and four things occurred. First the Scriptures came alive, as from Moses and the prophets Jesus showed them all that had been said about himself. How much do you know about the truths of the Old Testament revealed in the New?

This knowledge, which opened their eyes, gave them a message (v. 35). The reality of a person's faith is shown in their desire to share it with others. Is this true of you?

Meeting the living Lord gave them a purpose (v. 33). Instead of continuing their journey they returned to Jerusalem to tell the other disciples their amazing experience. Thus they were present when Jesus came among them, and their hearts were filled with joy (v. 41). From sorrow to joy! Such is the experience of those who walk in fellowship with Jesus Christ. May it be ours today and for all time.

JOY AND GLADNESS

John 20:19-23

It is hard for us to imagine the experiences the disciples were passing through during what we call Good Friday and Saturday, right through to Easter morning. Try to put yourself in their position of doubt, fear, despair, etc.

Suddenly he is with them, and '*then* the disciples were glad when they saw the Lord.' Is that a deliberate understatement?

They had the assurance of sins forgiven, 'he showed them his hands and his side', for the price was paid. There is no joy for the believer apart from Jesus risen from the dead, and knowingly alive in experience. If he had remained in the grave his death was worthless. A dead Saviour could not help those who trusted him; a risen Christ proves that his sacrifice for our sin was accepted.

They also had the assurance of constant companionship: 'he breathed on them...' His life given means a living Friend whose arm will hold us in weakness and defend us in temptation, whose presence will keep us from sin, who will plan our steps, order our lives, and because of his life in us, will bring that life through death. Do you know the Lord in such an intimate and positive way?

They had the assurance too of triumphant service. 'As the Father has sent me, even so I send you.' How had the Father sent the Son? To suffer on behalf of others; with holy love for all men; with authority over the powers of evil, and in many other life-changing ways. Are you willing for the Lord to use you in his service, as his witness, in this way?

THE ASCENSION

Mark 16:19

Only Mark and Luke record this momentous occasion. The Lord's work on earth is completed; his victory over death is confirmed in the presence of many people on many occasions (1 Corinthians 15:3-8). Now the next act in the drama of redemption is to take place. 'Jesus . . . was taken up to heaven, and sat down at the right hand of God.'

He is there as God's perfect man. Never had there been an arrival in Heaven as this. All others had found salvation through sacrifice, but Jesus came into his Father's presence in his own right. He needed no mediator to ask for mercy. He passed from earth to Heaven as perfect MAN, and stood unafraid in all the glory of eternity.

He is there as man's wounded God, for he bears the marks of Calvary. They tell of a penalty borne for the sins of the world. They tell of victory won over the powers of darkness and death. When work presses, burdens are greater than we can bear, days are weary and nights are long, how wonderful to know we face defeated foes, for the Son of man is in the place of power, and the Son of God is touched with the feeling of our weaknesses.

A Prayer: Lord Jesus, I thank you that you are today in the place of all power and authority. When my situation is dark, and events happen which I cannot understand, I thank you I can lift my eyes to see you as my victorious Lord, enabling me to do all things through your power within me.

APRIL 29

THE PROMISE OF POWER

Acts 1:8-11

How do you think Jesus felt when he knew he was about to return to his Father? He was leaving a few very ordinary men behind to continue to spread the Good News, so he devoted his final six weeks on earth to intensive teaching and training. The main message was concerning the coming of the Holy Spirit to empower and enable these men for the daunting task before them. His personal presence was required no more on earth, and a cloud of angels lifted him from earth to Heaven in the sight of his disciples.

Remember that through the merit of his blood and by virtue of his death, men are restored to God. Through his ascension and the gift of the Holy Spirit God is restored to men in order to administer the virtue of his life in all of us. The fellowship which sin ruined is restored, for not only did Jesus bridge a mighty gulf at Calvary, but he repaired a dreadful breach as he returned to Heaven in order to pour out the Spirit's power (John 7:39). In this way he created a fellowship never known before, 'Christ *in* us, the hope of glory' (Colossians 1:27).

What response can I bring to such a Saviour but to say I 'crown him Lord of all'!

APRIL 30

REDEMPTION COMPLETE

Revelation 5:1-14

This is the final picture of God's plan of redemption, and we are ourselves transported into Glory in this amazing account of John's vision.

First he saw a Book (vv. 1-5), which has to do with redemption, in the light of Jesus' words 'lift up your heads, your redemption is drawing near' (Luke 21:28), a yet future event when those redeemed through his shed blood are finally in the Father's presence. No one was found able to approach the Book, or worthy to undo the seals, and John wept in sorrow until an elder spoke to him, and he saw the only one able to fulfil the task. This mighty one was introduced as the Lion of the tribe of Judah.

As John watched to behold a Lion, he saw a Lamb, the one who had overcome sin, hell, the terrors of death, whom John had seen on that Easter day, alive from the dead, and had later watched as he returned to Heaven. The Lamb, who is also the Lion, has snapped every chain of sin, and is the Redeemer who presents himself before the Throne to claim back our inheritance, enclosed in the Book. He stood, though bearing the marks of death, the resurrected Christ alive for evermore. He alone was worthy to take the Book, and immediately a resounding burst of praise reverberated through the courts of Heaven. What rejoicing! All other sacrifice for sin is over, God's plan of redemption is complete. Jesus, our Saviour, Lord, Master, is the one worthy to receive the rejoicings of all the heavenly host and those redeemed by his precious blood.

'Worthy is the Lamb who was slain to receive. . . honour, glory, blessing' (v. 12). What does he receive from us? On your face before him, give to him all that is due to him from the limited expressions of a human heart and language.

THE SPIRIT OF CHRIST

MAY 1

THE PROMISE OF THE HOLY SPIRIT

John 14:15,16

The Spirit of Christ is the theme for the next two months, with the celebration of Pentecost. Therefore let us concentrate first on the teachings of Christ himself on the Holy Spirit as given to us in the Gospel of St John.

Christ is about to leave his disciples and he has much to teach them, but the concepts are so new the men find it hard to understand the implications so far as they are concerned. Many believers are like that too, so it is good to go back to the basics, the groundroots of faith.

First Jesus assured these apprehensive men that he had made adequate provision for them during his absence. To experience this the conditions never alter: love and obedience. These are counted on by the Lord as the basis of discipleship. Do we fail him on these two vital responses?

In verse 16 the Trinity is mentioned. As elsewhere Christ, without hesitation, associates himself with the Father and the Spirit in a way that can only mean that he too is God. Remember that when you are faced with doubters who deny his deity. Here is evidence also of the personality of the Spirit. Not an 'it', but 'he', the substitute on earth for the bodily presence of Jesus.

Here is the first promise of the Counsellor. The Greek meaning is 'one called alongside to help', a legal expression, hence the word 'advocate' in 1 John 2:1. The function of the Spirit is to convince (John 16:8), to bear witness to Jesus (15:26), to teach (14:26). How we need him to work in our lives constantly, that we are kept in tune with the purpose of God.

MAY 2

AT HOME IN THE HEART

John 14:17-24

As will be seen, Jesus refers more than once to 'the spirit of Truth', but in verse 17 a totally new concept is revealed. Jesus said the Spirit dwells *with* you, and will be *in* you. In Old Testament times the Spirit 'came upon' people, and up to this moment that too had been the experience of the disciples. At Pentecost they were indwelt by the Spirit, he was *in* them.

In verses 22-24 the Lord emphasized the truth he had stated in verse 15. The condition of heart for receiving the Spirit is based on love for him and obedience to him. If only we could really understand that these are the two responses Jesus longs for, and when he sees them then he fulfils his promise. This is so clear in verse 23: if a man . . . then we will come. So many Christians fail right here. They want the power, but are not willing to pay the price. They offer time, talents, money, and all they can think of (and rightly so), but neglect the first principles of total love and obedience laid at the feet of Jesus. Frances R. Havergal had it right in her great hymn of consecration, 'Take my life'. The following verses are an offering up of every part of the personality, but the crunch comes in the last verse, 'Take *myself*, and I shall be ever only, all for Thee.' Until Jesus has our SELF, he does not have all of us. Therefore he is not free to come and make his home *in* us. Until he is *there*, we will never experience all he is longing to give to us, and to impart the mighty power of his Spirit into our feeble lives. What love, what grace, what condescension! Oh Lord, enlarge our capacity for you, and may you be at home in our lives through your indwelling Spirit.

MAY 3

THE TEACHER

John 14:25, 26;15:26, 27

What a comfort to know that the Holy Spirit makes the Word of God clear to us! The Psalmist prayed in words we should all use as we read the Bible: 'Open my eyes, that I may behold wondrous things out of thy law' (Psalm 119:18). Ask him each day to show you his 'wondrous things'.

In John 14:26 the whole New Testament is the schoolbook of the Spirit. The Gospels were written because the words and work of Jesus were brought to the apostles' remembrance. The Epistles were written because the Spirit would teach all things. The final book, the Revelation, was written because the Spirit would 'declare . . . things that are to come' (16:13).

In days of disbelief and blatant atheism, when false cults and doubtful teaching abound, the Christian must be on the alert to avoid being deceived, and to test every new teaching in the light of 1 John 4:1-3.

It is the Spirit who teaches us to witness (15:26, 27). Our witness can be powerful only as it is informed and inspired. It is to *Christ* and of him that the Spirit, through the disciples, bears witness. To speak rightly and effectively of him it is necessary that we be *with him* (v. 27) and know him in an ever-deepening way. It was Peter and John who said, 'We cannot but speak of what we have seen and heard' (Acts 4:20). How often believers today omit the word 'but', and fail to witness to what they know of Jesus for fear of being challenged on what they don't know. If that is your problem read the study verses again, carefully and prayerfully, and seek the wisdom and love of the Holy Spirit to teach all truth.

MAY 4

THESE THINGS

John 16:4-11

The teachings Jesus was giving the disciples at this time were critically important, and his repetition of the words 'these things' emphasize that (14:25; 15:11; 16:4, 6). He now tells the disciples that the ministry of the Spirit is conditioned upon his own departure from them, and his teaching was according to their capacity to understand (v. 12). That is true in our situation today, and is in fact a fundamental principle of all teaching.

When Jesus ascended, his immediate presence gave way to his universal presence. Therefore his departure was 'to your advantage' (v. 7), hard though it was for the disciples to believe it. We have not lost, but gained, by his return to Heaven in the giving of his Spirit: 'if I go, I will send him to you', was his promise.

'And when he comes' (v. 8) he will commence his ministry to the world. His great work is in regard to sin, righteousness and judgement of the past. The Holy Spirit is essential to salvation, for the Christian life begins with the miracle of the new birth, and is intended to continue by the mighty power of the Spirit. The miracle is that Jesus became sin on our behalf so that we may be clothed with his righteousness (2 Corinthians 5:21). The only good thing about any of us is Jesus. He does not alter human nature; he alters the mainspring and gives us a new heredity.

Take good heed to these things that the Master taught, and allow him to work them out in your personal experience.

THE PRIORITY OF THE SPIRIT

John 16:12-15

In these verses is detailed the ministry of the Holy Spirit to the Christian, that is, to each one of us. Note carefully and prayerfully what it is, for it may be necessary to adjust one's life afresh to God's truth.

The Holy Spirit is essential to understand Scripture (John 14:26; 16:13). This has already been discussed, but the repetition shows the importance Christ places on a right interpretation of biblical truths.

The Holy Spirit is essential to make Jesus real to the believer (John 15:26,27; 16:14, 15). The Spirit does not bring glory to himself, but always points to Jesus. 'He will glorify me', said Jesus, and he emphasizes that point in both passages of Scripture, for 'he will bear witness to ME'. Yes, the Spirit makes much of Jesus, and the believer must open his heart increasingly to make that real in his own life.

The Holy Spirit is essential in evangelism to others (vv. 7-11). Because Satan has blinded men's hearts (2 Corinthians 4:4), only the revelation of the Spirit can convict of sin and reveal Jesus as Lord and Saviour. This happened in Peter's witness in Acts 4:8; with Barnabas in Acts 11:24; with Paul in Acts 13:9 – each of them was filled with the Spirit. Unless we have that empowering our words are weak and futile and then Satan is at hand to mock our efforts and discourage us until our lips are closed.

May the Lord open our understanding to see how dependent we are upon the ministry of the Holy Spirit in our lives, so that we may bring to Jesus the glory due to him.

MAY 6

FACING A NEED

Acts 1:1-14

A reading of the book of Acts raises the question, what was the secret of the apostles' power in their achievement? Before answering that, look at the situation prior to Pentecost.

Acts 1 is a watershed between dispensations, with Christianity about to replace Judaism, and worldwide blessing to take the place of national pride. Verse 1 unlocks the book as the writer, Luke, refers back to his Gospel where he told what Jesus *began* to do and teach. His birth, life, teaching, death and resurrection were only the beginning of God's purpose. Of course the work of redemption was complete, but the full plan in the mind of the Father was as yet incomplete. We do not worship a dead leader but a living Lord, who now works in power through his body on earth, the Church. He said it was necessary for him to leave earth and return to the Father. How confined he would have been had he remained here! But now in all parts of the world, in church and chapel, cathedral and grass church, in homes and wherever two or three gather in his name, he is there.

His departure was not sunset but sunrise! What Jesus accomplished in the Gospels and what he continues now to do is that once he worked on earth, now he works in Heaven by his Spirit in and through every child of God, his called-out ones. That is his way of saving the world, but oh, how we have failed. The believers in Acts 1 faced a need. So do we. Once substitutes are found for the Holy Spirit we are ineffective and helpless. May we heed the warnings, and seek earnestly to know his power, available for our need, so long as we recognize we are impotent without him.

MAY 7

EVANGELIZE OR PERISH!

Acts 1:8

The title has often been used as a rallying cry, and is needed again in these days. The Church's only reason for existence is to witness to the Lord Jesus in a lost world. That is true for every believer, but how to do this is the question.

The message of Acts 1 is the link between what Jesus began to do and teach while here on earth, and what he continues to do and teach after Pentecost. From now on the life and power of God would be within human lives. The Lord on the throne of Heaven becomes Lord on the throne of human hearts; that is his purpose, but how much is that being realized in the actual experience of Christians today? Are we really living in close communion with Jesus?

The purpose of the coming of the Holy Spirit is to give divine power for the task of witnessing to a crucified, risen Saviour. All that he was to be to his disciples personally in comforting, teaching, sanctifying, praying, was a means to an end – to endue them with power for service. That is the full impact of verse 8 and how we need to grasp it.

Waste of power is a tragedy. God does not waste the great power of his Spirit on those who want it simply for their own sake, to be more holy, or good, or gifted. His great task is to carry on the work for which Jesus sacrificed his throne and his life – the redemption of fallen humanity. Wisdom, goodness, holiness, gifts, are all part of the enduement of the Spirit to those who live in love and obedience to the plan of God. So often Christians are more anxious to know what the Holy Spirit can give *them* than they are to fulfil the task for which Christ has redeemed them, which is to evangelize or to see folk perish. May the Lord enable us even in these difficult days to rise up to the challenge of fullness in our lives in preparation for obedience to his will.

THE PURPOSE OF POWER

Acts 1:8

The word power is used so often in connection with the Holy Spirit that it is necessary to define its meaning and its effect in our lives. It is certainly not power for power's sake, like a generator or engine. We may want power for power's sake, but that is not what we need as Christians, nor is it what the Spirit has been given to impart to us. Man's search for power starts on the assumption that man is OK. God's offer of power assumes that man is all wrong, and only the Holy Spirit can effect a radical refit.

There are two words translated power: *dunamis*, from which the words dynamo and dynamic come; and *exousia*, which means authority. Jesus said, 'All power (authority) is given to me,' and 'you shall receive power (*dunamis*)'. So what is the power Christ offers, and how does it work in our daily lives:

There is power for weakness in Philippians 4:13, 'I can do all things through Christ who dynamites me'. There is no such word as *cannot* for the Christian.

There is power for warfare in Ephesians 6:10, again *dunamis,* while in 2 Corinthians 10:3,4 the believer is given authority in the battle.

There is power for a daily walk in Colossians 1:11, for we are strengthened with all *dunamis* – why? to walk worthy of the Lord (v. 10).

There is power for witness in Acts 1:8, and isn't that the power we need? For the Gospel is the *dunamis* of God to everyone who has faith (Romans 1:16). No wonder Paul was proud of the message he preached, and unashamed to glory in the name of Christ.

MAY 9

HIS WITNESSES

Acts 1:8

'You shall be my witnesses', said Jesus. These words graphically describe the purpose of his coming. It is the work of the Holy Spirit *in* us to be a witness *through* us to the risen Lord Jesus. Only the Spirit can make us witnesses because he is the supreme witness (John 15:26, 27).

A witness is, of course, one who testifies to what he has seen, heard, and experienced. We are to witness to our personal knowledge of Jesus. A person may know intellectually the history of the Bible, what it teaches about Jesus, whom he may admire immensely, but that does not make him an effective witness to the power and blessing of Jesus in his life. It is the presence of the Spirit now, at this moment, giving testimony to the presence of a personal Saviour that gives our witness that breath of life from Heaven, which alone can convince the listener of the reality of the truth he is hearing. You can only witness to as much of Christ as the Holy Spirit is witnessing to you in life and power NOW.

It is absolutely vital to have a moment by moment relationship with Jesus, and that is another aspect of the work of the Spirit. It is he who makes Christ real to us, who challenges us as we read the Bible, who is at hand to encourage our prayer life, and who equips us for whatever service he has planned for us. This is all shown in action through the early apostles in the pages of what should be called 'The Acts of the Holy Spirit through the Apostles'. May this be continuing even today, as the Spirit has free range to work in and through *our* lives.

THE EXTENT OF WITNESS

Acts 1:6-8

The disciples were still hankering after an earthly kingdom, hence their question in verse 6. NOW was important to them, for what was to be their immediate future? Jesus did not rebuke them, for the kingdom will come one day. He said, in effect, they were not to be concerned with a programme, but with power, which he was about to give them. They had no idea how he was going to fulfil his plan, no conception of the mission to which they were called. Only the events of Pentecost would teach them that they had a vital part to play, and that *through them* and all believers since, Jesus was going to win. No matter how hard the battle, we are on the victory side with Christ.

The first area of witness was their home situation, and everyone starts there, in 'Jerusalem'. To fail there can mean to fail elsewhere. But note that no Christian is to be parochial, but to have a worldwide vision. The commission the Lord gave had no 'or' but 'and' – Jerusalem *and* Judea. Not everyone can go into every part of the world in person, but the Spirit-led believer should know what God is doing in every nation, even though he may be based in his 'Judea' and not able to travel far. Those who work in, or have a great interest for say, Africa, should also be aware of the Spirit's working in the Far East or the Americas, for their encouragement, learning, and above all, prayer.

To think about: So many are content to stay in Jerusalem, and have never asked the Lord for his plan for career or service. The power of his Spirit is not given to enable a Christian to live an easy, self-centred life, but to witness to him – worldwide.

MAY 11

THE DAWN OF A NEW ERA

Acts 2:1-5

The book of Acts demonstrates first, that the Holy Spirit is sent to be to Christians all that the Lord would have been had he remained on earth, and could be a personal companion to each one. Secondly, believers are intended to be to the world what the Holy Spirit is to us. He comes to teach the truth, to testify to the Saviour, and to glorify him, and that is our job on earth.

Pentecost was the beginning of a new enterprise in God's programme. It was necessary because the redemption purchased by Jesus at Calvary was to be transmitted to the world, but this could only be done through those who knew and trusted him. For that task a special enduement of God's power was necessary in the lives of weak and spiritually ineffective men.

So in God's timing it happened, and the Spirit came on a group of very ordinary people who for days had gathered for prayer at the Lord's command. See the signs which were given, not for their sakes, but to draw the attention of the populace. 'A sound . . . like a mighty wind', 'tongues as of fire'. When the sound was heard the people rushed together (v. 6), and their attention was arrested. These signs were never repeated because they were never again necessary. The inward manifestation of Holy Spirit life in the lives of the disciples took the outward expression of his coming.

The disciples immediately spoke in other tongues, in order to communicate with the foreigners in Jerusalem at the time of the feast, to spread the Good News far and wide. Messiah has come! His Spirit is given to all those who believe, so praise him with Hallelujahs!

THE EFFECT ON THE CROWDS

Acts 2:6-13

As the people rushed to the area where the Spirit-filled disciples were, they exhibited various reactions. They were amazed (vv. 7, 12). For a brief time the people turned from other interests to listen, for something had happened which they could not explain. They were amazed and wondered: that is not worship, but it is the first step toward it. If wonder ceases, so does worship.

They were bewildered and perplexed, for they were in doubt. Amazement meant they didn't know; bewilderment meant they knew they didn't know. To be aware of ignorance is the first step toward the place of discovery. 'What can this mean?' (v. 12) was the enquiry which led to Peter's explanation.

They mocked and criticized. Because they couldn't understand, the people sought a logical conclusion – the disciples must be drunk. There was a new light in their eyes, a new urgency and passion in their words, therefore they were filled with wine! To be Spirit-filled can produce ecstatic effects, for Paul urged believers not to be drunk with wine, but to be filled with the Spirit (Ephesians 5:18), so there must be a similar behaviour pattern at times!

The signs on the day of Pentecost were never repeated, but the sequel was wherever the disciples went and preached – amazement, bewilderment, criticism. We need to ask if people react that way today in response to the Church's witness. Criticism maybe, but is there wonderment over changed lives, transformed characters, new believers in Christ? Or is our testimony so feeble and futile there is nothing for anyone to marvel at? May the Lord raise us from our sloth to be equipped for the battle outside the walls of the church against the world, the flesh and the devil.

MAY 13

THE SECRET OF THE NEW POWER

Acts 2:4

The few simple words explain everything: they were all filled with the Holy Spirit and began . . . It is only the church fellowship with Spirit-filled people that produces the sequel of wonder, bewilderment and criticism. If that is not happening it is because the Spirit is not filling. The disciples were not preaching, but praising God and pouring out the joy that filled them. There was a new vision of the Lord, and a new consciousness of his power. A new principle of life filled them, the 'victory life' of Jesus risen from the grave, and now seated at the Father's right hand in glory.

Do we experience this fullness of life? If not, why not? From personal experience and from years in the ministry, I believe that at conversion the Holy Spirit came into my life as Paul explains in Ephesians 1:13, the seal of my acceptance with God. But I knew so little, and it was not until some years later that I understood more of the work of the Holy Spirit and then opened my whole life for his filling. That to me was my 'day of Pentecost', a moment of crisis that transformed my life forever, changing my direction from a business career to a life in the ministry. That crisis, often called the baptism of the Spirit, is followed by many fillings (one might even say daily fillings), which happened in the lives of the early disciples as in Acts 4:31. Each sphere of service requires a fresh anointing for we cannot live today on the grace and blessing of yesterday, for God's love and mercy are new every morning (Lamentations 3:22, 23).

A Prayer: Lord Jesus, take my life today and fill me with your power so that I may be a true witness to you, that I may experience your presence and glory in the fact that I am your servant. Accept my praise and love and thanksgiving.

MAY 14

WHERE ARE THE PEOPLE?

Acts 2:6

The Church today sits and waits for people to come through the doors. In the above verse the crowd came to the place that had been shaken by the power of the Holy Spirit. What a difference! The disciples had been for days in prayer at the Lord's command, and the answer came in a dramatic way. When, may I ask, were we last in an 'upper room' as a fellowship of believers, seeking the mind of the Lord regarding his plan for forwarding his work? Where are the people surging forward in amazement as the Lord demonstrates his power? Sadly missing, for there is so little emanating from our witness to draw them to him.

People outside church doors are in roughly four categories, and we need to study these in order to pray for wisdom to know the Lord's strategy in reaching them.

There are those who completely ignore anything to do with 'religion'. To them neither God nor his followers exist.

There are those who have considered 'the Church' and choose to ignore us. To them we are useless, with no light to shine on their path, no power to help them bear their burdens. They had ideas of sacrifice being part of the Christian faith, but all they see is a self-indulgent Church. They thought we were devoted to Christ, but only see infighting, strife and lovelessness.

There are those who oppose with great determination, and seek to stamp out faith in a living Lord Jesus.

There are those who, with hungry hearts, look for reality and see some marks of it in a few who call Jesus Lord.

May he give us the sense of urgency to witness to him, as we live at the foot of the Cross for pardon and cleansing, and in the 'upper room' in prayer for the infilling of his Holy Spirit.

MAY 15

WHAT IS HAPPENING?

Acts 2:12-21

The events of the day of Pentecost crowd in one after the other.
First the disciples were gathered together, no doubt for prayer,
then the awesome coming of the Holy Spirit with signs like
wind and fire that brought the crowd running to the place. That
was followed by the ability of the believers to communicate
with foreigners in their own language to share the glad tidings,
and that brought sceptics to the conclusion that the men were
drunk.

Peter took charge and gave for the first time New Testament principles of witness. Study them carefully.

He established a point of contact: 'These men are not drunk,
but...' He showed how at that very moment the prophecy of
Joel was being fulfilled, and one can imagine the intense listening
of the people.

Peter then made a beeline for Jesus, for he was the all-
important One, the central figure. In the sermon Peter gave
there are twenty-two verses, twelve of which are Old Testament quotations, and ten explaining how Christ fulfilled them.
The Scriptures came alive to the disciples. Suddenly they saw
truths not only about history, or men and their needs, but about
God and Christ. How blind they had been before, but now with
eyes opened by the Holy Spirit, their testimony was aglow with
his power, wind and fire uniting to produce unheard of results.

A Prayer: Lord Jesus, may I too read your Word with eyes
and heart wide open to see yourself revealed within every page.
May the Holy Spirit prepare me today for whatever is before
me, and that I may be ready with testimony by word and life to
those I will be meeting.

AMAZING RESULTS

Acts 2:22-41

Peter's sermon is based on three Old Testament Scriptures which were fulfilled in Jesus Christ. Each of these is prefaced with the words 'this Jesus' (vv. 23, 32, 36 RSV).

Joel's prophecy foretold the amazing outpouring of the Holy Spirit and the universal salvation to be found in the Lord. Peter fearlessly preached the resurrection of Christ, who could not be held by death as he was the sinless Son of God. Calvary is the central point of history, as Peter made clear.

David foretold in Psalm 16 the truth of the resurrection, and Jesus is now risen from the dead and in the place of all authority in Heaven, pouring out on his disciples the promised Holy Spirit. The men who spoke were witnesses of all these things, and therefore could not be contradicted.

David had also seen the final outcome of history, the enthronement of God's perfect man (Psalm 110:1), and Peter quickly announced that this Jesus is both Lord and Christ.

Oh, to have heard that sermon given by a transformed, Spirit-filled man! The people who did hear reacted quickly. 'What shall we do?' they cried. 'Repent,' Peter replied. They had first asked, 'What does this mean?' and when they heard the explanation were eager to respond and get right with God. When we read that over 3000 people were baptized at that time, we can rightly ask why that doesn't happen today. We expect people to ask how to become Christians without them seeing evidence in our fellowships, and our individual lives, to make them ask first, 'what does this mean?'

Let that challenge our hearts and change our lackadaisical approach to the urgent task of making Jesus known to the world in our generation. After all, it is the only generation for which each one of us is personally responsible.

FULLNESS OF LIFE (1)

Luke 4:1

How Jesus met the tempter illustrates the fullness of Christian living. Jesus went into the wilderness as *man*, having the same spiritual equipment each child of God can have today. Think now of five areas of Holy Spirit life we share with him.

It is life in the Spirit: 'Man shall not live by bread alone' (v. 4). A Christian is born from above, and is therefore fed from above, and he quickly learns where soul-satisfying food is found, the Word of God, for material things only satisfy the body and mind, but not the Spirit.

It is a life of faith: 'by every word of God' (Matt. 4:4). Faith comes by hearing and hearing by the word of God (Rom. 10:17). Live by the truth of God's Word, as Jesus did, for that is victory.

It is a life of worship: 'you shall worship the Lord your God' (v. 8). Whatever or whoever we worship is a god, an idol. Jesus must have first place in heart and life, for if he is not Lord of all, he is not Lord at all.

It is a life of service: 'and him only shall you serve' (v. 8). The will of God must be supreme in the believer's life as it was for his Son, Jesus. Doing all for him lifts the possible drudgery into glory and transforms the commonplace.

A Prayer: Father, make me daily more like your Son, that by his indwelling Spirit I may show to a lost and desperate world the true meaning of life in Christ.

MAY 18

FULLNESS OF LIFE (2)

Luke 4:12,13

To continue yesterday's thoughts on the fullness of the Spirit in the life of Jesus, in the closing verses of Luke's account of Christ's temptation in the wilderness are found the final two areas of spiritual victory.

It is a life of obedience: 'you shall not tempt the Lord your God' (v. 12). The sins of the children of Israel were disobedience and tempting God in the wilderness. They treated him like a stranger, and were discontented, grumbling, and unbelieving. We may be critical about the behaviour of these people, but how often we are just like them in our attitude to our heavenly Father. We need a right-about-turn of behaviour in complete obedience to his word and will, which in turn brings joy and peace of heart. We only *prove* that when we *do* what he commands.

It is a life of victory: 'The devil . . . departed' (v. 13). The sword of the Spirit is the Word of God, and Jesus teaches us in this passage how to use it against a subtle enemy. To know victory over evil within our hearts, and that which comes upon us from outside forces, it is essential to read God's Word, study it closely, compare Scripture, memorize, and be so acquainted with it that it becomes easy to use it as a weapon to rout the enemy. Laziness in this vital area of spiritual preparedness will result in constant defeat, which will grow into a severe slipping away from a close walk with the Lord. Remember, if this should happen, that God never moves, he is the unchanging one, and the fault is always on our side. The old cliché is true: backsliding is the result of slack abiding. Be warned!

MAY 19

THE SOURCE AND THE OVERFLOW

John 7:37-39

It was the Feast of Tabernacles, and on the final day Jesus spoke these words. On the previous days the priests had carried water from the Brook Kedron in procession to the Temple, recalling God's supply of water during the wilderness journey. On that final day there was no procession or water, indicating God's purposes were not yet fulfilled, so Jesus announced that he himself was the answer and the fulfilment of God's promise.

Man's basic needs are breath, food and water. Only Jesus can supply our spiritual needs, for he is both the source and the overflow.

John 3:5	Except a man be born of water and spirit – that is the source.
John 4:14	Whoever drinks the water I shall give him will never thirst – that is satisfaction.
John 7:38a	If any one thirsts, let him come to me and drink – that is all-sufficiency.
John 7:38b	Out of his heart (inner man) shall flow rivers of living water – that is overflow.

The Holy Spirit within us checks the thirst for peace and life's meaning, and promises not just a trickle of his grace and power, but a full flowing river of freshness, which is totally satisfying and thirst-quenching. It is there for us to receive as we open our hearts to him.

A Prayer: Lord Jesus, fill my life with your joy and power, so that you may be seen as the only source of true and meaningful living, and I praise you for your abundant supply in the fullness of the Spirit.

MAY 20

A ZEST FOR LIFE

Matthew 5:13

Salt is the worldwide ingredient for adding flavour and stopping corruption. When Jesus said his disciples were the salt of the earth he implied they were to have the same effect on people as he himself had. The Living Bible says, 'You are the world's seasoning to make it tolerable.' If you lose your flavour, what will happen to the world that is your immediate sphere of influence and witness?

Jesus talks of salt and light, both small items but able to spread their blessings afar. You may think of yourself as just a speck of salt, a tiny candle, but each can influence the immediate area. In a house where we once lived the outside bell had a tiny light in the bell-push, and it was amazing to see this shining in the darkness across two fields! Such is the influence of light in darkness, of salt in a corrupt environment.

What if the salt becomes savourless, and the light goes out? What keeps a Christian alight with love for Jesus, and filled with the savour of his very presence and power? Only the Holy Spirit within can reproduce the life of Jesus, and – if one can say it – he is as salt in the container of our bodies, the glowing light in the lampstand of our lives.

A Prayer: Lord, for today may I bring the zest and light of your love to someone, that they too may share the joy of your salvation.

MAY 21

ONE GRAIN AMONG MANY

Mark 9:50

The second reference Christ made regarding the believer as salt concerns relationships within his body, the Church. 'Have peace with one another' is the important phrase, one to be repeated constantly in our fellowships, and sought after by every member of Christ's body on earth.

How fragmented is the body of Christ! On every subject under the sun there is discussion and division, from eschatology to church government and mode of worship. Take warning from verse 50: if we, as grains, lose our savour, the tang has gone and the fellowship becomes prey to dissent. No wonder the Lord urged us to live at peace with each other (see John 13:34, 35).

How do we cope with 'difficult' people? How does Jesus cope with us? One answer is given in Philippians 2:1-11, especially some of the early verses. These stress real Holy Spirit love, selflessness, humility: in fact the very nature of Jesus himself. Humility is the ability to take hurt without resentment, and the secret of unity in the Church is for each grain of salt to covenant, when there is the possibility of differences of opinion, to disagree agreeably, and not break fellowship. That attitude will turn away the darts of the evil one, and keep the salt grains fresh and full of flavour.

MAY 22

THE SALTINESS OF DISCIPLINE

Luke 14:34, 35

The final reference to salt by the Lord Jesus is given in connection with himself, as he states his terms of discipleship. The full reading is from Luke 14:25, and we will look at these terms in reverse order.

Verses 28-33 give the challenge of complete renunciation of *all* to the Lord, for he has first claim on all we possess, physically and materially. We are only stewards of life and possessions.

In verse 27 we are commanded to bear his Cross. What does that mean? Certainly not some physical or material hardship, but a much deeper following of Jesus himself. He was sent into the world, he lived a perfect life, but the final act was the yielding of his body to death on the Cross. Meditate on that in relation to Romans 12:1, 2. Are we ready to yield up our very selves to him daily for the fulfilling of his perfect will in and through us?

Finally, verse 26 seems to give strange directions: 'hate' our loved ones? Never! The word has the meaning of 'reject', and human love has to take second place to love and devotion to the Master. If we reject our claim on our own lives and give them unreservedly to the Lord himself then we will know the savour of life that is typified as salt, because he daily restores its saltiness and tang. Loving him with all our heart and soul enables us to know what it means to love family and friends in a deeper, purer way than ever before.

MAY 23

WE ARE ONE IN THE SPIRIT

Ephesians 4:1-6

What is the outcome of the ascension of the Lord Jesus? What is he doing now? He received the promise of the Holy Spirit (Acts 2:33), not for himself, but for his followers on earth, to make it possible for him to perpetuate his life and work here through each one of them. Pentecost was the beginning of a new heavenly enterprise. Jesus is no longer localized in one place, but indwelling a multitude of lives in a multitude of places, for where there is a Christian there is Jesus! To quote Major Ian Thomas, 'Deity has clothed itself with humanity.' A stupendous thought on which Paul throws light in the passage for meditation, to enable us to grasp the object, strength and basis of what Christian living is all about, a life worthy of Jesus Christ.

A unity is established (vv. 3-6). Unity exists, for we are all one in Christ, but it has to be preserved. It is fragile and so easily broken by those who seek to assert themselves and their ideas. The character of unity exists in the fellowship of the life of Jesus into which every convert is introduced, and is sevenfold, the number of perfection (vv. 4-6), so note each one carefully. The central 'strand' is the Lord Jesus himself. At Pentecost the 'one body' was formed by the Holy Spirit – not one group or sect, but a united body, indwelt by the same life. The Head is in Heaven, the members here on earth, and each is united to the others. Every believer has one hope, a common destiny to be like the Lord, lifting up Jesus as Lord, and to know the Father who is Sovereign, above all; who is transcendent, through all; who is in all, incarnate in the lives of those who know and love him. This glorious unity is for us in our day to maintain with all the strength we have, so that the good news of salvation may spread without hindrance from those who call themselves by the name of the Lord Jesus.

MAY 24

GOD'S GRACE GIVEN

Ephesians 4:7-12

Unity is not uniformity, but the gift of the Spirit to unite believers in the bond of peace. What a travesty the Church today makes of this! How it must delight the enemy as he sows discord among believers! Unity is maintained by a truly Christlike spirit outlined in Eph. 4:1-3. As you read, make the words your prayer and heart's desire.

Grace is given to us to live in unity because there is a wonderful diversity. *Every* believer is given grace, but to some there are special callings (v. 11). It is grace according to calling, for God's grace only flows into the life which is using the gift he has given. If you are called to preach, then his grace is available as you give your life for that purpose. Likewise grace is given to those in every sphere of life, some in 'up-front' situations, others in the humdrum but very necessary activities of daily living. Whatever you do, wherever you are, God's grace for your work makes Christian service a luxury. To attempt work to which you have not been called creates strain, tension, burnout.

To covet the gifts of others also brings stress and unhappiness, for God's gifts are *given*, bestowed, and are for specific purposes outlined in verse 12. The underlying sense is for each Christian to adjust his life constantly to the plan and purpose of God in the building up of each member of the fellowship, so that everyone shares in the overall ministry. Gifts are given so that there is no rivalry or bitterness, no self-seeking or self-aggrandizement, but a loving, gracious, kind and generous merging together of a diversity of people and gifts into the united body of Christ.

THE OBJECTIVE

Ephesians 4:13-16

There is usually a reason for a certain gift being given to a certain person. A businessman would not appreciate a baby's rattle any more than a toddler would enjoy a briefcase! God's gifts are tailormade for everyone who receives them, for he has an objective in mind, given in these verses: 'Until we all attain to the unity of the faith.' The NIV gives verse 13c as 'attaining to the whole measure of the fulness of Christ.' It is important to remember constantly that that is God's reason for the gifts he bestows, not that we should bask in a feeling of superiority because we think we are more gifted than others. Heaven forbid!

Unity of the spirit (v. 3) is something to be striven for and maintained *now*; unity of the faith is something that will be seen when every Christian is made perfect in Christ – and that does not mean when we get to Heaven! The sum total of every believer, possessed by the Holy Spirit, is required to achieve that objective. No one person can ever reveal Christ to perfection: the Lord is too big for that. But all together, the body of Christ, anointed and filled by the Holy Spirit, can attain this objective.

How then is this achieved in practical terms? Paul leaves us in no doubt in verses 15, 16. To gain maturity in Christ requires the maturity of every believer. Every member of the body, joined and knit together by the contact of each part with the Head, the source of life, derives power to grow in proportion to the vigour of each individual part, and so it is built up in a spirit of love.

What a picture! What a glorious organism is the body of Christ, his true Church! May he give each of us grace for our appointed task as we unite to achieve his great objective of being salt and light in this sad and weary world.

MAY 26

BE FILLED!

Ephesians 5:18

The Spirit-filled life is normal Christian living. The Holy Spirit is not an optional extra for some who become super-spiritual giants, but he is an indispensable necessity for ordinary, everyday living. 'Be filled with the Spirit' is a command to be obeyed. So many Christians have unsatisfied needs in their lives, an unquenched thirst for God which he only can satisfy. When he does, then we can love him with greater understanding and intensity, and lean on him more completely. What, therefore, does it mean to be 'filled'?

At our new birth we are *indwelt* by the Spirit (1 Corinthians 12:3), but we can be far from being *filled*. These are two different things. For a few people (e.g. Acts 10:44-48) these events occur simultaneously, but with most of us there comes a later experience of fullness. At conversion we are filled to the limit of our capacity, and every act of faith and obedience increases that capacity, while unbelief and disobedience shrink it. An easy to remember thought on this is that at conversion I have Jesus; at his filling (my personal experience of Pentecost) he has me. Is that true of each one of us?

Fullness is not a once-for-all experience but an increasing habit of life. Ephesians 5:18 is literally 'be being filled with the Spirit'. We need to be, because we leak! The apostles were constantly experiencing fresh anointing of power for particular tasks to be undertaken. The fullness of the Spirit is characterized by a daily walk with God resulting in increased capacity for the indwelling of Jesus Christ. May this be the desire above all of each of us.

LIFE AND LIBERTY

Romans 8:1-4

The apostle Paul devotes much space – a whole chapter – to the doctrine of the Holy Spirit and how it is worked out in the life of every believer. It is a vital chapter, which begins with 'no condemnation' ends with 'no separation', and in between teaches there is no defeat, for victory is inevitable.

The position of the believer is made clear that he is in Christ Jesus, and equally the Holy Spirit is in the Christian. So first he is the Spirit of life, for there is no spiritual life in any person until the blood of Jesus cleanses from sin and the Spirit indwells to give life. At that moment the old grip of sin and death is loosened and so, in the second place, he is the Spirit of liberty, of freedom.

Two masters tug at the believer: the law of the Spirit of life, and the law of sin and death and every person is under one or the other. Submit to the fleshy nature and we are under the latter. But if we yield to the Spirit we know freedom: we are now under new management!

We are not free, however, to indulge ourselves, for that is licence. We are free to do the will of God, living in a right relationship to him. We certainly cannot do that by ourselves, in our own strength or willpower, but praise God, the Holy Spirit *in us* (v.4) enables us to accomplish what we can never do.

This is not a recipe for 'instant holiness'. If we ever think we have got the formula, therefore all is going to be easy and straightforward, we are in for many sad shocks. God expects nothing from us but failure, but he has given his Spirit that we *need* never fail. It is never impossible for us to sin, but it is always possible for us not to, for the Holy Spirit's work is to deliver us from the law of sin and death. So in which are we living right now?

THE BATTLE FOR THE MIND

Romans 8:5-9

Cults, ideologies, anti-God systems, all fight for the mind, for that is the hub of human actions and reactions, the base of the will. Here Paul contrasts the fleshly mind and one controlled by the Spirit. To understand the word 'flesh', delete the H and spell it backwards: SELF.

What do you 'mind' most of all? What are the important things in life? The heart is set either on selfish, worldly matters, or on the things of God – there is no half-way house. A person who continues on the first way of life will find it ends in death, eternal separation from God, whereas life in the Spirit is peace (v. 6).

The test is, how much do we *mind*? What are the reactions when one is overlooked, criticized, misunderstood? Is it to say, 'but it's only *natural* to react like that'? That is the problem, and such a reply proves that person is 'after the flesh', and knows little of the peace God can bring into a trying situation when he is in the place of control.

If we 'mind' and are concerned with the things of God, then we know his peace, which only comes from fellowship with, and dependence on, his Spirit. See the contrast of verse 9 to the darkness of verse 7, the grim picture of the hostile mind, rebellious against God, lawless, and in no way able to please him. Thank him now for the peace, life and liberty he can bring to your heart as you gladly submit to his authority and indwelling.

MAY 29

THE LIFE-GIVER

Romans 8:10,11

To become alive in Christ is to experience the life-giving power of the Spirit. The body may hamper and be a drag, but it is the inner life of heart and soul that, when touched by the wind and fire of God's Spirit, generates a totally new source of strength and ability.

How does this weak body of ours express the life of the Spirit? As Jesus was raised from the dead by the mighty power of God, and appeared in bodily form, so that same Spirit quickens, makes alive, our bodies also. Fantastic! The dynamic power that brought the once dead body of Jesus out of the tomb ALIVE is the power that lives in us. Let that sink in.

That is the Spirit's power, but what about our side of the matter? It is he who enables us to yield every faculty we possess to be 'instruments of righteousness' (Romans 6:19). How many Christians are slaves to their bodies? Lax and undisciplined, they listen to the demands of the physical and disregard the promptings of the Spirit. Too tired to pray; too hungry to go from work to a Bible study; too lazy to go to Church, for that might prove to be a painful and challenging experience.

Paul fought with his body to keep it under control (1 Corinthians 9:27). If you do not learn discipline, you will find the body dominating your walk with Jesus. Allow the resurrection power of the Holy Spirit to flood into your heart, penetrating every nook and cranny, until you can say in honesty before the living Lord, 'Christ lives in me!' (Galatians 2:20).

MAY 30

IS A VICTORIOUS LIFE POSSIBLE?

Romans 8:12-17

It has been shown how the Spirit makes alive. In verse 13 he counteracts the downward pull of the carnal, fleshly part of our make-up. He enables us to put to death the works, the impulses of the body, but he can only do that with our cooperation, for we are not robots. It is for us to claim voluntarily his power to do all his will in and through us. This is real victory, a simple reminder being constantly to count on his presence, reckon on his victory, and draw on his power.

The ministry of the Spirit is not yet finished, for in verses 14-17 we learn it is through him we become sons of God. Note the vivid contrast: once slaves to sin, now sons of the Father. We are adopted into God's family, and can call him 'Abba', 'Father dear'.

At new birth we are made children of God, having kinship with him. When we grow in grace and understand more fully what new life in Christ involves, we find we are led by the Spirit, and are among those who alone can call themselves 'sons', denoting growth in character and awareness of family blessings and responsibilities. The Spirit gives witness to this great fact, and assures us of the reality of our salvation. While we must always cling to the Father as children, we must also grow in grace, and glory in that assurance of life, of Heaven, of full redemption, because of the inner witness of the Spirit.

What more could God do to enable us to live as victors, not as slaves to sin and self? It is for each one of his children to enter into a closer and deeper walk with him daily, led by the Spirit to appropriate all that is ours in Christ, deaf to the comments and criticism of those around, who may be far from understanding the good and perfect will of our God.

MAY 31

THE HOLY SPIRIT AND PRAYER

Romans 8:26, 27

Prayer is, alas, so often the weakest area of Christian living, providing the chink in the armour through which the enemy can attack. Often a new believer does not know how to pray, thinking it has to be in a special type of 'holy' language, or in a special voice! He feels very helpless and threatened, and often gives up trying, which is a tragedy.

Read the two verses carefully, and let the truth sink in. It is the Spirit who helps us in all our weakness, who prays through us and prays for us. Prayer is not a one-sided monologue of me speaking to God; it is a conversation, a communion, and I must allow him to speak to me. Many times of prayer can begin with a sense of coldness and deadness, then the Spirit takes over with sighs too deep for words or, as in the AV, with groanings that cannot be uttered. Human language breaks down, and often one can only breathe out 'Jesus'. In the same way a grief is shared more with a tear than with words. Love finds expression in the light of an eye or the clasp of a hand. So often words are unnecessary, yet usually all we know to do is to rush in with them.

So in prayer. The Spirit *in* you knows the will of God *for* you, so allow him to pray *through* you. Then prayer will be in the will of God, and he will hear you. 'The mind of the Spirit' is the channel God uses, and as he guides in our praying, so he will guide the direction of our lives step by step. He leads by the Word of God and by the inner witness of his life in us. Study of the Bible together with prayer are the two legs that take us along the path of God's will and the experience of his constant presence with us.

JUNE 1

THE MIGHTY SPIRIT

Ephesians 4:30

In this letter Paul outlines three areas of the Spirit's work. We are sealed by him at conversion (v. 30; 1:13); he can be grieved, and he continually fills us (5:18). The first and last of these truths have been considered already. Now we think of the Spirit being grieved, wounded.

First, however, let us think again of all the Spirit does for us, to see afresh how it is impossible to live the Christian life without his power, which will make us see more plainly the awful fact that we can cause him grief.

Whatever work of God done in this world is through the Holy Spirit. It is he who convinces and convicts of sin (John 16:8). He enlightens the mind so that the youngest believer can begin to understand spiritual truths (John 14:26). He empowers the Christian for service and for living in a way that delights the Father (Acts 1:8). He guides into truth (John 16:13), for he directs each step in the way of life that is pleasing to God. He glorifies Christ, and makes us holy by bringing us into union with the Lord. All the apostles experienced at Pentecost is the privilege of every believer.

All that is the work of the Holy Spirit in our lives, but God does not drag us into any experience of his grace apart from our earnest desire and heart-hunger to know and enjoy everything there is for us to claim of his goodness and grace. Man is free to work out his own mode of salvation, but it is only God who can work *in* us to lead us into the way everlasting (see Philippians 2:13). We can resist, or we can yield. We can put out the fire, or cause it to glow. In short, we can wound God in a way deeper than Calvary, because we do so as one of the family through deliberate sin, not from ignorance.

JUNE 2

THE SENSITIVITY OF THE SPIRIT

Ephesians 4:25-32

It is necessary at times to banish a child from the room because of persistent bad behaviour or disobedience. Is that child no longer a family member? Of course not, but probably loved and longed for more than ever by the parents at the time of banishment, for they may suffer in heart far more than the child. When the tearful apology is finally made, what love and joy there is in the restoration of family relationships! All the sweeter, maybe, by the lessons learned.

What are the things that wound and grieve God's Spirit, and cause that feeling of being bereft by the erring believer?

Falsehood (v. 25). Not necessarily a deliberate lie, but conveying a wrong impression, twisting a story, blackening someone's character.

Anger (v. 26). Not all anger is sin. 'If you would be angry and not sin, then only be angry at sin.' When the cause of Christ is being attacked, it is not a sin to be angry; when you yourself are wronged, it is. That is the moment to step aside and let God's anger operate on your behalf.

Stealing (v. 28). Not necessarily open theft, but perhaps robbing your employer of time for which you are paid. More often we rob God by our disobedience in tithing, stewardship of money, possessions, time.

Wrong use of the tongue (vv. 29, 31), which so often betrays the fact that self is on the throne and not the Spirit of Christ. More damage is done in Christian fellowships by idle gossip and chatter than by anything else. No wonder James wrote so strongly about the tongue in the first half of chapter 3, as well as here and in Colossians 3:8-10.

Check your life by this incisive list of that which wounds the Spirit, and claim the grace and power to put right all that is wrong.

THE HEALING OF THE WOUND

Ephesians 4:22-25, 32

How much easier it is to offend someone than to apologize! The price of blessing in restoring a relationship with God is a step involving self-crucifixion: NO to self and YES to him.

The first step is confession to God. 1 John 1:9 is gloriously true, and we claim that cleansing every time we make confession of sin. But often that is not enough. We are not to continue in sin that grace may abound (Romans 3:8 AV). Confession does not prevent recurrence. So the second step is restitution to others.

Where fellowship is broken, when lies have been told, or anger has been demonstrated, or whatever unchristian attitude has been shown toward another person, then confession to that one is a condition of forgiveness and the healing of a wounded Holy Spirit. Jesus' words in Matthew 6:14, 15 are very apt in this connection, for not only do we confess our wrong to those we have wronged, but we are to forgive those who have wronged us. Do you say you cannot? You MUST, or you yourself cannot claim God's forgiveness, and by your hardheartedness you show you have no real experience of his forgiveness and the meaning of Calvary.

That is the impact of verse 32. The healing of the wounded Spirit releases an inflow of his love and power into our hearts, and we immediately demonstrate this by being kind, loving, forgiving, toward our friends. These are not demonstrated by our own efforts, but are the outflow of the kindness, love and forgiveness God showed toward us when he gave his Son to die for us. Get on your knees and pray that this may be true in your daily experience, as you seek to walk with God.

JUNE 4

EARS TO HEAR

Revelation 2:7

The Holy Spirit is the substitute on earth for the bodily presence of the Lord Jesus. In Matthew 17:5 the Father said, 'This is my beloved Son, hear him.' In the verse for this meditation the message is to listen to the Spirit. This phrase indicates that he has something to say to every fellowship and every Christian, for the phrase is repeated to all the churches in Revelation 2 and 3.

It also tells us that he must be given time and room to speak, and it is sufficient if there is only one person, 'he who has an ear...' That person must have the capacity to hear what the Spirit is saying: 'he who has an ear, let him hear'. All fruitful service begins and continues with what the Spirit is saying. That has little to do with the outward ear, for he has many ways of getting his message through to those who are ready, firstly through the Word of God. The Word without the Spirit is dead; the Spirit without the Word is dangerous; the Word plus the Spirit is dynamite!

The Spirit speaks through a message, when he seems to single out a person as being the only one to whom the preacher is speaking. The Spirit also speaks through outward circumstances, as in Acts 16:6-9.

All these means of speaking to us are useless unless we have ears to hear, a willingness to be still, to abandon our own plans and preconceived ideas, and just meditate on all He brings to our notice, and then relate them to our own situation. Prayer and Holy Spirit enlightenment is his way to reveal the will of God to each one of us, and to his Church, the body of Christ.

JUNE 5

THE SPIRIT'S DISCIPLINE

1 Chronicles 12:38

There is a discipline in fellowship, and the story of this passage illustrates the fact. After the long list of names it is said that these men of war knew how to 'keep rank' (AV). That is true of all soldiering, but alas, not so in the Lord's army, where the 'men of war' are so often very strong individualists, and know little of working alongside each other.

This discipline has to be applied first in one's own life. God does not give 'ears to hear' in order to criticize other people, but first and foremost to adjust one's life to his will. The Church, the body of Christ, should be a harmonious organism, every part oiled by the Holy Spirit, united in fulfilling the mission of the Founder, the evangelization of the world. Sadly that is so rarely the case, and in place of harmony and oneness of mind and purpose there is discord and breakdown. How little Christians know of the discipline of the Spirit in their lives.

It is A. W. Tozer who said, 'If the Holy Spirit was withdrawn from the Church today, 95 per cent of what we do would go on, and no one would know the difference. If the Holy Spirit was withdrawn from the New Testament Church, 95 per cent of what they did would stop, and everyone would know the difference.'

The modern Church substitutes programme for Holy Spirit strategy, and Christians slander God in their eagerness to work for him without knowing him. May he draw us up short to look at our own lives and motives for service, and then put ourselves under the Spirit's discipline to learn to keep rank, and march under HIS orders unitedly.

JUNE 6

MEETING THE HEART'S DESIRE

John 16:7-15

What do Christians need and desire most of all? Three basic things in all probability: assurance of salvation; understanding of the Bible; ability to make Jesus known to others. Do you say Amen to that?

This is just what Jesus said when he introduced his teaching on the ministry of the Holy Spirit, because first, he is essential to salvation (vv. 8, 9). The Christian life begins with the miracle of the new birth, and is intended to continue as one. Unless this happens you have a church member on your hands, but not a Christian. This is the exchanged life as given by Paul in 2 Corinthians 5:21, and the only good thing about any of us is Jesus. The Lord does not alter human nature, but he alters the mainspring to give us a new heredity.

The Holy Spirit is essential to our understanding of Scripture (v. 13). Then he is essential to making Jesus real in the heart of the believer (vv. 15, 16). As you read and meditate on the Word, allow the Spirit to do his mighty work in you, as Jesus promised. It is our haste and disobedience and lack of discipline that hinder him, leaving us cold of heart and unfulfilled in our quest for spiritual maturity.

When we have claimed the Spirit's sovereignty in these areas, then we realize he is essential in the work of evangelism (vv. 7-11). He alone can convict of sin and bring folk into the knowledge of Jesus as Lord. We need a fresh infusion of the Spirit for every new situation, every day, and he abundantly answers if this is our heartfelt prayer.

JUNE 7

LEARNING BODY LIFE

1 Corinthians 12:4-26

This chapter has to be understood in relation to the sovereignty of the Holy Spirit in Christian service. Only as we grasp what is said here can we hope to 'keep rank'.

Paul launches straight in (v. 4) with clarification of the gifts of the Spirit, for while there are many gifts it is the same Spirit who distributes them to each person as he wills (v. 11). He knows what is best for each of us in order that we may fit into his body, the Church (vv. 6, 7). It is very important that these verses are fully understood. We must also understand that, because the gifts are given by the Spirit individually, we should never be guilty of envying the gifts of others, or demand that everyone should have what we possess. Every gift is needed within the fellowship of the body (vv. 14-21), just as foot, hand, eyes, etc., make up the human body and are necessary for wholeness.

Each one of us should know that our place in the body is not of our choosing, and neither is it the result of the appointment of other people. We are where we are and what we are by the sovereignty of the Spirit, and to realize this will keep us from dissatisfaction with our place and gifts, without envy of the position of others, and when things get tough we will be slow to resign unless specifically shown to do so by the Spirit.

Take time to read the portion, and allow him to do his work in your heart regarding this most important aspect of Christian living and service.

JUNE 8

THE FULLNESS OF THE SPIRIT

1 Corinthians 12:12,13

It is clear that at conversion every believer is 'overwhelmed' by the Spirit, baptized into new life in Christ. At Pentecost the disciples had this experience as Jesus told them in Acts 1:5, and thereafter they were constantly filled by the Spirit. We all need this, for baptism into a new relationship occurs once, while the filling of the Spirit in the growth and maturing of that relationship occurs over and over again. Every step of faith and obedience enlarges our capacity for more of him. If you are feeling dry and barren, look into your heart to find the moment of doubt or disobedience, acknowledge your sin to the Lord, then claim his cleansing and a new anointing of his Spirit.

The prophet Zechariah was given the promise 'not by might, nor by power, but by my Spirit' (4:6), and when we acknowledge that truth and claim the Spirit's power to replace our feeble resources, what a release of tension floods our hearts! Until that happens, the Lord is resident in our lives, but not President. With Satan crowding on all pressure these days, unless we know the fullness of the Spirit alive in our hearts, we are defeated before we begin battle with the enemy. We cannot win against him with second-class weapons but only by those given by the mighty Spirit within us (2 Corinthians 10:4).

A Prayer:
O fill me with your fullness, Lord,
Until my very heart o'erflow
In kindling thought and glowing word,
Thy love to tell, thy praise to show.

F.R. Havergal

JUNE 9

THE BEST GIFT OF ALL

1 Corinthians 13

It is impossible to meditate on chapter 12 without proceeding to the next chapter, especially as Paul had no such division in his letter! 12:31 goes straight on into chapter 13.

The hallmark of the Christian faith should be love. It was for the love of Christ that in ages past his people opened hospitals and all charitable organizations. The great social reformers of the last century were men of God who shared his love for the outcast, the disabled, the orphan.

Other 'religions' know very little, if anything, of true love. Some are governed by pure hate, others by fear and abject slavery to rules and observances. The anthropologist goes to a heathen tribe and is enthralled by their culture and tribal ceremonies, little knowing they are governed by fear of evil spirits, fear of witchcraft, fear of offending the dead. Only the love of Jesus flooding their hearts can bring joyful release from such bondage.

So Paul calls love the greatest and highest gift, and he was of course echoing the words of the Lord Jesus who said emphatically and repeatedly that Christians are to love one another and share that love with lost humanity.

Great eloquence, amazing knowledge, faith leading even to martyrdom – all mean nothing if performed without love. And the quality of love is all-important: it is certainly not a human passion, but a divine infilling of Holy Spirit love, life and power. Claim that for your own life and witness today.

JUNE 10

LOVE IS THE WAY

1 Corinthians 13:1-3

Look more closely at the meaning of 'love'. One Greek word, *philio*, means friendship, natural affection. The other is *agape*, from which we get the word 'agony', and is the word used by Jesus and Paul. Deep love can produce an agony in the heart, for it is the actual absorption of every part of our being in one great passion. It is a word used most often in relation to God, for he is the embodiment of *agape* love.

Agape has little to do with emotion, for it indicates love which, deliberately and willingly, through thick and thin, goes on loving continually, eternally. How much of such love have we experienced, or given to others, in particular to God himself? God so loves us (John 3:16) and we are to love the Lord with *all* our heart, mind and strength. How tragically far short most of us come from that sort of love!

Such love speaks of complete self-denial, never thinking of oneself. We are even called to love our enemies with *agape* love (Matthew 5:44)!

The pre-eminence of love given in these opening verses opens our eyes to the fact that the talented, gifted person without *agape* love in his life is empty and worthless. The man or woman with strong emotional or intellectual powers really has nothing if there is no love in the demonstration of these powers. Like the pealing of a bell come the repeated words, 'but have not love', for that all-powerful, all-pervading gift of the very love of God is the mainspring of Christian living, and the only channel by which the love of God is transmitted to a lost and weary world.

THE SOVEREIGN ON THE THRONE

1 Corinthians 13:1-3

Love must be sovereign in the heart. Ability to speak with the gift of tongues, Paul has been saying in the previous chapter, is a wonderful expression of emotion, praise and worship. In verse 1 Paul imagines a person having the tongues of angels also, but without love such a person even in prayer, or the silver-tongued but loveless orator, become nothing but a big noise. The power behind speech is not one's vocabulary but the depth of heart, the capacity to love. Eloquence without love can possess power to do devastating damage, and its hiss is as full of venom as a serpent. *Agape* love alone is a universal language.

Love must be sovereign in our intellect. There are four things here that belong to intellect as distinct from emotion and will. Prophecy is the gift to declare the things of God, to interpret life, to bring the word of the Lord to bear upon earth, to bring eternity into time. Mysteries probably mean understanding God's secrets, spiritual discernment. Knowledge is intelligence in the truth, understanding Scripture. Faith is firmness of belief that takes a person through all the complexities of life because he trusts God.

You may have all these, but without love you are nothing. Balaam the prophet had no love, and betrayed God's people. Caiaphas had discernment but no love, and he delivered Jesus to death. Judas Iscariot had knowledge, having been with Jesus for about three years, but he turned traitor, for he had no love for his Master.

Where do we stand? Is love sovereign, ruling our lives – mind, will, heart – from the throne of our being?

JUNE 12

THE LOVE LIFE

1 Corinthians 13:4-7

Pause in this vital chapter to allow the warmth and glow of love to flood your heart and mind. Having looked into what might be a very uncomfortable mirror in verses 1-3 and acknowledged your failure to know and exhibit true love, see now the picture of a life of love. It is a picture of Jesus, and should be a picture of Man, but Satan and sin have robbed humanity of all likeness to God's character. Only his grace and the power of the indwelling Holy Spirit can renew us and make us what God longs for us to become.

In verses 4-6 the power of love holds a life in restraint that it may do no evil. In verse 7 love is active and positive. See the ingredients of love, and meditate upon each one in the life of the Lord Jesus and the fact that it is his purpose that we should be like him.

Love suffers long, is patient. It refuses to give way to anger and resentment. Though wounded and injured it does not strike back. See 1 Peter 2:23: how do we react?

Love is kind, and not only takes injury but shows positive grace and kindness to the person responsible. Do we?

Love makes no parade (Moffatt). To boast is to advertise emptiness and ignorance. Love is too big to swagger. Jesus never showed off, but laid aside his glory and humbled himself (Philippians 2:6-8).

A Prayer: Dear Lord, in view of your demonstration of *agape* love, make me a reflector of your grace, love and humility.

JUNE 13

THE HUMILITY OF LOVE

1 Corinthians 13:4-7

Love is not puffed up or arrogant, but humble. 'Love gives itself no airs' (Moffatt). The Lord never showed contempt of others – do you?

Love is not rude or ill-mannered, but always courteous. This is God's love expressed in the little, everyday things of life. Do you lack real Christian goodness and courtesy?

Love is not selfish, but self-forgetful, and therefore finds joy in serving others.

Love is not easily provoked or bad-tempered. No sin ruins a life, a home, a church, more than sheer bad temper. It demonstrates a complete lack of love. Jesus was against sin and hated it, but was never vindictive when hate was directed against him. If you are temperamental, touchy, easily offended, then claim once again an infilling of the love of Jesus.

Love thinks no evil, and while acknowledging the many kindnesses received, will keep no record of wrongs. God not only forgives, he forgets, and our sins are remembered no more against us. Never, never bear a grudge; that would show a complete misunderstanding of redemption.

'Love is never glad when others go wrong; love is gladdened by goodness' (Moffatt, v. 6). Love weeps over sin and condemns it, but always seeks to restore the sinner.

Love bears, believes, hopes, and above all, endures *all things*. There is no retaliation but a constant seeking after truth. There is no despair in disappointment or in people who fail, because love cannot be conquered – it endures! If your life is the reverse of what Jesus is, then know grace can triumph, and yield yourself to him.

JUNE 14

LOVE NEVER ENDS

1 Corinthians 13:8

How powerful and permanent is *agape* love! It never fails, for God is love, and his love is shed in our hearts by the Holy Spirit. The reality of our Christian faith is not so much what we say we believe, but how much we love (1 John 5:1,2).

Love never falls to the ground, like a wilted flower, for there is no decay in love. Love never loses its strength, like a weary athlete or traveller, because love is inexhaustible. Love never leaves its place, because it is immovable. Love never drops out of line, like an exhausted soldier on a route march, because love is absolutely tireless. Love never fails, and can outlast anything and everything.

True worship is not in the beauty of a building or a psychological atmosphere. It is a congregation who have given themselves to God, and in whose lives there is love and sacrifice to the limit. Such a fellowship is lit up with the glory of the indwelling Christ.

To allow enduring love to flow in our hearts and through our lives, we must live simply and hold the things of the world lightly. Be active and mobile in the Lord's service. Determine priorities and put God's things first, share responsibility and exploit opportunities. In short, be on the attack for Jesus!

A Prayer: First read verses 4-7, replacing the word LOVE with JESUS. Then, if you dare, read the verses again replacing LOVE with I. May the Lord's response be a fresh infilling of his unending Holy Spirit love and power.

THE VICTORY OF LOVE

1 Corinthians 13:8b-13

'Love never fails', Paul says, 'follow after love – make love your aim.' Love is contrasted with gifts and compared with other virtues, and the conclusion is a shout of victory, 'the greatest of these is LOVE!'

Ultimately all things will pass from the earthly scene, and only love will remain. Knowledge and prophecy are imperfect, but one day in God's presence all will be revealed and made perfect.

As childhood is based on growing into manhood, so spiritual life on earth is based upon spiritual life in eternity. We begin that life now, at conversion, and are moving towards the goal of when that life has its fullness and perfection in glory. Make Heaven your goal, maturity your aim, Christ your object, but never boast of your attainments. At present we are a reflection, but one day we will see God in his glory.

Faith, hope, love are put alongside in verse 13, and compared; you cannot magnify love by minimizing faith and hope. Faith is trust that rests on evidence and leads to action. Hope is confidence in the future. Christian hope is not a vague guess, but an absolute, confident assurance based on the eternal purposes and promises of the Word of God. Faith and hope are related to love and cannot be separated. Faith possesses the past, and makes Calvary real in my life. Hope looks into future glory, while love dominates my life now, and enables me to experience the daily joy of living for Jesus, with him ruling in my life.

JUNE 16

THE PROMISE OF HARVEST

Galatians 5:16-25

Harvest is sure, after the sowing, and that is true not only in agriculture but in our lives. We reap what we sow, and these verses show the two possible harvests. The two ways of life are utterly incompatible (vv. 16-18). They are diametrically opposed, and we walk in one or the other.

Note the description of each: *works* of the flesh; *fruit* of the Spirit. The first indicates effort, and what a horrific list of evil Paul gives, but the way of life produced is unstable and insecure. How true this is in our modern world, with the high rate of crime and debauchery, and of suicides. The second way of life is governed by the Spirit, and there is harmony.

Look at the cluster of fruit, and remember Jesus said, 'I chose you and appointed you that you should go and bear *fruit*' (John 15:16). He also spoke of the Holy Spirit coming to indwell his disciples, so here is the fruit *of the Spirit*. The flesh cannot produce this, only the Spirit, and he can only transform character when a firm relationship has been established. You must have the root within you before you experience fruit. That is vital.

The ninefold cluster produces fruit in three relationships:

Our relationship to God — Love, joy, peace
Our relationship to others — patience, kindness, goodness
Our relationship to — faithfulness, gentleness,
ourselves — self-control

Before we look into these more closely tomorrow, pray over each 'fruit', and think of your concept of each one in your own experience. Is a harvest being reaped, or are there too many weeds?

JUNE 17

HEAVENLY FRUIT

Galatians 5:22-25

Love, joy, peace, all spring from a right relationship to God, because they are virtues and grace given by him to us. God's love has been poured into our hearts by the Holy Spirit when first we committed our lives to him (Romans 5:5). Love can never be worked up, whether it is love for God or for other people. It is stimulated within us and imparted by the Holy Spirit. Joy is a special promise from Jesus himself (John 15:11; 16:24), and is experienced as we grow in ever closer fellowship with the risen Lord. Peace is his parting gift (John 14:27; 16:33), and the promise that in a world full of tribulation the trusting heart knows his peace. What an example was the life of the Lord Jesus!

All this of necessity affects our relationship to those around us. Patience, long-suffering, mean we are slow to anger, for it takes two to make a quarrel, and no one living in the power of the Spirit can be one of them. Kindness is a reflection of God's attitude to us in Titus 3:4-7, and should cause us to be slow to criticize others. Goodness is in opposition to everything evil. So the results of the life of the Spirit are to be seen in daily conduct.

Toward myself there must be a walk of faith, a gentle spirit toward others, and self-control at all times.

Here then are the two harvests: that of the flesh is tragedy, that of the Spirit is life to the full, the abundant life of which Jesus spoke in John 10: 10b. The three steps toward the fullness are given here also: walk (our daily mode of life) in the Spirit (v. 16); be led by the Spirit (v. 18); live in the Spirit (v. 25). Think on these things, and pray that they may come to fruition in your life.

BREAKDOWN

Psalm 51:1-9

Not every Spirit-filled Christian is constantly rejoicing. What happens when there is a spiritual breakdown? To sin is never necessary, yet it is always possible, and most of us, at some time or other, have been humiliated as Satan has brought us low in some area of battle. But does God desert us then? Of course not. Yet what about those who are in despair and saying a truly overcoming life is not for them?

To know the background of Psalm 51 read 2 Samuel 11 and 12. David found the path away from the blessing of God was easy to follow, but the way back is so difficult to tread that, were it not for the ministry of the Holy Spirit, no one would ever make any headway. As God's Spirit worked in conviction in David's life, he felt his tragic condition to be as if all his bones were broken, and moreover that the Lord himself had done the breaking. His sin was so flagrant, but his repentance was overwhelming. The opening verses show how crushed he was by his chastisement; life had been so good, but now it was bitter. A child of God cannot sin cheaply, and he soon finds the way of transgression to be hard.

David was a man after God's own heart, and the Lord would not allow him to be at ease in sin. When Nathan confronted him with the sin of both adultery and murder, he trembled before the Lord he loved so deeply, and whom he had failed so despicably. Now the Holy Spirit convicts him to such an extent he feels his whole body has disintegrated.

Can you identify with that experience? At a time of spiritual breakdown, may the Spirit be free to work in our lives as he did in David's, and may our response be as honest and open. Only then will there be healing.

JUNE 19

BROKEN BONES

Psalm 51:8

To understand the power of Holy Spirit conviction, see first what lies behind the statement 'broken bones'. They are very painful. A scratch on the skin is nothing, but the grim pain of broken bones shows the intensity of David's pain of mind and the torment of his soul. Broken bones are serious. It is always a relief to hear after an accident, 'no bones are broken'. When broken they cannot be taken lightly, and something has to be done immediately. Genuine sorrow for sin is no mere sentiment, and a real sense of guilt can have disastrous effects on a person's body and mind if not dealt with adequately. The blood of Jesus cleanses from all sin, and his Spirit is there to do his mighty work of renewing and filling.

Broken bones are dangerous, for if they are not attended to properly a limb may have to be amputated. When a life is broken by sin, remorse and unbelief and despair all threaten to take possession and cause a person's heart to harden against God. If you can live in known sin and be happy about it, there is cause for trembling. If you can continue day after day without prayer, or Bible reading, cold and indifferent to the Lord, there is reason to question the reality of your conversion. But when the conviction of the Spirit drives you back to God, there is hope.

Broken bones are hopeful when they have been broken by God, for he who wounds will heal. God can do wondrous things with a broken heart if he is given all the pieces. He has infinite power, and if in his infinite wisdom he breaks, then in mercy he will reset and renew. He is the one who heals the broken heart and hears the cry of the contrite. Look to him for all this in your time of need.

JUNE 20

CONSOLATION

Psalm 51

David turned to God in a torrent of prayer and confession, and how often this Psalm has been a special blessing to those who have fallen down in the battle. Vv. 7, 8 are particularly poignant, as David begins to see light at the end of the tunnel, and can talk of joy and gladness. David's need and ours, is much more than forgiveness. It is for complete deliverance from the pollution of sin (vv. 2, 7, 10), and Calvary is God's all-sufficient answer. Living at the foot of the Cross brings unending consolation.

The opening phrase of verse 8 is 'make me hear joy and gladness'. David was sure of a full pardon, a clean heart, and a right spirit within him. However, when the Holy Spirit convicts, he points to the wounds of Jesus for our cleansing, and then floods our lives with life-giving power. Hear what he has to say, open your ears to his voice and his truth, and receive the consolation he longs to bring you.

The enormity of sin can never exceed the merit of the sacrifice of Calvary. Without injury to his justice or smear upon his holiness, God can forgive us NOW. Believe it, for it is true.

'Lord, make me to hear', not to hear a preacher with an outward ear, but to hear God's word deep down in the heart. Understand how a broken heart before God is the outcome of broken bones that he has healed. Never be ashamed of tears as you confess your sin and failure, for the Spirit of consolation is there to wipe them away.

A Prayer: Lord, please cleanse the ears of my soul that they may hear your words of grace, and may my heart be restored as the throne room of the Lord Jesus.

FICKLE OR FAITHFUL?

2 Corinthians 1:12-22

The reason Paul wrote this passage is a very practical one. In verses 15-17 he states a reason known to all who live by their diaries! He found he could not keep an appointment to visit Corinth, and the church there accused him of being fickle, changing his mind arbitrarily.

His reply to that is very firm, and he challenges the Corinthians to look at his character, a bold thing to do (v. 12). The charge of inconsistency is absurd because God's unswerving grace in giving his Son as his YES to Calvary, had been met by Paul's AMEN in total commitment of his life. Truth had gripped him to such an extent that obedience became the only possible course of action – even to changing his travel plans. What a contrast is our often halfhearted AMEN, 'so be it', to the Lord's commands. Often this is because we are moral cowards and hate to be thought narrow or eccentric. So we lapse into fickleness and say 'perhaps', 'I hope so', instead of 'this one thing I do' and 'one thing I know'. God grant that we accept his love and his standards without hesitation.

The contrast in this passage is between the fickleness of so many Christians and the eternal faithfulness of God. So how can we stop double-talk? Communion with a faithful God makes faithful people. As believers we are established, commissioned, sealed, guaranteed, all because his Spirit is within us to make us his own, and to enable us to bear the likeness of our Father (vv. 21,22; Ephesians 1:13,14). Think on the meaning of those four words and how their importance in your life is worked out: rooted, sent, sealed, guaranteed.

CALLED BY GOD

Acts 13:1-4

Do you believe in the Holy Spirit, not as part of a creed or as a question of intellect, but as a matter of personal experience? Every born-again Christian is indwelt by the third person of the Trinity, the executive on earth of the Godhead, therefore God actually lives within us. He is there to order, to control and govern, to direct and channel every Christian, as well as groups of believers, into effective service for him. God's business is the concern of the Holy Spirit and can only be done in this way.

'The Holy Spirit said, Set apart for me...' (v. 2). The Spirit spoke and made known his will so clearly that there was no doubt or uncertainty in the minds of the assembled men. It is not told how he spoke, probably through some of the prophets and teachers present, but the human instrument is unimportant. There was absolute conviction among them that they heard the authoritative voice of the Spirit of God.

The command was to set apart two of the company for a special assignment. 'Put a circle around those men' is a free translation, for they were wanted by God for special work to which he was calling them. There was a real closeness between Paul and Barnabas, and it could be that the Lord had already spoken to them about a new area of service. It was, however, on this particular occasion when this strategic company of men were gathered that the Holy Spirit made public the plans of God's heart, for they all had to share in the commissioning of these pioneer missionaries.

Happy is the worker who sets out from a fellowship knowing he or she is called by God, sent out in the power of the Spirit, and supported fully and faithfully by the fellowship of the Church. Does this happen in your own Church?

JUNE 23

THE CHURCH IN ACTION

Acts 13:1-4

This is a picture of the Church acting corporately at the bidding of the Holy Spirit, for it is through the body of Christ that the Spirit of God reaches out to the world. He did not speak to Antioch, but to the Church at Antioch, and the same is true today. We must therefore, as individuals and as a Church, be open and alert to hear his voice and respond, not in isolation from other fellowships, but as 'all one in Christ Jesus.'

Now see *when* the Spirit spoke: while they were worshipping the Lord and fasting. The word 'worship' here is the word from which 'liturgy' stems, giving a special emphasis on praise. They were answering the precious ministry of the Lord to them with their praise to him. It is the praising, thankful Christian to whom God speaks, for he is obviously living in fellowship with the Lord Jesus and therefore can be trusted to receive his secrets. 'The secret counsel of the Lord is for those who fear him, and he makes known to them his covenant' (Psalm 25:14, and see Mark 4:11a).

Not only did the Church pray and praise, they also fasted. If prayer is the outward sacrifice, fasting is the inward sacrifice, the denial of self, living at the foot of the Cross, and taking time to do so, free from the most legitimate needs such as food, drink and leisure.

When problems arise that are too great to solve easily, time must be taken to wait on God, unhindered and undistracted. The Spirit does not guide or control fleshly energy, but speaks to those who wait in expectancy and faith in the presence of the Saviour, in absolute commitment to his will. If we have never understood these things before, let us begin to act upon them now, for our enrichment and his glory.

JUNE 24

THE CONFIRMING OF A CALL

Acts 13:1-4

How far removed are we from the place where the Holy Spirit can speak to us? How can this be rectified? Each of us must answer for ourselves.

After the Lord's command came to the assembled company, immediate action took place. The early Church leaders did not take time to hum and haw, to question or form a committee. They had fasted and prayed, then they laid hands on Paul and Barnabas and sent them off. How simple, how glorious, how unique!

Here is the whole body of believers working in fellowship with the Holy Spirit. The call of God was confirmed, the two men were *sent away* to the task by the Church, and at once were *sent out* by the Spirit. There is an important difference, for the Church loosed them, released them as a ship is launched from the dock into the ocean. As the Church let them go, so the Spirit sent them forth to the task prepared for them by God, while the believers took the responsibility to care for them as they went.

This is a wonderful picture of any call to service, with a working together of the authority of the Holy Spirit and the obedience of the local Church, resulting in spirit-filled service and overflowing blessing. The outcome in the lives of Paul and Barnabas in verses 5-12 illustrates this fact.

The modern Church, by and large, needs to learn these lessons, that the most necessary adjustments may mean more prayer and less work, more silence before God and fewer words on our part. It is time to scrap a busy, barren life, and give God time to speak, and when you hear his voice, GO TO WORK!

JUNE 25

SPIRITUAL CONVICTION

Acts 5:27-32

Read from verse 12 of this chapter to get the full thrust of Peter's bold words. Twelve men had turned Jerusalem upside down in a matter of weeks. Is your town stirred to such a degree through the witness of Christians? Thousands meet in their churches to worship God, but what impression is made on the nation?

These men had a deep spiritual conviction. Peter declared three things concerning God: he raised Jesus from the dead; he exalted Jesus to his right hand; he gave the Holy Spirit to those who obey him. Peter clinched his bold words by saying, 'we are witnesses to these things.' Yes, he had seen the empty tomb, he had met, eaten with, touched, talked to and heard the living Christ, and who would dare gainsay these facts? Peter did not preach Christ as a martyr, but as the risen, reigning Saviour who wants to pardon even members of the Sanhedrin! It was no human power that enabled these 'uneducated, common men' (4:13) to preach so convincingly, but the Holy Spirit within them. Evangelism is not a doctrine, but an outpouring of passion implanted by the Spirit of God.

These men were governed by an unshakable principle, 'we must obey God'. This is the secret of their fearlessness, because they had been brought to a place of unqualified submission. Tomorrow the implications of this submission will be the theme.

A Prayer: Dear Father, as I compare my life with that of the early believers I feel so ashamed. May your Spirit so deal with me that my one desire may be to be your obedient servant, with no regard to the cost.

JUNE 26

WHAT EXAMPLES!

Acts 5:29-32

'We must obey God,' said Peter, speaking for the others also, and every word needs emphasis:

We must obey GOD. All other demands and authority must be swept out of our lives. He above all demands our all.

We must OBEY God. No theorizing or arguing, or procrastination, but total obedience.

We MUST obey God. There are no two ways about it. It is not 'we may' or 'we ought to', but a recognition of obligation to share our faith, and then we receive the power to do so. It is easy to confess that we *ought* to obey, but that means we don't and won't. Determination of the Holy Spirit is required.

WE must obey God. Responsibility rests on those who read at this moment, and who heed God's word. We do not place the onus of obedience upon others. Obedience to the call of God gives us the power to win victories in his name because:

These men possessed an irresistible power (v. 32). They had seen the events of Easter and the Ascension, but their witness also testified to the facts, together with the Holy Spirit. Is that true in our lives? As we go into a lost world each day, is the Spirit free to testify to the glory of Christ through us, by life and lip, because we walk in obedience to him? This is a glorious partnership, and it only breaks down when we deliberately shut our ears to the Lord's word and close our hearts to the Spirit's urgings. It is not our relationship with the world that is at fault, but our relationship with the Spirit. The testimony of those men bore the Spirit's confirmation, and that made their witness irresistible. May the Lord grant that this is true for us today and every day that lies ahead of us.

THE CHURCH'S MARCHING ORDERS

Matthew 28:16-20

The series on the Holy Spirit ends with the outcome so far as our individual lives are concerned, in the commission which Jesus gave to his people prior to his ascension. We have studied the person, work, ministry, resources of the Spirit; now look at his power through our obedience.

These verses in Matthew are so important, yet are often ignored by Christians today. There is little real commitment in this modern world, both secular and Christian, in a 'me first', 'I do it my way' society. How easily the world traps a believer into its mould.

Turn back to Matthew 26:31, 32, where the three greatest events in history are seen: 'I will smite the shepherd', the crucifixion; 'but after I am raised', the resurrection; 'I will go before you to Galilee', where he gave the great commission. This latter command was repeated in 28:10 after the resurrection, and the study passage opens with the assembling of the disciples at Galilee as Jesus had instructed them.

Without the commissioning of the disciples to preach a crucified, risen Saviour, the crucifixion and resurrection would have been pointless. Why should Jesus suffer all that if the new life now available through his work of redemption is not made known worldwide?

The eleven apostles were there at Galilee, some with much trembling, no doubt. Thomas had had his doubts removed, Peter had repented after his denial and been restored, so the band of first pioneers for the Gospel assembled to receive from their Master their marching orders. Are you too prepared to present yourself before him for the same reason?

THE CONTEXT OF THE COMMISSION

Matthew 28:18-20

As you read these words you will see it is not a question of 'Have I received a call?' but 'Have I an exemption?' Not all are called to leave home and country, but not one believer is exempt from telling out the good news of salvation by faith in Jesus. Evangelism is the preaching of a whole Christ to the whole man in the whole world by the whole Church. If you are not doing that task in your area of 'the whole world', then you are not a missionary but a mission-field. Jesus gave his entire life to redeem us from sin and death; can we offer less to him than our entire lives, worthless though they may be in our eyes? As the task of evangelism is faced, three questions need to be answered:

1. When Christ died, did he provide adequate redemption for all men? The answer is an emphatic Yes: adequate for all, effective in those who repent, believe, and obey the Gospel, for God is not willing that any should perish, but that all should reach repentance (2 Peter 3:9).

2. If it is adequate for all, is the result automatic redemption for all men so that all will be saved? This is a popular concept on the pretext that a loving God would send no one to Hell. Men send themselves to a Christless eternity by rejecting the only way of salvation, so the answer to the question is No.

3. Can anyone be saved without hearing the Gospel? No. Read Romans 10:14, 15 and recognize that each one is responsible for sharing what we know with those who are ignorant of their lostness, whether they live in our home, our street, or the uttermost parts of the world.

JUNE 29

THE CONTENT OF THE COMMISSION

Matthew 28:18-20

The word ALL occurs four times here: **all** power is given to the risen Lord; make disciples of **all** nations, the purpose of the risen Lord; teaching them to observe **all** things, the precepts of the risen Lord; I am with you **all** the days, the presence of the risen Lord.

Consider first the power of the one who is commissioning his followers, not only the eleven men, but every believer of every country throughout the ages since, down to you and me today. All authority from heaven is given into the hands of Jesus. Therefore giving to his people that knowledge, there can be no dispute or debate about his authority in your individual and personal life. 'Am I not allowed to do what I choose with what belongs to me?' asked Jesus in Matthew 20:15.

The purpose of preaching is not to make converts but disciples, and that is where much evangelizing fails to have lasting effect in changed lives, filled with the Spirit, and purposefully following the Master. It is comparatively easy to make a convert, but much harder to see that convert become a disciple. The Lord does not see his authority complete or his purpose fulfilled until he has our voluntary submission to his rule over our lives, and our will made one with his. It takes a disciple to make a disciple, for only those whose lives are committed and obedient to the Lord and inspired by his Holy Spirit can reproduce another disciple who in turn will learn to live only for God's praise and glory.

JUNE 30

THE FINAL MESSAGE

Matthew 28:18-20

Everyone coming to faith in the Lord Jesus needs to learn so much, therefore Christians are to teach the precepts laid down in the Word of God. Jesus himself spelt them out firmly and succinctly in the Sermon on the Mount, and he does not change his standards of morality to suit the whims and fashions of every generation. He does not water down his terms of discipleship and discipline. However, before a person can teach others, he must be living in obedience himself to the Lord's precepts, and that is possible only by the indwelling of the Holy Spirit who is our Teacher.

Finally Jesus promises his abiding presence, which is more a fact than a mere promise. The Christian is never alone, never commissioned to go on his own. And that is not for certain special times, but *all the days* – good and bad, glad and sad, days of sorrow and trouble, anxiety and temptation.

Jesus is about to return to Heaven, but he had already given the assurance of 'another Counsellor' who would be *in* every believer (John 14:16). What more do we need?

There is, however, the conquest of the world yet to be undertaken in the name of Christ. Each of us has a place in this. A missionary once said at a meeting, 'The Lord said 'Go into the world'. Can you prove your commission to stay at home?' A challenging word, much needed today with an altered world situation, but still a world full of needy, lost men and women. If we are exempt from *going* to another land, are we world-minded and therefore praying, and concerned so much that we are giving that others may go?

VICTORY IN CHRIST

JULY 1

WHAT A PRIVILEGE!

Ephesians 6:10-24

For the next two months our thoughts will be centred on victory in Christ. This is based, of course, on his own victory at Calvary over all the powers of darkness and over Satan himself. The glorious truth is that every Christian can share this in his or her own life, but how few claim all the resources that are theirs in Christ.

It is a great privilege, yet an immense responsibility, to live as a Christian in a world like this. Satanic forces are increasing in subtlety and power, people are living Godless lives yet are full of doubt and fear, the world moves rapidly toward judgement – and in such conditions the Christian is a representative of Christ, the pivotal point of resistance in his name against all the powers of hell. That is our privilege. Our responsibility is to stand our ground, to fight to the end in a relentless war with no respite, and to remain victor on the field with all enemies vanquished.

Cheer up, because you are not alone in the battle! You are part of a great company who have been redeemed by the blood of Christ, an army committed to victory over Satan, with the power to win through depending on the personal victory of each of Christ's soldiers. If God's purposes are to be fulfilled today, then *every* Christian must be living in the light of Christ's victory, and committed to waging war with the enemy whose design is to hold sway in our lives (Mansoul, as Bunyan says) and in the whole world. Let us all be among those who raise high the banner of the Cross, and follow Christ fearlessly, knowing victory is assured through him.

JULY 2

FACING THE FOE

Ephesians 6:10-13

A recruit for the armed services is provided with all that is essential for his part in any conflict. He leaves behind his civilian job, his clothes, even his home, and he does this knowing his government will make provision for his needs.

So with our heavenly Commander. He calls us into his service, and he provides all our equipment, and he commissioned Paul to write about the supplies given us in our battle against evil. And what evil it is! It has never changed since the serpent tempted our first parents in the Garden, and Paul outlines what we are up against in today's passage.

If we read only verse 12 our hearts could well fail for fear at such formidable enemies. Keep your eyes on them and you are defeated before you begin. However, Paul commences this section by making us look to the Lord, 'the Lord strong and mighty, the Lord mighty in battle' (Psalm 24:8). He is the God of the impossible (Matthew 19:26), and the question asked to Abraham still challenges us: 'Is anything too hard for the Lord God Almighty?' (Gen. 18:14), and we answer a resounding NO!

Yet in day to day living just where do we cast our eyes? Are we like the ten spies who could only see giants in the land, or like Caleb and Joshua who knew God was strong enough to overcome the enemies and give his people the land he had destined for them (Numbers 13:27-33; 14:6-9)?

It has been said that Satan is a roaring lion (1 Peter 5:8), but his teeth were drawn at Calvary and his power is limited. May the Lord give us the eyes of faith that can see the foe is active and dangerous, but above all to see Jesus the Victor on the throne in glory.

GOD'S ARSENAL

Ephesians 6:13-17

The command is to put on the *whole* armour of God, not one piece today and another for tomorrow. The Roman soldiers guarding Paul in prison as he wrote this letter were no doubt his models. God's provision for our battles is complete and perfect, forged by the Victor himself, for it is 'the armour of God'.

The Girdle of Truth speaks of the psychological need of the Christian. The mind is to be made strong in the truth that is in Christ Jesus, strong to act and think for him. We all need to be filled with the truth of the faith we believe in in order to scatter all doubt and fear, and making us speak out what we know.

The Breastplate of Righteousness covers the whole body. There must be a rightness of life and conduct, the ministry of the Holy Spirit, which protects the joy and peace he gives us as the fruit of his indwelling. Our lives must be pure, causing no offence to God or man, otherwise our arms are weak and we are totally unfit for battle.

The Shoes of Preparedness signify our readiness to do God's will and obey his commands, and to be fearless in testimony to the power of the Gospel. Read Isaiah 52:7, a wonderful word picture of the tirelessness and urgency that should be shown by every messenger of God's Good News.

The Shield of Faith is 'above all', because the Roman shield covered the soldier from head to toe. The faith of the Christian should be so deep and unshakeable that he has absolute confidence in God's ability to overthrow the enemy.

Pray over these pieces of armour as you go out into today's battle, and remember that **FAITH** means Forsaking All I Take Him.

JULY 4

VICTORY IN BATTLE

Ephesians 6:10-20

The Helmet of Salvation is needed to protect the head from false teaching, and to give assurance of salvation. A soldier who is immobilized by fear and doubt is a menace to his entire company. The Christian who has no real assurance that he has been born again by God's Holy Spirit is unfit to serve in the King's army, for he can lower the morale of the entire fellowship. The 'hope so', 'don't know' person is no witness to the truth of the Gospel.

The Sword of the Spirit, the Word of God, is the only offensive weapon the Christian possesses, so he needs to know its message and content. Jesus used its power when tempted in the wilderness by Satan, and through it was victorious with the enemy routed.

Here are the means of conquest, and each one can be seen in Christ himself: truth, righteousness, preparedness, faith, salvation, the Word of God. Jesus forged them all when he came in obedience to his Father to Bethlehem, and proved them as he travelled the road to Calvary.

Finally see that we must maintain a position of faith as we are equipped with God's armour. We are to stand firm (vv. 11, 13, 14). We can only stand *against* (notice the repetition of this word in verses 11, 12) evil as we know ourselves to be cleansed from sin, justified by faith, and set apart for God's service.

We are to wrestle as individuals, for it is a personal conflict we endure each day, and we cannot hide in the army. Satan never lets up, so we must always be prepared mentally, physically and spiritually, for we are to pray at all times as we shall see in future meditations.

Meanwhile thank God for all his wonderful provision, and pray you will use his heavenly arsenal rightly for his sake.

THE CHURCH AT PRAYER

Matthew 18:19, 20

What encouraging words these are! In these days when numbers are everything the Lord shows his delight and concern for the individual. Some things to him are not important, such as the need for a crowd. Two or three meeting together find him in the midst— husband and wife, two friends, a few concerned over a special need, a 'prayer triplet'. Nor are titles important, for it is not necessary for pastors or teachers to be present, or for participants in prayer to be among the Church elite or the most mature. Anywhere can be a place of prayer, for God listens to those who seek him in spirit and truth at any time, in any place.

The important matter is to meet 'in his name', to have fellowship with him and each other, to carry out his will as shown in his word, to honour and worship him, and to meet together because he commands us to do so. As we follow these simple directions then we experience his glorious promise, 'there am I in the midst'.

A Prayer: Dear Lord, make me a child who loves and longs for every opportunity of meeting in your presence with a friend or two, and to know that you are the unseen Lord at the very centre.

JULY 6

THE BREATH OF LIFE

Luke 11:1; Matthew 6:7-14

Prayer has rightly been called the Christian's vital breath, and is such an important aspect of Christian living and of victory over the evil one that we now consider what the Lord Jesus taught on this subject. Luke's Gospel records many occasions when the Lord went off alone, usually to the mountains or a desert place, to commune with his Father. If it was necessary for him to do this, how essential it is for us to learn to pray effectively (see Luke 3:21; 5:16; 6:12; 9:18, 28).

In Luke 11:1 the Lord was praying and the disciples asked him to teach them to pray, and he gave them the 'pattern prayer', which is recorded more fully in Matthew's account, from which our meditations are taken.

Its structure is interesting: it begins with worship and ends with praise. It is so simple a child can understand every word, yet so profound its depths of meaning are unfathomable. As a principle of life it shows how sin can be overcome, and where deliverance lies. As a basis for social relationships it lays the only foundation for true fellowship.

There are seven petitions, and the first three concern God: his name, his kingdom, his will. Then there are four petitions concerning ourselves: our daily needs, sin, temptation, evil. We so often come into God's presence bursting with our needs and requests, and then stop briefly to praise and thank him. The Lord taught that worship must come first to enable us to come into God's holy presence, recognizing *who* he is, and *how* to know his good and perfect will for our immediate needs.

So as we see this prayer in greater detail, come to it with the request of the disciples upon your lips and in your heart, 'Lord, teach *me* to pray.'

APPROACHING THE THRONE

Matthew 6:7-9

So often we almost barge into God's presence with our 'many words', and forget we are coming to the Lord God Almighty, Creator of Heaven and earth. At the same time, Jesus has revealed to us the Fatherhood of God, and teaches us to come to him as our own Father.

A name signifies character. Mention one friend's name to another, and immediately the person comes to mind. To call God 'Father' indicates we are in his family, for we can only claim that relationship through Jesus Christ, the only-begotten Son, and we receive the Spirit of adoption, and call him Father (Romans 8:15). So this is a family prayer, and only loving hearts will approach the throne of grace with the word 'Father'. It is doubt and fear and sin that dry up prayer, and make us avoid the place of prayer.

God our Father is in *heaven*, a place free from earth's conflicts, uncertainties, perplexities, but he is not remote. He is not only at our side, but is now within us through his life-giving Spirit. Yet to understand where God is, in the realms of glory that our finite minds cannot comprehend, saves us from over-familiarity, and should give us that respect and awe and worship that is due to his holy name.

He is *our* Father, and this whole prayer is very personal. True prayer is aloneness with God, as the Lord Jesus stole away at night to be with his Father. There is a glorious relationship with God our Father, which also claims responsibility, for he is not only *my* God, but yours also, and we are bound up in a bundle of life with him and all who are in his family. What a warm and comforting thought, but may we be delivered from disgracing his almighty name.

JULY 8

HOLY IS HIS NAME

Psalms 19 and 20

These exuberant Psalms show how God's holy name is revered in creation, as Paul explains in Romans 1:20. Look outside on a spring or autumn morning; hear the birds' dawn chorus, see the glorious colours God spreads before our eyes, and we are bound to say in the words of an old hymn, 'Shall all nature be vocal and sing, and no psalm of rejoicing from me?'

In our personal relationship with our Father, to pray that his name be hallowed is to pray at the deepest level of which any of us is capable. It means that we desire first and foremost his glory to be seen in everything we are and do. It expresses our concern that whatever form of service we undertake will be for his glory. As we prepare programmes and schedules for work in the church, can we write 'hallowed be thy name' over them? Is his name glorified in the books I read, the friends I make, the TV I watch, the habits I form, the money I spend, my thoughts and ambitions, my attitude to joys and sorrows? Let us see to it that in everything we honour our relationship with him, so that he is not ashamed of us, his children.

To fail to do this can have disastrous consequences, for the world expects a high standard from those who profess the name of Christ. Careless conduct and speech can do deadly harm. It is surely of little value to pray in church 'hallowed be thy name', and then be responsible for the name to be dishonoured at home or at work.

A Prayer: Loving Father, as I recognize that I am your representative where I live, may your Spirit give constant grace to honour your name, whatever the cost, so that my friends will see Jesus in my behaviour.

JULY 9

KNOWING KINGDOM LIFE

Matthew 6:10; Romans 14:17

The prayer, 'Thy Kingdom come', is answered in three specific ways. Prophetically, the kingdom has been long promised, as in Isaiah 9:6, 7; Luke 1:32. We pray for the fulfilment of God's purposes on earth, for his kingdom consists of those acknowledging his kingship in their lives. It will never come about by striving to live good lives, doing good works, creating a better world, as was once the Utopian dream.

It is the kingdom of grace, as Paul writes in Romans 14. Unless Christ reigns in our hearts by his Spirit now, we can never reign with him then in the kingdom of glory. By righteousness, joy, and peace, our lives should make known the blessings of union with Jesus, and make people envious of what we possess in him. But do we show all that to others? What is really seen of Christ in our lives?

The kingdom of God is his personal reign within us. He is King, we are his subjects. We cannot pray 'Thy Kingdom come' until we have prayed 'my kingdom go'. It is an earnest prayer, for we acknowledge we cannot *go* to it, it must *come* to us, and that happens when Jesus comes into our hearts, for he said 'the kingdom of God is within you' (Luke 17: 20,21), and he is our strength for life (see Matthew 6:33).

In that strength each Christian is to go out into the world to proclaim the Gospel of the Kingdom, and continue doing so until those of every tribe and nation are gathered in. It is only those who have claimed the Lordship of Jesus in their lives who have the power to witness effectively, for if he is not Lord of all – our King – he is not Lord at all!

JULY 10

THE OBEDIENCE OF LOVE

Matthew 6:10; Luke 19:11-14

In praying to our Father we claim a family relationship through Christ. Now we pray for his will to be done. To reverse this order would be sullenly to submit to the will of an unknown God. He has not only a name to be revered, a kingdom to be established, but a will to be done, and true obedience always springs from love. Think on these statements.

One day God's will is to be done on earth, therefore the obedience of his people is his desire for them and for the world. Rebellion in our hearts against the rule of Christ makes obedience impossible (Luke 19:14). Look within your own heart, for the centre of all unrest is a will that is off-balance.

The manner in which we are to obey God is 'as it is in heaven'. There it is never rejected or questioned, being done instantly out of love and devotion and worship.

Only one man has ever done the will of God completely, and that is the man Christ Jesus, for he knew no other will than his Father's, and the deepest revelation of doing the will of God was at Gethsemane, when he prayed, 'Not my will but thine be done.'

How often we argue and query God's will and even dare to say No. Only the power of the Holy Spirit can change rebellion and argument into obedience. First there is God's will for all believers shown in sanctification (1 Thessalonians 4:3), thanksgiving (5:18), right living (1 Peter 2:15), and you can find more. If we obey the specifics, then God will reveal his daily plan to each one of us individually. May our response be 'the will of God: nothing more, nothing less, nothing else' as we also meditate on Hebrews 13:20,21.

JULY 11

DEPENDENCE ON GOD

Matthew 6:11; John 6:35-51

From adoration, a desire for the kingdom of God and his will, to our daily needs – what a contrast! The first part of this prayer has gone from the inward shrine of worship to the outward sphere of service. The second half is the reverse, from outward wants, through sin, conflict and temptation, and ends finally in praise. It deals with present needs, past sins, and future evils.

The unknown battles of life await us, but we can know the One upon whom we can depend for *all* our needs. We rely on him to reveal himself as our Father, to make us a member of his kingdom, to fulfil his will. Therefore we can face the future with confidence, because we believe with all our hearts he is able to meet our every need, for we can pray, 'Give us'. It is his delight to give, as Paul points out so vividly in Romans 8:31, 32.

This little prayer expresses our belief that he will supply the great necessity of life, bread. While we think of material food, remember spiritual sustenance also. The wheat that makes flour for bread has first *died* (John 12:24), and Jesus, crucified and risen, is the source of our life. Therefore he could portray himself as the Bread of life, the only one who can supply the deepest needs of every human heart. He promises 'daily bread', which never grows stale, just as the manna had to be gathered in the wilderness and used each day before it went rancid. God's grace is not to be stored; he does not give us his supplies to be banked or refrigerated until needed. No, they are new every morning (Lamentations 3:22-24). We do not win today's victories with yesterday's supplies of grace: there is always so much more from God's storehouse of love and power.

JULY 12

THE FRUIT OF FORGIVENESS

Matthew 6:12, 14, 15; 18:15-35

Daily bread is for the present; forgiveness concerns the past, and in the prayer the two phrases are linked by the word 'and'. As we need daily to draw upon his resources of grace to meet our need, so daily we are cast on him for his forgiving mercy.

This is the family prayer, and we are praying as a child to his Father. Any sin in our lives is a sin against him, and when we sin we wound God. We can annoy a stranger, but wound only those who love us. How many of us are really conscious of sin? We rejoice in the fact of 'no condemnation', of our position in Christ, but are careless in our experience. We cannot glibly say, 'The blood of Jesus covers all my sin', because atonement only covers sin that is confessed. We *cannot* disobey and hurt God with impunity. Unconfessed sin results in loss of fellowship with him.

'Forgive us' is a heartcry in recognition of desperate need. Daily heart-searching, confession, and the Lord's cleansing and forgiveness – that is the pathway to victory. As has already been said, keep short accounts with God.

'As we forgive' is the crunch, and Jesus enlarges on it in verses 14, 15. It is not the sin of the unbeliever that is in question, but the sins that bar God's children from fellowship with him and with one another. If we want to know God's forgiveness, we will seek it in vain unless we show forgiveness to others, hence the question of Peter in Matthew 18. The evidence that the Lord has forgiven me is that I forgive my brother and sister. That is the victory of love, with pride humbled and bitterness replaced by grace.

TEMPTATION AND DELIVERANCE

Matthew 6:13

This pattern prayer is a picture of growth in Christian experience: from the cry 'our Father', through worship, service, surrender, dependence, conviction of sin, conflict, warfare, victory, to Heaven itself!

Now we look at the future, the days of conflict that lie ahead. Temptation is not sin, but to yield to it is to sin. So how does temptation begin? It is Satan's greatest ploy to separate the believer from God by bringing doubt, unlawful desires, and all manner of sins into our minds. God uses temptation to test our faith while Satan attempts to achieve our downfall. God never in malice tempts us; he does in mercy try us. See the distinction in these words in James 1.

The evil from which we are delivered is both internal and external. The first assails our character and circumstances and all our inner feelings; the other is that which comes as darts against us, that makes us unhappy, gives us pain and sorrow. At the bottom of all this is Satan, the evil one, whose design is to blot out totally the image of God in men, to bring about their eternal ruin, and so prove himself to be more powerful than God. Paul understood the machinations of the evil one and wrote, 'we are not ignorant of his designs' (2 Corinthians 2:11). But is that true of Christians today? They are often trapped by the thought patterns and actions of the world, and are caught by Satan in his iron grip: we see this happening so often and so tragically. But in Jesus there is deliverance, and he prayed to his Father to keep his own from the evil one in John 17. One day that prayer will be fully answered when each redeemed soul is with the Lord in glory. In the meantime we must arm ourselves with the power of God, for in Jesus we stand in victory!

JULY 14

PRAISE GOD FROM WHOM ALL BLESSINGS FLOW

Psalm 34

The doxology of the pattern prayer is often omitted and given as a footnote in many Bibles. It is too wonderful to be treated this way, for it is the shout of victory concluding the prayer which has expressed such confidence in the faithfulness of God the Father.

All praying should begin with worship, continue in intercession, and end with praise and thanksgiving. See how in this prayer praise is essential in every petition. When we pray for daily bread we magnify his goodness. When we pray for forgiveness we exalt his mercy. When we ask for guidance we honour his wisdom, and when we pray for deliverance we glory in his strength.

'For thine is the kingdom, the power and the glory': note the word 'for'. We expect to be heard in our praying, not because of what we are or promise to be, but because our hope and confidence are in God, in his character, his name, his promises, summed up in the words: kingdom, power, glory. When we praise God for his love and mercy, we do so because we realize his name and glory are linked inseparably with our every need. The glory of God is linked with our salvation; never forget that now, as a redeemed sinner, you are his representative on earth. The character of God is linked with our happiness, so be sure to find your joy in the Holy Spirit living out the life of Jesus through your body. The promises of God are linked with the supply of all you need. Therefore praise is the very foundation of prayer.

Now pray the words of this prayer, and if you can, give praise to him after every phrase, to make the petitions real and active in your life.

JULY 15

CROWN HIM WITH MANY CROWNS

Psalm 96

Thine is the kingdom! Jesus is King now and has been since before the foundation of the world (v. 10). Satan is the prince of this world, but he is already defeated and in his death throes, even though his final activities have the world by the throat. Ultimately he will meet his doom, when Jesus the King of kings establishes his reign over earth and Heaven.

The old hymn says 'the crowning day is coming', and we praise God for that. In the meantime his kingdom is in our hearts, we are subjects of the King, and our experience of this is righteousness, joy and peace in the Holy Spirit. Do we really know that in our lives? If not, it is because the throne of our being is not fully occupied by the living Lord Jesus. How easily his place can be usurped by 'puppet self', and while we might profess that 'Jesus is Lord', our actions may be in utter contradiction to his authority. He is King by right, but as yet uncrowned so far as our will and surrender are concerned.

A little girl was given a birthday present of a fully furnished doll's house by her father. She showed it off to her rather envious friends exclaiming, 'Look at my dolls, my toys, my doll's house!' Yet they were only hers as a gift, for she had not chosen or bought one thing herself. How often the words me, my, mine are on our lips! When Jesus is on the throne of our lives then everything I have is mine because they are his and from him; most of all my life is mine only because it is his, for not only did he create me, but he bought me at the cost of his own lifeblood. Is that true of you? Crown him Lord of all now!

JULY 16

THE POWER AND THE GLORY

Revelation 21:1-4; 22:1-7

How best can be expressed the supreme authority of the living God? Who else can claim to receive power and glory forever, and receive the paeans of praise recorded in the book of Revelation? None other than God the Father, Son and Holy Spirit. At the same time his supreme authority searches out our every motive and tests to the utmost the sincerity of our praying.

The power and glory of God run through the whole Bible, and are seen supremely in the coming of his Son to Bethlehem, and expressed to its full extent at Calvary and the resurrection. There was no answering power on earth as God demonstrated his mighty authority through the redemption that is ours in Christ. There was no answering power in our lives as we received the regenerating power of the Holy Spirit at conversion. Day by day we are kept by the power of God (1 Peter 1:3-5), and because his power is so great, so is his glory.

How rarely the Church today exhibits both these symbols of the Lord's authority. His promise to the first disciples was power through the Holy Spirit in Acts 1:8, and they attempted nothing until that power came. The disciples waited for the power, then witnessed, then won. Where have we failed? We don't wait, we don't witness to Christ, but often to ourselves; we don't win, and the whole thing becomes a burden, so we give up.

It is a costly way, for it means death to our own esteem of ourselves that his life may move within us. If, however, we allow him to fill us with all the power of the Spirit then we sense a glow of the glory that we shall one day experience in Heaven itself, and taste the reality of the glimpses given us in Revelation.

JESUS CHRIST, GOD'S AMEN

Revelation 1:4-8; 3:14

Martin Luther said that the family prayer is one of the world's great martyrs: it is used so frequently without thought or feeling. And that is true of the 'Amen', perhaps because people do not understand its significance. It dates back to Deuteronomy 27, and the great praise Psalms conclude with Amen in Ps. 106:48 'Lord, let it be as you say.'

It is the name given to Jesus in Revelation 3, for he is Alpha and Omega, the beginning and the end, the Amen. Yet prayer is not just saying glibly, 'for Jesus' sake, Amen.' His name is not an 'open sesame', a magic word to open the treasury of Heaven. Yes, he answers prayer that is one with his desires through the Holy Spirit; so can he endorse all we ask? See Romans 8:26, 27.

Amen is a word of faith, and as we pray so the angels seem to wait until the reality of prayer is sensed, then God sends deliverance, because the angels are his ministers (Hebrews 1:14). However, we often mistake God's answer to our prayer, for there are times when he does not remove the problem but gives strength to cope with it. Can we say Amen then?

Amen is a test of our sincerity, because prayer is so often off-centre, as James 4:1-3 points out, and we do well to listen to him. Now go through each phrase of the family prayer and from the heart add your Amen: is he your Father in Heaven? do you hallow his name, and pray for the coming of his Kingdom in your life and in the world? do you desire his will to be done always in your life? is he the supplier of your daily needs, the forgiveness of your sins, and your victory over Satan? If so, praise him with a resounding AMEN!

JULY 18

THE BATTLE OF TEMPTATION

1 Corinthians 10:13

From the heights of prayer, wherein lies the source of victory against Satan, we now consider a subject that can bring us down remorselessly. When asked how we are, most of us reply with a smile, 'Fine, thanks', regardless of the true state of our inner lives. A friend who was getting tired of this stock answer said, 'One day I'll say, 'if you have fifteen minutes to spare, I'll tell you how I am'!' Do you sometimes feel like that? Take heart, as we consider God's perfect way to overcome our weaknesses by his strength.

Temptation is common to all, and God does not say he won't allow it, or that he will not allow us to fall. But he does say we need never succumb. As Jesus resisted the subtle ploys of the devil in the wilderness, so we are enabled to resist and come through victorious, though maybe battle-scarred.

Paul gives insight into temptation and the way God enables those tempted to cope. In this verse we see that God has no favourites, but he is faithful to all. While temptation is the common experience of us all, it is graded to our fibre (not beyond our strength), and is sent to prove and humble us and bring us to repentance.

If you are in the midst of severe testing at this moment, read and re-read this verse to understand God's answer to the problem. This answer is continued in tomorrow's thought.

A Prayer: Lord Jesus, while I do not understand the pressures and trials that come my way, help me to remember that my life is in your hands, and I know that as I abide in your love, all things will ultimately work out for my good and your glory.

JULY 19

THE WAY TO SAFETY

1 Corinthians 10:13; Hebrews 4:14-16

If we understand something of the universality of temptation, and in particular God's reasons for allowing his people to experience it, then we must find his answer.

In this verse Paul states that the way to escape is guaranteed alongside the temptation, which is not necessarily removed, but help from on high is promised. The 'way of escape' can be twofold. First, the only course is to run for your life (v. 14, 'shun'). Resist the devil and he will flee from you, says James 4:7. Where do we flee? Into the arms of Jesus, for if we draw near to him, he is right with us (James 4:8).

Secondly, there are times when God releases the pressure, as an engineer will cause steam to escape when it threatens to blow up a motor or engine. The testing is still there, but the pressure is removed by the hand of God. In either case the result is the same: that you may be able to endure it. It is a wonderful thing to experience the moment when the urgency and torment of severe testing is removed, and while the problem remains, to know that God is in control and his love is never-failing. He understands because of what his Son endured on our behalf, for he was tested on all points, as we are.

A Prayer: Thank you, Lord, for your ever-present help in trouble, because you yourself endured and overcame the onslaught of the evil one.

JULY 20

COPING WITH TENSION

James 1:1-4; Psalm 91

Again God's word reminds us that we are to expect trials, 'when (not if) you meet various trials'. One translation says we 'fall into' trials. It is not deliberate disobedience to God that is causing problems here, but the fact that every day we 'fall into' difficulties and trials. When Paul faced persecution he could testify that the Lord delivered him (2 Timothy 3:11), and this is our great hope. Either physically or spiritually God never fails to deliver when we trust him completely to do his perfect work in our lives.

Our reaction to trial, strangely, is to be joy (v. 2a). The reason given is in verses 3, 4. The trial of faith causes patience to grow, provided we act aright and allow it to have full effect. To bear all God brings into our lives, even if they come crowding one after another – so long as he appoints them and they are not our own foolish doings and disobedience – then we can rejoice to see his deliverance and undertaking, and give glory to him. This is the source of joy, and is a strong testimony to those looking on to see a Christian having a hard time, yet exuding the joy of the Lord which is his great strength. Like the ocean, when in a time of storm the waves may be twenty feet high, in the depths the water is unruffled.

If you are in the depths of overwhelming tension, take heart from the promises of God, and learn to rest in his arms of love as you cast *all* your burdens on him (1 Peter 5:7).

THE NEED OF PATIENCE

James 1:4, 12; Ephesians 6:18-20

As by God's grace we accept that trials and temptations come to us as they do to all men, then we can seek to find out the reasons for them. Not only do they produce patience and perhaps make us the more earnestly anxious to wait on God for his word, but they make us mature, lacking nothing. What a place trial has in the manufacture of a saint! Our circumstances are God's tools, and he uses:

a) the gardener's knife; every branch that does not bear fruit he prunes (John 15:1-8)

b) the refiner's fire to purify, so that the molten gold and silver finally reflect his likeness (Zechariah 13:9; Malachi 3:2, 3).

c) the carpenter's cutting edge, and is Jesus not the Carpenter?

Be patient, and allow the daily trials of life to do their perfect work in your life and character. If you do not understand, tell the Lord so and then trust him (v. 12). Remember the Cross is but for a while, but the crown is for eternity.

Patience and perseverance are part of Christian living, as Paul stresses in Ephesians. This is only brought about through earnest prayer, not only for oneself, but broadening out to include friends and loved ones, those on special service for the Lord at home and overseas, who may be experiencing exactly what you are going through, and need support and intercessory prayer. Therefore, pray at all times in the Spirit.

JULY 22

ARE YOU BEING TESTED?

James 1:12-15

Check the source of trials and testings. God never brings them upon us to cause us to sin— always remember that. He does not tempt, but he tests us in order to bring out good (vv.12,13). So many people, Christians included, immediately blame God for any sorrow or trial that comes into their lives, and fail to look closely at the root cause of the experience.

All testings have an outer and inner area, seen in verse 14. 'Lured and enticed' is the outward attack; 'by his own lust' is the inside attraction. The root of sin is within us. Lust means the desire of the heart toward anything evil. 'Lure' and 'lust' are in partnership, and we must all recognize that there is combustible material within us, but it need never take fire. When the mind gives assent to the allurement, then sin is born, leading to death of soul as well as body.

The answer is to read on to verses 16-18, where the antidote to failure and sin is to see again our relationship to our heavenly Father, who bestows upon us every gift and grace to combat the downward pull of our sinful nature. The only place of safety is to walk closely with the Lord Jesus, claiming the power of his Holy Spirit to make real within us the life and power of the living Saviour, and to be strong in his strength alone, for, as the old hymn rightly says, 'the arm of flesh will fail you'.

Praise God for his unfailing love and ability to meet our every need as we confess our inability to cope with the pressures of life.

JULY 23

OUR GREAT HIGH PRIEST

Hebrews 4:14-16

If prayer is the key to victory in spiritual warfare, whether we ourselves are in particular need, or are ministering in prayer for others, or are interceding on behalf of friends in their time of need, let us consider the ministry of Jesus NOW, and see how men through the ages have known divine deliverance through prayer.

To understand the letter to the Hebrews it is necessary to have a background of O.T. worship. The verses for today's meditation have the Day of Atonement (Leviticus 16) in mind, when the High Priest went once a year into the Holy of Holies with the blood of sacrifice, to atone for the sins of the people. Jesus, our High Priest, is also the sacrifice for sin, and therefore on his own merit has passed through into Heaven – not through a curtain as did Aaron, only to come out again to show the people atonement had been made.

Because Jesus was man, he knows all about our weaknesses because he experienced them. Because he was also the Son of God he had no root of sin within him to be tempted by sin, for had he once fallen to even one sinful thought, he could never have been our Saviour. But he was tempted from without, as we are, by Satan, by mankind, by the effects of sin in the world, and he never yielded one inch. So he can sympathize with us in our struggles, and above all, provide his protection for us. The throne of grace, the place of prayer, is where we can draw near through the merit of his shed blood, and find mercy and grace to help in times of need. Are you fully availing yourself of this unique and marvellous provision? Or do you complain and grumble at the hardness of the way? God forbid.

JULY 24

THE LORD'S PRAYER

Hebrews 7:23-26

The writer of this letter is stressing the supremacy of Jesus Christ over all the O.T. priests and rituals, which were 'a shadow' of what was to come (8:5). There was an ever changing army of priests because of death depleting their ranks, but the high priestly office of the Lord Jesus will never be vacant, he continues for ever. There is never a moment when his watchful care for us, his loving sympathy, his complete understanding and his working in us, are not in full operation. Therefore 'he is able for all time' to save the worst of us. The AV rendering is 'save to the uttermost,' which speaks not only of time, but from the lowest to the highest, the outcast and the millionaire.

The Lord cleanses by his blood, refines us by his discipline, renews us by his Spirit, and ultimately will present us faultless before the throne of God. Is he allowed to do his full work of salvation in your life, or are you hindering him by disobedience and unwillingness to surrender to him?

Now Jesus lives to intercede for us – amazing thought! No wonder we can go to him at any time, in any place, and make our needs known, and find his sustaining grace and power to make us strong in the battle against the enemy. For see the Lord's qualifications in verse 26: 'separate from sinners' shows he is their friend, but free from their sin, and this is clearly shown as we study his life. He was accused of being the friend of sinners, but when he asked, 'Who accuses ME of sin?' no one answered.

Come to him now in prayer, telling all your needs, fears, aspirations, for as Intercessor, he shares with you and then supplies all that is needful.

THE PERFECT REDEEMER

Hebrews 7:26-28

See Jesus now made higher than the heavens, exalted above them, in order that his life may be communicated to us. It is hard for our finite minds to realize that all God's planning from before the foundation of the world was to redeem you and me. The life of Jesus from Bethlehem to Calvary, from the tomb to the ascension to his place on the throne – all this was to make it possible for us to have a living relationship with God our Father. Let these stupendous thoughts sink into your heart and life, to give you a new glimpse of the greatness and majesty of our Lord Jesus Christ.

The sacrifice of Calvary never needs repeating, for unlike the daily monotonous, tedious, unending sacrifices of the O.T., Jesus gave himself *once for all*. Sense the contrast of verse 27 and read 10:10-14 to get the full impact of the monotony of the temple sacrifices and the work of the priests, and the once-for-all (all time and all people) offering of Jesus, never to be repeated. Something that is to be repeated is imperfect, but that done 'once for all' is for ever. The priests offered sacrifices; Jesus offered himself.

It is therefore easy to see how Jesus is the only way into God's presence. If there were any other way he need not have died. As you see in a fresh way the wonder of your Redeemer, no longer hesitate to come before him with all the love and adoration of your heart, to share every area of your life, and rejoice in his gracious and willing ability to be more than you can ever ask or think.

JULY 26

RESTORATION IS AT HAND

Mark 14:26-31; Luke 22:26-34

Here is Jesus personally dealing with one man who is about to fall. It is a foretaste of his intercessory ministry after he returned to Heaven.

The Mark passage comes just before the Luke version, which accounts for the lack of connection between verses 30 and 31 in Luke's story. 'I will *never* be offended', Peter had boasted, and Jesus who knew him inside out, gently told him what was about to happen.

Satan was about to rock the world of those few disciples. The 'you' in verse 31 is plural, while that in verse 32 is singular. Their great Friend was leaving, and Satan was prepared to leap in upon them. Jesus must have heard the enemy's plans, for he said, 'Satan demanded to have you' (See Job 1). Jesus uses a fan (Matthew 3:12) to separate the saved from the lost; Satan uses a sieve to shake and disturb the people of God and cause them to be confused and unbelieving, which happened in Peter's experience.

Then Jesus added a mighty '*but* I have prayed for you'. What victory in those words! Yes, Peter would be in Satan's sieve, on one side of the balance, so to speak, but the Lord's intercession was on the other side, so the sifting experience was short-lived, and the effect of Christ's prayer led to a transformed life. Even at this moment he gave Peter a glimpse of the future usefulness and service he would have (v. 32b).

No matter how hard the struggle, how far you may have sunk in disobedience, how much you have been shaken in Satan's sieve, the prayers of Jesus are for you: you are on his prayer-list, and the answer will come, for you are never forgotten by him.

A MEMORABLE VICTORY

Joshua 5:13-6:2

It is always encouraging to see the varied ways in which God worked in the lives of his people, and to see their response to his word, whether they found victory, or doubted and suffered defeat. Let us look at some Old Testament heroes.

The great leader, Joshua, confronts Jericho, a walled city seemingly impregnable, which cannot be left uncaptured. No doubt he was assessing his resources and plan of campaign. Suddenly a man confronted him, his sword drawn in his hand, and Joshua challenged him: see verse 13 and the reply in verse 14. This majestic stranger said, 'No, I am neither for you or the enemy, *but* I am commander of the Lord's army. So, Joshua, if you are for the Lord you are for ME.'

Joshua's response was immediate as he fell down and worshipped the heavenly commander. His first, almost automatic reaction was total acceptance of a superior power. Do we recognize that in our commitment to the Lord Jesus?

The next words sound strange to us: take off your shoes, you are on holy ground. Moses was given the same instruction in Exodus 3:5, and it is a sign of servitude and obedience. Here Joshua was consenting to be a bondslave to this mighty Commander of the Lord's army, for it is stated succinctly, 'And Joshua did so.' No question or argument; is this the way we obey the commands of Jesus?

The next words spoke of victory: I have given into your hand Jericho, its king and people. And that is what happened. What if Joshua had demured and argued about battle strategy? No, he believed the word spoken, obeyed to the last letter the commands given him, and saw a mighty victory. What a lesson for us all!

A GOD OF FAITHFULNESS

Joshua 14:6-15

Caleb is a great character, a true 'Great-Heart', and as we get to know him in these verses, three things are said about him which will challenge our own lives and commitment.

At the age of 85 he stepped out to address Joshua, who was apportioning the newly claimed land among the tribes. Caleb had a faith that never wavered, for in Numbers 13 and 14, 45 years previously, Caleb with Joshua returned with the ten other men who had spied out the land of Canaan, and the gloomy report of the majority overcame the positive words of the two men who knew God would give the land to the nation. Caleb had a special word from God at that time (Numbers 14:24) which he treasured in his heart.

Caleb had strength that never weakened (v. 11). It is always a challenge to see an older person who is filled with the power of God's Spirit, and remains young in heart, alert to the up-to-the-moment work of the Lord, and who is proclaiming loud and clear the truths of 2 Corinthians 4:16 and 12:9, 10. Read these verses and pray God will make them true in your experience, no matter what age you are.

Caleb's love never waned. Of him it is said more than once that he wholly followed the Lord his God. When he had first seen the land it was not its fruitfulness that impressed him, but Hebron, a rugged mountain stronghold. The name means fellowship, love, communion, and that was the longing of Caleb's heart. So after 45 years, during which time Hebron was always before him as his goal, this desire was granted. God's faithfulness was shown not only in Hebron, but because Caleb inherited the 'milk and honey' in the form of springs of water and fertile land (15:19b). Our faithful Lord rewards his people's faithfulness by the lavishness of his love and grace (Ephesians 3:20, 21).

JULY 29

GIVE ME A MAN!

1 Samuel 17

The battle against the enemy is an individual one. Basically we each go into combat on our own, even though there may be others around us.

In the historic confrontation between Israel and Philistia, the giant stood up to defy the people of God with the words in verse 10, 'Give me a man!' and then issued his challenge.

The devil comes in various guises – an angel of light, a lion, a criminal or a sophisticate. But he is still the same underneath, and is always challenging his authority over God's people (vv.8-10).

Enter David (v. 17), a youngster working for his father, but obedient to his will. At once David met opposition from his brothers (v. 28), and was accused of shirking his work to see the battle – what battle? God's people were in such a state of panic they could only huddle in fear and try to close their ears from hearing Goliath's repeated challenge, while King Saul sat in his tent. When David was taken to him the King asked him questions, and the lad gave a clear testimony of his experiences and God's great faithfulness toward him. Do you know victory at home and in your work place, to which you can testify and give God the glory?

Then came the conflict, and Goliath was nonplussed to see not a man but a boy; but with David's ringing challenge (vv. 45-47) Goliath is slain and victory is won. When the giant came against the Israelites the soldiers thought, 'He's so big we can never kill him.' David looked at the same giant and thought, 'He's so big I can't miss him!' How do you view the enemy: with the eyes of logic or of faith? The battle is the Lord's, and it is he who overcomes IF we look to him for victory.

THE CROWNING DAY

2 Samuel 3:6-21

Stirring days of intrigue and power-struggle follow the death of both Saul and Jonathan, but the house of Saul loses against the might of David. Abner, the central figure in this passage was a cousin of Saul, and therefore committed to seeking the establishing of Saul's son on the throne of Israel so he 'made himself strong' in the palace. It did not take Abner long to discover that Ishbosheth was a weakling with no chance of overcoming David and gaining undisputed kingship. The dynasty of Saul was finished. Saul's failure to put God first in his life had sealed the doom of himself and all his family.

The scene was dark, but Abner saw one rising star, the conquering David. Maybe into Abner's memory came the story of David's anointing as a young lad by the prophet Samuel and as an opportunist, Abner turned from allegiance to Saul's house to that of David, and realized the only hope for Israel was a united nation under the leadership of King David. So the outcome was the challenge to the nation's elders in verses 17, 18a: 'In time past you sought David as king over you; now then do it!'

Does that speak to your heart? It is time for Jesus to be acclaimed Lord and Saviour to the nation, in church life, in our lives. How often we have been challenged to give him his rightful place in heart and life: now then do it! As individual Christians crown Jesus as Lord, so the Church should become charged with Holy Spirit power and go out to witness to the authority of Jesus as King of kings. God grant this may happen before it is too late, and it all starts with you and me: now then DO IT!

A Prayer: King of my life, I crown thee NOW; Thine shall the glory be. Lord, give me grace to do this NOW, and every day of my life.

JULY 31

REJOICE ALWAYS!

2 Chronicles 20:1-30

Here is a stirring chapter, with wonderful lessons to teach us as we enter into the battle of life daily.

King Jehoshaphat was a godly man, and on hearing of an approaching enemy, though outnumbered and fearful, his first thought was to seek the Lord in prayer and command the nation to join him.

Study his prayer in verses 6-12, for his approach to God then is our way to the throne now. First he reminded himself, his people, *and God,* how great the Lord was and how precious his promises, for not one had ever failed. In the present situation God's power and honour were at stake, for the enemy was coming to drive his people from the land he had given to them. The king knew his army was inadequate, and so came the ringing assurance of verse 12, as he cast himself, his reputation, his army, his nation, into the hands of the Lord.

Sense the hush of verse 13 as the people waited to see what would happen. Jahaziel stepped forward with a message from God, in the amazing words of verse 17. This was the Lord's battle, and he would fight it his way and win. See the complete trust the king had in this message, his praise and worship, and his orders to the people. This was not a question of 'marshal the army', but 'gather the choir and band'! No doubt there were many hearts beating somewhat fearfully, but the people obeyed and broke into praise and rejoicing. As they did so God worked against the enemy, and the victory was won.

Give thanks, praise, rejoice, are all words a Christian should understand, and when a situation has been committed to the Lord and prayed through, then the outcome of Philippians 4:4-7 is ours.

AUGUST 1

HOLY GROUND

John 17:1-5

It is recorded that Jesus spent hours and nights in prayer with his Father. John now gives his very words, spoken at a strategic time, immediately prior to his arrest and death.

As we approach John 17 we may feel we are eavesdropping. The outpourings of the soul of the Saviour are for our worshipful contemplation, not for critical analysis, nevertheless we can see the thought patterns in his mind and the burden on his heart. Every word is vital, and the opening paragraph is one that cannot be hurried through, but read on one's knees in worship and adoration, for Jesus is praying to his Father concerning himself.

The hour which had not come in John 2:4; 7:6; and which was drawing near in 12:23, has now come. It is the hour of his glorification through death. He prays that, by completing the act of redemption that will secure man's salvation, glory may come to both Father and Son. Just what is eternal life? It is knowing God the Father through his Son, Jesus Christ. Think of the times Jesus claimed deity, and that to see and know him is to see and know God.

That Jesus pre-existed before Bethlehem is made clear in verses 5, 24, and is like a thread running through the whole prayer. That he glorified the Father during his life is self-evident, as he revealed God's character to his disciples and to us. His final request in verse 5 was honoured by his Father in enabling the Son to endure the agony of the coming hours in such a way that one person, maybe expressing the thoughts of many others, exclaimed, 'Truly this was the Son of God' (Matthew 27:54; Luke 23:47, 48).

AUGUST 2

SET APART FOR GOD

John 17:6-19

Jesus directs his praying to the disciples and their great need at this hour of history. What he prayed for them has relevance for his people today, though he continued his intercession for them in verse 20. This section of the prayer shows the concern of the Lord that his disciples should be kept firm (vv. 14-16), and sanctified, which means consecrated, set apart (vv. 17-19).

Notice a progression of thought: the disciple is saved out of the world (v. 6), set in the world (v. 11), separated from the world (v. 14), sent into the world (v. 18). What then is 'the world'? It is of course the planet on which we live, in which we are placed by birth, and into which we are sent as witnesses to the Lord Jesus. It is, in another sense, the kingdom of the enemy, who is the ruler of this world (14:30), and from his power we are saved and separated.

Sanctification is a misunderstood word, being associated in thought with 'sanctimonious', a word used by cynics. A true believer is one who in thought and attitude sets himself apart from the trends and influence of the 'world' dominated by the power of the enemy. John outlines this in 2:15-17 of his first letter. Read it carefully to comprehend the full meaning, and lay your own life along that yardstick. Above all see how Jesus himself set the pattern for us to follow in verse 19 for though he was completely in the world which he had come to redeem, he was completely 'set apart' from the spirit of the world, dominated by the evil one.

It has been said that a boat is built to be in the water, but if the water gets in the boat it sinks. The Christian is to be in the world, but if worldly ways become part of his mode of living, he is utterly out of step with the mind of Christ and useless as a witness.

AUGUST 3

THE FOLLY OF IGNORANCE

John 17:1-23

How often we say, 'I *want* to do the will of God, but how can I know what it is for me?' If we do not get an easy answer, some turn away because they do not take time to wait on God, and then complain that he does not answer prayer. Such is the folly of ignorance.

In his prayer to his Father Jesus leaves us in no doubt, for what he asks the Father for us must be his will for us. So for what then does he ask?

1. It is God's will that we are **saved** by the giving of his Son for our redemption (vv. 2, 3). Then that we are kept (v. 11), as we considered yesterday.

2. It is God's will that we are **sanctified** (v. 17). It is not enough that we are safeguarded, and sanctification is not to be interpreted as isolation. Separation is a mark of holy living, in a right relationship with the Lord, and holiness is spiritual health. See 1 Thessalonians 4:3

3. It is God's will that we are **witnesses** (v.20) in order that others may be saved. Every saved person should be a proclaimer of Good News, otherwise how are unbelievers to be reached? See Romans 10:14.

4. It is God's will that we all become **missionaries**, sent ones (v.18). The Sent One has sent you and me, and we are not told how far anyone will be sent, but we must recognize our commission and respond to God's call, even if it is just to the house next door, or halfway round the world.

5. It is God's will that **unity** should characterize his Church (vv. 22, 23). More of this later, and further signs the Lord gave us in this prayer.

Have you taken note of the revealed will of God? If you still profess ignorance that is sinful folly, not bliss.

AUGUST 4

LOVE AND GLORY

John 17:24-26

The two final areas in which God's will is shown are in these concluding verses of the Lord's prayer.

It is God's will that we should *love* one another as he has loved us (vv. 23, 26). Christ's love for us is to be the standard, though it cannot be the measure, of our love the one for the other. How amazing is the possibility, but how tragic is our failure. The Lord had high hopes for his followers, that we would grasp the implication of all that he taught, and for all that he prayed. Let the truth sink in that we *cannot* love others with our puny, human, somewhat self-centred love, in a way that would reach the standard set before us. No, the love Jesus longs to see is equal to the love between the Father and the Son. Think about that as you refer also to John 13-16, and John's first letter. Only the Spirit of God within us can enable us to love others – even the unlovely and unloving – for it is the love of Christ in our hearts shed abroad towards those we know to be lost and without hope.

Finally it is God's will that we spend eternity with him in Heaven (v. 24; 14:1-4). In these days we are so wrapped up with mundane and material needs we spend little time thinking about eternity, so do so now, for it is then and there we will see Jesus in all his glory, and 1 Corinthians 13:12 will be true. Life has its problems for us all, its ups and downs, difficulties, sorrows and stress, but by God's grace, as we obey his will in what he has shown us here, we can say with the old hymn, 'It will be worth it all, when we see Jesus.'

THE STANDARD OF CHRIST

John 17:20-23

It is God's will that unity should characterize his Church, but how rarely this happens. Paul writes to the Ephesians about unity of the Spirit and unity in the faith (4:3, 13), and we should have agreement on both counts, but that too is sadly lacking among believers today.

How wonderful that Jesus should look down the centuries and pray for his people *now*! His will is that we should all be one in him, with a bond as close as that between himself and his Father, because we are indwelt by his Holy Spirit.

The Lord does not talk about uniformity, for we are not robots, but about unity that has variety. See how this happens in the Godhead: one in essence, but the Son does not act independently of the Father nor the Father of the Son, and the Spirit comes from both. The Father sends, the Son is sent; the Father creates, the Son redeems. So in the Church, the body of Christ, there is diversity in unity, as Paul outlines in 1 Corinthians 12. There are many 'sheepfolds', but one flock (John 10:16); many regiments, but one army; many stones, but one temple (Ephesians 2:19-22).

The object of unity is that the world might believe, but there are now so many conflicting voices and views that the unbeliever is confused, and dismisses the Church as being irrelevant to modern life. Surely the glory (v. 22) is withheld because the will of God shown in verses 20, 21, 23 is not being taught, regarded, understood or obeyed by those who claim to follow Christ. We cannot censure others before taking a long, hard look at ourselves to see how we measure up to the Lord's standard. Make this your aim and your urgent prayer, that you may be among those in these strategic days whose desire above all else is to be a reflector of the glory of the Lord Jesus.

THE SHORTEST PRAYER

Luke 18:9-14

Two men went to the Temple to pray, and as Jesus sketched them for us, let us study and learn from their attitude and reaction.

See first the Pharisee. In his time he was reckoned a good, moral, upright man, a religious leader, highly respected. But his attitude and prayer reveal his true character, and the first thing Jesus says of him is that he 'prayed thus with *himself*'. So he enumerated all his good points: 'I ...I... I...' and in his mind those virtues placed no obligation on God. And that was the end of his pat on his own back. He made no request to God, sought no blessing, revealed no love, and interceded for no one. There was no sense of sin, of need, of wrongs to confess. May the Lord deliver us from any trace of such fearful self-righteousness.

The tax collector did not even raise his eyes, but beat his breast as he uttered a three-word prayer: God – mercy-me – Sinner. The prayer was addressed to Almighty God and signed 'sinner', with the simple request 'miserere', mercy-on-me. This man was on praying ground, for he recognized that God was holy yet merciful to sinners. He knew he could do nothing to save himself, so cast himself on the mercy of God.

See the Lord's verdict in verse 14. The second man's prayer was heard, and he went away justified, for God had heard and answered. Like the Psalmist in Psalm 34:6 he could say, 'This poor man cried, and the Lord heard him, and saved him out of all his troubles'. The Pharisee went away with his head held higher in the air, unchanged and unblessed.

Pray that the Lord will help you to see the true meaning of prayer, so that you leave his presence blessed and enriched through fellowship with him.

AUGUST 7

SEE, HE IS PRAYING!

Acts 9:8-18

Saul the persecutor of the Church, met the risen Lord on the way to Damascus, and immediately recognized the divine authority of Jesus upon his life. The vision of Christ blinded him, but God had a wonderful plan to open Saul's physical and spiritual eyes. He enlisted the help of a humble disciple, Ananias, who, though fearful, was obedient and was God's instrument in setting Saul's feet on the pathway of God's will (vv. 5, 15, 16).

It may have been the four words in verse 11 that quelled Ananias' fears: 'Behold, he is praying'. What was significant in those words? They show there is both a right and wrong way to pray. Saul, as a religious leader, had probably spent hours each day praying, but it was never real, being wrapped in formalism and repetition. It was never right, for not knowing Christ, he could not approach God in the name of Jesus, who alone is the Way, the Truth, and the Life , and our sole claim to come into God's presence.

Further, Saul the Pharisee knew nothing of repentance. His rage against the followers of Jesus showed he was ignorant of the Master's teaching. Saul knew nothing about humility, or the way into the presence of God through faith. So a miracle had taken place, and the Lord said of him 'Behold!' be amazed and see, for 'he is praying'. For the first time God was hearing the prayer of the once proud now penitent man, and it was such a strategic moment it is in the Word of God for all to read and learn. Can those words be said of you and me?

AUGUST 8

THE HEART OF THE MATTER

Matthew 11:16-30

Looking at the passage as a whole, the sequence of events throws light on the well-known promise with which it ends. The Lord has pronounced in severe tones the doom of the impenitent and the cities which had seen the working of his power, but which were rejecting him. He understood this, for nothing came to him by surprise; and it is a great encouragement to us in our daily struggles, disappointments, and all that life throws at us, to know that Jesus experienced these enemy forces too, and showed us yet again how to cope victoriously.

He turned from showing the people the danger of their way of life and upbraiding those with hardened hearts, to praising his Father. This is a truth we all can learn, for there is power in praise, as it discomforts and routs the enemy, and brings liberation and the joy of the Lord into the praising heart.

The opening words of Christ's prayer show the contrast between the unheeding cities and people, and those with a childlike faith. It is something to marvel at that an illiterate, humble person with faith in the power of Jesus Christ shows more wisdom and understanding in the things that really matter than many Ph.D.s with their purely worldly wisdom. Jesus used a visual aid to stress this point (18:1-4), and showed that the simplicity of a child, its acceptance of things taught and the example of the loved ones who teach, are the ingredients needed in our attitude to the word of God. Jesus longs to see a simple childlike faith in his followers which out of love obeys him, but never a childish spirit, showing petulance and argument instead of acknowledging that because God knows the end from the beginning, 'Father knows best'.

AUGUST 9

THE VICTORY OF HEART'S EASE

Matthew 11:25-30

The trouble with so many people is that they do not know the Father (v. 27), therefore they are restless and dissatisfied. To all such Jesus says, 'Come to me, and know the Father; I can bring you to him, and in finding him you will have rest and ease of heart.'

Jesus gives a two-fold promise, 'all who labour and are heavy-laden,' and 'I will give you rest.' The first term expresses active toil, the other a passive endurance. The burden to which Jesus refers goes deeper than problems, but to sin that dominates life. No amount of effort can release the weight of sin, so the Lord tells his hearers to cease their puny efforts which will avail nothing, and come to him.

Jesus gives a two-fold invitation, 'come to me, learn of me'. The first is the initial step of faith at conversion, the second is life-long discipleship. In order to learn we must be prepared to be 'yoked' to Christ, to submit to his authority, and live in joyful obedience to his will. Salvation in Christ is not an escape route from hell, but the entrance to a whole new way of life, linked to the living Lord who is gentle and lowly. Have you put yourself among those who are heavy-laden, and now accept his invitation to victory over sin?

Jesus gives a two-fold promise of rest, 'I will give you rest; you will find rest.' The first is the rest of ceasing to work out one's own salvation and finding rest of soul in Jesus. The other is the continuing rest as we 'trust and obey'. When peace, love, forgiveness pour into the life of one who has for years been struggling with sin, what an immense rest of soul and heart's ease is experienced! This continues so long as we submit to the Lord's yoke and follow him gladly.

AUGUST 10

THE REST OF FAITH

Hebrews 4:1-13

Chapters 3 and 4 should be read together as they are one continuing subject: chapter 3 is the O.T. incident to illustrate the unfolding truth of chapter 4. The subject of 'the rest of faith' is maybe a new concept to some readers, but of vital importance to us all if we seek to live in victory according to the will of God. Faith is resting on what Jesus has done for me, but this form of rest is not laziness or inactivity, nor *laissez-faire*. The more we accomplish for the Lord the greater should be our repose in him, for it is not we who labour, but his Spirit. It is not motion but effort and friction that break restfulness.

Chapter 3 warns against the danger of unbelief and disobedience, which keep the Christian back from the experience of the rest of faith which God has promised (v. 11; 4:5).

Repose is part of the character of God, a calm in everlasting strength. At creation he rested on the seventh day, not because he was wearied by the work, but because it was accomplished. Therefore in his love and mercy he commands one day in seven as a day of rest, because he knows we need it. The human body is not an automaton, but a structure which needs periodic relaxation and change of pace and interests. Christian workers and clergy in particular should heed this, for to disobey is sin.

There is rest in redemption, for with the world ruined by sin, Jesus came as Redeemer, and having accomplished his great work at Calvary, he rose from the dead, ascended to Heaven, and *sat down* at God's right hand. What majesty, and what a glorious finale to his mission of love!

AUGUST 11

THE WAY IS OPEN – ENTER IN

Hebrews 4:9-11

The rest of God after creation; the rest and enthronement of the Lord Jesus after Calvary – both point to a rest the Christian may enjoy here and now. It is a present tense experience (vv. 3a, 10), as well as something we finally enjoy in Heaven (Revelation 14:13). We are concerned about the here and now, our daily living in a way pleasing to God.

It is a rest of *faith*, which is different from belief. Belief accepts a proposition to be true and that brings peace to one's understanding. Confidence (3:14) and obedience (5:9) have similar connotations but are not necessary to belief, but are essential qualities of faith. We experience faith in Christ, but that can be an assent of the mind, a belief. When our hearts go out to him in trust, and our wills submit to him in obedience and surrender, then we begin to experience the rest of faith.

All anxiety is swept away. We need never heed the fiery darts of the enemy as he whispers, 'Has God said?' to disturb our peace and assurance of the faithfulness of God and his word.

All our burdens are now on the shoulders of our mighty God.

All our desires are satisfied when our hopes and aspirations are centred in the will of God. Soul hunger and thirst are quenched.

How then do we enter into this rest? Read verse 11: 'strive' is not a call for effort and good works, but to diligence in our walk of obedience. Refer everything in life to his supreme will, relax in the sure knowledge of the finished work of the Lord Jesus, and your acceptance before God is now made real by the Holy Spirit's indwelling and empowering.

AUGUST 12

SAVED BY HIS LIFE

Romans 5:6-11

A further aspect of the rest of faith is in this passage. Some years ago my friend, Major Ian Thomas, wrote a book he called *The Saving Life of Christ*, and it has been very widely read and proved life-changing to so many, including myself. What a relief it was to understand for the first time that it is not I but Christ who alone can live the Christian life in me!

God showed his love to us that while we were still sinners Christ died for us, and we are now justified, made fit for the presence of a holy God (vv. 8, 9). As *enemies* we are reconciled to God by the death of his Son. It is as if on the Cross one outstretched arm held the hand of the rebels – all of us without exception – while the other arm gripped the hand of God, and so Jesus brought peace and reconciliation. What a glorious new life is ours because Jesus died for us! How much more is there for us now he lives! Yes, we are saved by his life risen from the grave, ascended into Heaven, and poured into our hearts by the Holy Spirit (v. 5). Pray that you receive not just a trickle because of your lack of commitment, but the full outpouring he longs to give.

No wonder we rejoice in this amazing full salvation. By the shedding of his precious blood Jesus delivers and saves us *from* the uttermost: from the depths of sin and rebellion. By his resurrection life that overcame sin, death, and Satan, now resident in our hearts by the Spirit, he saves us to the uttermost: a life that overcomes the downward pull of sin, and lifts us to the heights of union with himself by faith, which will one day be fully experienced when we see him face to face.

AUGUST 13

WHO GOVERNS YOU?

Romans 6:1-23

As there is no short-cut to a life of victory, we will study Romans 6 and 7, because Paul tackles the problem head on, and shows there *is* a way of life whereby we are not constantly in a state of despair over the shallowness and failure of our Christian living. These chapters are not easy to understand, but are inescapable if we are to enter into the joy and blessing of chapter 8.

Chapter 6 is a Charter of Freedom, so note the references as you read it through. In particular see in verse 7 we are free from sin's condemnation, in verse 18 we are free from sin's domination; in verse 22 we are free from sin's fruit.

To experience all that we must understand Paul's terminology. First he shows that we have been delivered from the power of death, for now the Lord Jesus is enthroned in the believer's life over the dominance of SIN (5:18-21). So Paul asks a rhetorical question in 6:1, and then launches into his thesis. If we are justified without being 'good' or working to merit salvation, does that mean we can live as we like? NO! Read verse 18: the tyrant over us still is SIN, but to those in Christ sin is forced to yield to his righteousness which clothes the believer. The slave is released, and the way of deliverance from sin is revealed.

Paul is speaking here about SIN, not sins. We are delivered from the guilt of our sins by the shed blood of Christ, but we still have a tyrant within, the principle of SIN, the root from which the fruit, sins, spring. That evil does not easily yield the throne to Jesus, and is the battle we all face. In Christ we are delivered from the slavery of sin, but in experience we are so often overcome by it.

Assess your own heart's condition in the light of these words, and pray for understanding of the Lord's solution to the problem.

AUGUST 14

HOW MUCH DO YOU KNOW?

Romans 6:1-4

At our conversion we are brought from the rebel's camp into the Lord's army, for there is a battle to wage against the power of SIN within, and the onslaught of Satan all around. That enemy within is the greatest obstacle to progress in Christian living, as no doubt you will acknowledge. So often we are told that because Jesus died for our sins and we are therefore delivered, now we must go out and do something for God. We then perpetuate defeated living because we have no answer to failure in our own lives that we can pass on to others.

Paul says there are three things we must know in verses 3, 6,9. First, do we understand the symbolism of baptism? We are all baptized by the Holy Spirit into the body of Christ at conversion (1 Corinthians 12:13). Water baptism is the symbol of the experience of dying to the old unregenerate life and rising into resurrection power. In effect we say, 'Lord I have died, now bury me!' (v. 3), and then we are raised up to walk in newness of life.

In verses 5-11 we see the pivot of this chapter. We know (do we?) that we have died with Christ, but we feel very much alive! Our old sinful nature was redeemed at Calvary (v. 6), but the 'body of sin' lives on in our experience. The word 'destroyed' is not annihilation, but 'made inoperative'. If the mainspring of a watch is removed, the watch is not destroyed but is of no effect. God in Christ renews the mainspring, and in place of the SIN principle is the power of the Holy Spirit. This is not sinless perfection, but the way to overcome the downward drag we all feel within us. We live under either slavery to SIN, or freedom in Christ, and that is the arena of daily, personal conflict.

FROM THE GRAVE TO GLORY

Romans 6:7-14

In the opening verses we learn Christ died *for* sin; in verse 10 he died to sin. Do we know and understand that (v. 9)? Jesus has dealt with SIN forever, and therefore we must experience his victory on our behalf, and count on his power within us to lead us out of temptation and deliver us from the evil one.

So many Christians are content to paddle in the shallows and never venture into the deep waters of God's grace, mainly because they cannot understand the language of passages like Romans 6, or they feel that to be saved is all they need.

A not-so-young woman, eager to get married, is courted by a wealthy man and they marry. After the wedding day is over she says, 'Goodbye, dear. I've all I want now.' She didn't want to change her status or mode of life, but she wanted the Mrs to her name and the kudos of being married. Far-fetched, perhaps, but that is how many people treat Jesus. There is no evidence of his grace in their lives, and they have no idea that he is waiting for them to experience his victory through their union with him at the Cross in death and into resurrection life (vv. 9, 13) and the promise of Glory. Because of Christ's power we need no longer be under the domination of SIN (v. 14). The secret of this transformation is the total commitment of our whole being to the control of the Lord Jesus, a specific act that can be done NOW.

AUGUST 16

EXPERIENCING DELIVERANCE

Romans 6:11-23

Three further words of importance are in today's reading: consider (v. 11, 'reckon' AV), yield (v. 13), obey (vv. 16,17). Faith reckons on the work and purposes of God that we are to walk in newness of life (v. 4) because the Cross enables us to do that as we are delivered from the power and penalty of sin. We are to consider the old nature to be *dead*, for the all-victorious, indwelling life of Christ within does not respond to the onslaught of the enemy. We assent to the death of sin within us, to ambition, pride, self-pleasing, because a 'dead' person cannot feel hurt or criticism, and cannot respond unkindly to unkindness. Thus we yield all our faculties to Christ. Everything that once responded to the urge of Satan and sin is now laid at the pierced feet of Jesus. Hand over every part of your being to him now, from head to toe, from inside to out.

The outcome of this is the obedience of fellowship with the risen Lord. The choice is simple, either slavery to our own sinful nature, or devotion to Christ. For the goal of deliverance from sin's power is fruitfulness of life and service (vv. 20—23). The power of evil pays those who serve, and the wage is death. Almighty God rewards those who yield to him and obey him by the gift (no wages from him) of eternal life through Christ.

The obvious question is, whose slave are you? One thing we *cannot* do is to wear the uniform of one master and do the bidding of another. Therefore reckon yourself free from the old master, yield all you are and have to your Lord, and obey him with glad and grateful heart.

LAW AND GRACE

Romans 7:1-12

To help understand Romans 5-8, notice that in each chapter there is a ruling monarch who impedes the progress of the man justified by faith, and each is deposed by the Lordship of Jesus Christ.

Ch. 5 The reign of death bows to the life of Jesus.
Ch. 6 The tyranny of sin is broken by his righteousness in us.
Ch. 7 The grip of the law is overcome by grace.
Ch. 8 The pull of the flesh is replaced by life in the Spirit.

Romans 7 is a difficult passage, for to whom does it relate, the saved or the unsaved? Does a Christian go through chapter 6, then chapter 7, and finally arrive at chapter 8? No, because all three are the record of the believer whose experience swings from one to the other. However, they show us the nature of the conflict in chapters 6 and 7, and the secret of victory in chapter 8.

Law is pictured as a Jewish husband (vv. 1-6) to whom his wife is bound until his death, when she is free to marry again. The grace of the Lord Jesus liberates us from the grip of legalism, so that new life in the Spirit can be experienced. The law of God is given to provide guidelines within which we can walk and please God, for to break them is sin. Paul testifies that he felt comfortable with God's law until he read the tenth commandment, and was convicted of covetousness, and then he realized his sinfulness. Guilty on one point made him guilty on all (James 2:10), and this realization brought him to faith in Christ.

AUGUST 18

INNER STRUGGLES

Romans 7:13-25

Paul testifies to the inner struggles he had between his old nature and the new life in Christ, and how they speak to our hearts if we are honest! It is comforting to know a man of Paul's stature was once beset by such heartaches and struggles.

These verses are not Christian experience, but the experience of a Christian, for Paul realizes he is not always on a spiritual 'high', but can be carnal, 'fleshly' (v. 14). He could not keep himself from doing that of which he disapproved (vv. 14-17). He could not do that of which he does approve (vv. 18-20). Then he came to the conclusion which this experience forces on him in verse 18, 'nothing good dwells in me'. Isn't that the story of your life too?

How Paul longed for a holy life, free from all the battles with himself (vv. 21-24!) No doubt that is your heartcry too. It is caused by failure to grasp the truth of our union with Christ, sharing his resurrection life by his indwelling. It is failure to reckon that our self-life is 'dead', that we live either dominated by the old nature, or by God's Spirit, and there is no fence between on which to sit. Therefore breakdown is due to the fact that he is not in control of our whole life, every facet of it.

When Christ is enthroned there can be no civil war, but when he is not, all our faculties – mind, conscience, emotions, will – are at loggerheads. We may never doubt our new birth, yet Romans 7 may be our experience, though it is not what God intends. Make verse 25 your prayer and commitment, and end the struggling against his Lordship to experience his grace and power.

AUGUST 19

ACQUITTED

Romans 7:21-8:4

After reading chapter 7 one might ask just what is sin? First the negative: sin is *not* a weakness, infirmity, tendency that we can just shrug off. It is not inherited temperament, whereby I only blame myself, nor the power of environment, when I can blame outside influences. It is not merely being self-centred, nor is it separation from God – that is the result of sin, for he is always near and longing to work deliverances in the heart and life of the sinner.

Sin is a voluntary breaking away from God's will, a conscious violation of his order. The result is wrong living because of a wrong relationship with God. It is this fact that caused God to thrust our first parents out of Eden, because that precious fellowship with him had departed once doubt and disobedience came into their lives.

Jesus did not come to describe sin, but to remove it. We can do nothing about it, though inwardly we are in the wrong (7:21-24). To acknowledge the fact that we are fighting God and deliberately going against his revealed will, the Law, is the first step to victory. Once we cry, 'wretched me, what can I do?' then we find the Lord Jesus alongside to proclaim deliverance through his sacrifice on our behalf.

Therefore we can pass from the pit of sin to peace with God, into the area of 'no condemnation' because Jesus has borne the penalty of sin on the Cross, and now comes the promise of his Spirit within to overcome the downward pull of sin within us. Read Romans 7:21 to the end of chapter 8 until the message becomes real in your life.

SETTING THE SCENE
1 Samuel 25:1-13

To illustrate the truths in Romans 7, turn to a lovely O.T. story. David the outlaw, fleeing from King Saul, was in the southern-most area, Paran, and his presence and those of his men was a great help to the farmers, as the narrative reveals. One of these was a wealthy man, Nabal, who also had property in Carmel. David had helped him in times past (v.21) and now sent his servants up to Carmel to ask for payment for services rendered (vv. 5-8).

Look at this man Nabal. He was rich, but of such a nature that even his servants spoke against him (vv. 3b, 17b), and later his wife said the same (v. 25). He was a vicious, churlish man, as was shown in his response to David's request in verses 10, 11. The point behind his remarks is that, in spite of what he knew about David and his previous help, and also the fact that David was fleeing from Saul's unwarranted wrath, Nabal spoke as if he had never known the young man and virtually called him a brigand.

David's response to this humiliation was untypical, yet the Holy Spirit paints the heroes of faith truly, warts and all. Here was the man after God's own heart overreacting in a violent way. He had on more than one occasion spared the life of his enemy Saul, trusting in the Lord's final victory and vindication. Now, on receiving an insult from a violent man, David in a blazing temper set out with four hundred men to kill Nabal, and all his male relatives (vv. 21, 22).

What a picture of the sudden rushing of sin upon a Christian! David, who had shown patience and deep trust in God's guidance, is now suddenly inflamed with anger and thoughts of murder. Let those of us who think they stand take heed lest they too fall into deep sin. The onslaughts of the devil are always awaiting those who find themselves unprepared for his attacks.

AUGUST 21

A WORD FROM THE WISE

1 Samuel 25:13-35

Enter Abigail, Nabal's wife, a woman of understanding and beauty (v. 3). The contrast between her and her churlish husband is remarkable, for one asks why did she marry him? Was it a parental arrangement between the two families or was she flattered by his wealth? Whatever the background, she was united to this man in an utterly incompatible marriage.

In God's gracious planning a servant told Abigail about Nabal's latest iniquity, graphically given in verses 14-17, and the lady went into action to forestall the angry young man, David. Picture the events in verses 18-22: Abigail and her servants with supplies coming from one direction, David muttering dire and ungodly threats coming the other way with four hundred men. Then they met (v. 23), and Abigail immediately pleads with David to think again about his pending actions. Her torrent of words show how understanding she was, as she gently told David he was acting contrary to his character, outside the will of God, and against a man who was not worth bothering about! What a humbling thing for her to have to say that her husband's name meant 'fool', and that was exactly what he was! Read this paragraph carefully to get the thrust of her argument, and you will not be surprised to read David's response in verses 32-35. How this beautiful woman had pierced his bitter heart, as she reminded him of all God had in store for his life (v. 29), for the Lord and David were one in the commitment of both to each other: 'David, don't wreck all that by one foolish act. You are as a stone in a sling in God's hand against your true enemies.' Was that reminder of his great victory over Goliath the barb that struck home to David's heart, and brought him to his senses?

AUGUST 22

THE GLORIOUS OUTCOME

1 Samuel 25:36-43

When Abigail returned home she found a great feast in progress. This fact speaks of the rift between husband and wife, the total lack of communion and understanding between them. Abigail never told him about her intended meeting with David: Nabal did not appear to have told her about the celebration.

Nabal went to bed in a drunken stupor, and when he awoke Abigail told him of David's intended attack and her intercession. The effect on Nabal was probably a violent stroke, from which he died after ten days.

David, having melted at her pleadings, had gone back southwards. His heart must have been rejoicing as he praised God that Abigail's intervention in his life at that moment had delivered him from an act that would have ruined him and left a stain on his life forever. He must have thought much about that beautiful, gracious, and godly woman, for when he heard of Nabal's death we read he 'wooed Abigail to make her his wife' (v. 39). The domineering husband now dead, Abigail was free to marry the man soon to be king. What a picture of Romans 7:1, 2!

Tragedy came, however, and chapter 30 recounts the story of a raid on David's home town, Ziklag, during his absence, when Abigail and another wife were taken prisoner. David responded swiftly and regained his possessions and the two wives (v. 18). From freedom, through fear, to fruitfulness is the story of Abigail's life, for she had a son, the crowning joy of her union with King David (2 Samuel 3:3).

Some of you may have been in bondage to fear, but through faith in the Lord Jesus have come to know freedom in the Spirit, and therefore are now knowing the joy of fruitfulness in your life and in your service. If so, give to him all the praise, for he alone is worthy.

BEATEN BUT BLESSED

Genesis 32:22-32

Jacob had two life-changing encounters with God, the first at Bethel after he fled from home (ch. 28), the other at Peniel. Twenty years separated these events, during which Jacob had grown little in the knowledge of God, but much in trickery and deception. Jacob at last felt the time had come to return to his own land, even if it meant confronting his brother Esau.

On the journey the family group came to Peniel, and sending everyone over the brook Jabbok, Jacob was alone in a place of solitude. He was scared of his brother, of the future, of his responsibilities, and no doubt his mind went back to that vision of God at Bethel. One can assume Jacob was an ashamed and defeated man, full of fear, and longing for God.

Then came a man to wrestle with him, and Peniel became a place of sight as Jacob saw God face to face (v. 30). What a picture of Jacob now clinging in desperation to this angelic visitor! What a contrast from the two-faced deceiver who now pleaded for the blessing of God and would not let go until he received it! He was forced to confess his name was Jacob – deceiver – and in God's mercy was given a new name, Israel – prince of God. The result of the contest was a broken man. The angel touched Jacob's thigh, and he limped for the rest of his life. His pride was shattered, his strength gone, so no longer wrestling he clung like a child to the mighty Victor.

Peniel became a place of sunshine, for after the long dark night the sun rose upon a limping man with bowed head and humble voice. What a transformation! Maimed but mighty in the power of the Lord who had won the victory over such a rebellious, but desperately needy man.

AUGUST 24

THE POWER OF PRAYER

Acts 12:1-24

The pressure of the enemy (vv. 1-4) was becoming evident in arrests, imprisonment, death. To the Jews, the capture of Peter was a victory, and one can hear the prison doors shutting one after another as he was taken to the most secure place with constant surveillance.

The power of prayer (v. 5) is significant. Peter was in prison, BUT PRAYER, persistent because it was without ceasing, prevailing for the whole Church was involved, pointed because directed to God, personal for it was all on Peter's behalf. What do we know about this kind of praying? The answer to that question reveals the spiritual state of the believer as well as the church fellowship.

The plan of deliverance was put into action, almost at the eleventh hour (v. 6), and how exciting it was as Peter was taken by the angel out of all the locked doors into the street! Note that Peter slept, perhaps the only Christian in Jerusalem to do so that night. Would you do that in such a situation? I like to think he was recollecting his conversation with Jesus (John 21:18) who said, 'When you are old. ..' And Peter thought, 'I'm not old yet!' so he slept on the promises of God. It was the believers who limited God's power as seen in verses 12-16, when they were so amazed to find Peter at the door. How astounded we often are at the way God answers our prayers, far beyond the limits of our thoughts or dreams!

God sometimes allows tragedy (v. 2) or delay (v. 5a), but every situation should encourage us to pray (v. 5b). Then God acts at the critical moment (v. 6a) in his own perfect timing, overcomes insuperable obstacles (v. 6) and brings victory and joy into the hearts of all who have borne the burden in prayer.

AUGUST 25

A SLIPPERY SLOPE

Luke 22:54-60

Peter's life is very interesting, and in a way, very comforting, for he is so very human. We can all identify with his ups and downs, his actions and reactions, and learn deep lessons as we see how Jesus dealt with him.

The passage for meditation is, of course, the story of Peter's denial of his Lord, referred to in all four Gospels. To his credit Peter was not with the main group of disciples who fled when Jesus was arrested. Instead he went with John into the courtyard of the High Priest's house. Try to imagine Peter's thoughts at that time, his emotional state and complete bewilderment at the events, and stand by his side as he tells the story. The steps he took have been trodden by most of us at some time, therefore we listen to him speak in order to learn, not to condemn.

'I was taken by surprise', he says, for in verse 33 he had made bold statements of loyalty, even to imprisonment and death. No doubt he pictured himself a great hero, but now the comments of a servant girl around a fire caught him unprepared. It is in the commonplace and not the crises that Satan trips us up, so beware and learn from Peter.

'I slept instead of praying', he says, recalling the hours in Gethsemane of missed opportunities to share the burden with his Lord. No doubt we all spend more time asleep than in prayer, so we must heed Peter's warning.

'I never accepted the Cross', he says, recalling his words to Jesus in Matthew 16:21-23, and the Lord's rebuke. Peter's zeal and enthusiasm stood in the way of his recognition of his need. We are glad to accept Christ's forgiveness, but do we too fail to accept the true meaning of the Cross?

AUGUST 26

THE UPWARD CLIMB

Luke 22:60-62

Peter's denial is so often quoted, and many of us follow his downward path, but he did not stay there. So how many follow his steps back to fellowship with the Lord Jesus?

His return started with Jesus, with the eye-to-eye contact they made. When the cock crew all Peter could do was to remember that Jesus foretold the moment in which he was living. How fast is the way down, how laborious the way up.

We can be sorry for sin because our pride is hurt and our ego is punctured. No look from a friend can help to raise us up because we are looking at ourselves and not at the Lord. When Peter saw Jesus looking at him, his whole soul was torn open, and he wept bitterly. He saw himself as God saw him, and he craved mercy, grace and forgiveness.

Peter was a rough, blustering fisherman, but inside that exterior the Holy Spirit had planted the seed of eternal life. When Peter failed he did not need a thunderclap to gain his attention, but the silence of a look of love from his Lord. Then the tears came flooding, and Peter stumbled out of the crowded place to be alone with his thoughts and prayers, recalling Jesus' gracious words in verse 32.

It was the face of Jesus that brought the transformation in Peter's soul. One can inwardly picture the look Peter received, but no artist can ever convey it. Surely there was no resentment or condemnation in that gaze, but it searched into the innermost recesses of Peter's heart, and he could never be the same man again.

We have been with Peter, stood where he stood, but have we felt the eyes of Jesus on us in love and understanding and desire for our repentance and restoration?

AUGUST 27

NEWNESS OF LIFE

John 21:1-14

Put yourself in the place of these fishermen. They had been part of the most dramatic period in history, they had seen their Master killed, buried, and then risen from the dead. What was happening? When would they see him next? Endless questions with no answers, so they went back to what they knew best, fishing. The important thing to notice is that they did this *together* (v. 2). The recent events bound them together in a special way, and they clung to each other for support and fellowship. Soon they would be scattered, but now in their need they wanted to share the excitement and uncertainty of those days together. Is that the situation in our fellowships, the sense of much needed togetherness?

They were unsuccessful in their night's expedition, but at dawn what an experience awaited them! There on the shore was someone preparing breakfast, and of course they recognized their Risen Lord. Imagine their emotions as they rowed back with their boat full of fish, knowing the source of that miraculous catch (v. 6), and who was their host at the meal. As he prepared the bread and fish did their thoughts go back to a hilltop some few years back when Jesus fed over 5000 people with a few rolls and small fish? Or were they thinking more of the bread and wine at the Last Supper?

They all knew now their fishing days were over. A new life was opening up before them, for Jesus had long ago told them they would be 'fishers of men' (Mark 1:16-20). Even so, the Lord had not yet finished with Peter's heart condition, and while this was dealt with there by the lake, praise him, in his love and patience he still continues to renew a right spirit within *us*, so we may daily experience newness of life in him.

AUGUST 28

HUMBLE AND LOYAL

John 21:15-19

The moment of reckoning for Peter had come as the Lord gently drew him away from the other men, and opened the conversation with the searching words, 'Do you love me more than these?'

Peter experienced a new humility. His defeat was in public and his name and witness discredited. No doubt you and I also fail the Lord both in public and in private, but had the record of *our* failure received the same publicity as Peter's, our reputation would share the same fate. Yet we can be so critical of the faults of others and over-sensitive to criticism of ourselves while we carry in our hearts such a record of sin, which, if it were made known, would strike us dumb with confusion. What does Jesus hear in confession from us? Humility is the silence of the soul before God, when there are no more arguments with him. Peter never forgot that lesson, and years later he wrote about it in 1 Peter 5:5.

Peter also experienced a new loyalty: 'Do you love me more than these?' It had been a good experience to be back with old and close friends in a boat fishing. The pressures of the immediate and the future were released as every faculty concentrated on the task at hand. It was a good life for Peter, one he knew and where he was the boss.

Jesus shattered this dream: 'Do you love ME more...?' At that moment the love of a fisherman's life died in Peter as he cried, 'Lord, you *know*..' Years later he wrote, 'in your hearts reverence (set apart) Christ as Lord' (1 Peter 3:15). Is this a lesson you need to learn as the things of the world and daily living press in on you? Hear Jesus say to your heart, 'Do you love ME more than these?' and give him your answer.

AUGUST 29

HOW REAL IS YOUR LOVE?

John 21:15- 17

After the re-assessment of his life and his future goals, Peter experienced a new intimacy with his Lord. He had thought his days of close fellowship with Christ were ended, and now he was being asked, 'Do you LOVE me?' Jesus, who is Love, is appealing for the affection of his wayward disciple, for intimacy is the hallmark of love (see John 14:21).

The fact that two words translated 'love' are used in this interchange between Jesus and Peter is no doubt well known. The Lord used the strong word *agape* in verses 15 and 16, while Peter could only bring himself to use the word *phileo*, meaning a deep affection, brotherly love. When Jesus came down to that word in verse 17 Peter was upset and grieved, and cried out, 'Lord, you know everything!' Peter was trusting the Lord to look into his heart and see the strong desire there, the deep love that he couldn't bring himself to articulate for fear of further failure. How like him we can be, so slow to show our inmost feelings, yet longing above all for a real and lasting intimacy with Jesus, unbroken by sin and defeat. Peter points the way when he wrote, 'Grow in grace and knowledge of our Lord and Saviour Jesus Christ' (2 Peter 3:18).

This is a testing paragraph for we each have to ask ourselves, 'how real is *my* love for Jesus?' and then a further question, 'how sincere is my love for my fellow-men?' May the Lord pour into our hearts pure Calvary love, coming from his heart through our renewed lives and out to others.

AUGUST 30

A NEW RESPONSIBILITY

John 21:15-19

God never lets love lie idle. If you have known failure in your life, and have confessed that deep down in your soul you truly love him, I am sure he will have a task for that love to do.

The Peter of verses 1-3 was not the type of man churches would be after to fill their pulpits. He would not have been a featured preacher anywhere. But when the hour struck for the most important and vital sermon in all history to be preached, God chose Peter to do it.

There is a close connection between the question 'do you love me?' and the command 'feed my sheep'. Our sick society could be transformed within a short time by love to bring true spiritual revival, but first the lives of God's people have to be transformed by his love within them. This is his will for us all, and he has made it possible for us to love as he loved, and yet . . . How can we ever afford to be as we are in the light of his forgiveness and saving mercy? No wonder years later Peter wrote, 'Tend the flock of God' (1 Peter 5:2; 3:8).

He also experienced a new serenity (vv. 18, 19). Can you see the new light in Peter's eyes as he and Jesus faced each other before rejoining the group? As Peter gazed into the eyes of his Master he saw the brightness of a new day planned for him, but he also saw the shadow of a cross, and in that shadow he was to live and serve all his life (Acts 12:4). No wonder in his later years he wrote so much about suffering, and the response of the disciples to prejudice, hate, and death. Yet his challenge to them was to rejoice (1 Peter 4:12-14), for like himself they were called to follow their Master, who had himself walked that way and triumphed.

AUGUST 31

FOLLOW ME!

John 21:20-25

Peter, being Peter still, was momentarily distracted from his deep thoughts and commitment following his precious moments with the Lord Jesus. Rejoining his fellow disciples he saw John. Jesus had given to Peter a brief glimpse into the future concerning himself, but he still had to blurt out, 'And what will this man do?' Once again the Lord rebuked his impetuous follower, because it was none of his business – he was responsible only for his own commitment to and service for his Master.

To follow Christ is the main business of life. First a person must seek him, to make the quest for peace with God a first priority, and having found salvation and fallen in love with Jesus, then to follow him faithfully so long as life shall last.

To follow Christ is to lay aside all that hinders true heartfelt obedience (Hebrews 12:1, 2). Peter wanted to know what John was destined to 'do', and that was nothing to do with Peter. He learned later, after Pentecost, that his old life, his way of thinking and acting, was transformed by the motivation of the Holy Spirit within him, and his main concentration was personally to leave the trivia of life, and like Caleb of old, wholly to follow the Lord.

Praise God, we know this came to pass, and Peter's life and letters bring hope and faith to those who blunder and fail in their walk with the Lord. What a note of triumph and encouragement to end this brief series on victory in Christ!

LIVING FOR CHRIST

SEPTEMBER 1

I AM THE LORD YOUR GOD

Exodus 20:2, 3; Matthew 5:17-20

The next two months will consist of meditations on living for the Lord Jesus, and to start at basics we look at this subject from God's point of view as outlined in the Ten Commandments. It is possible Exodus and the three following books of Moses have been neglected by some readers as being of no concern to modern Christians. This is incorrect, for all is part of God's Word, for 'the Old is in the New revealed; the New is in the Old concealed.'

The Lord Jesus recognized and observed the Law of God, and proved his deity by turning strict ritualism into heartfelt obedience as in Matthew 5:21, 22: 'It was said. . . but I say to you. . .'

In the first commandment we are brought face to face with Almighty God, Jehovah, 'He that will be, he that is, he that was.' Past, present and future are all known to him because he lives in all at one and the same time: he is timeless and eternal.

He is our God, the supreme object of worship, therefore no other idol is allowed. If he is who he claims to be, then it would be very unreasonable to have another god beside him. As there cannot be two who fulfil the description of endless life, any other 'god' must be limited and, indeed, man-made.

Because of man's need to worship there must be a God to accept that worship. There is a shrine in every human heart that must have an object of worship, because man made in the image and likeness of God is dependent upon him for the satisfaction and supply of the deepest needs of the human heart. Idolatry is anathema to a holy God, who loves each one of us to the extent of Calvary, therefore our heart's response should be to fall at his feet and worship only him.

SEPTEMBER 2

NO GRAVEN IMAGE

Exodus 20:4, 5; Psalm 81:1-16

The first commandment forbids us to have any 'gods' other than the One who made himself known by his eternal name Jehovah. The second forbids the creation of anything material to assist in worshipping him. The key reason for this law is in verse 5a, 'you shall not bow down to them or serve them.'

The tribes surrounding Israel illustrated the need for such warning, for their idol worship led them to fearful extremes of bondage and savagery, of human sacrifices and abominable behaviour. Sadly this happened to God's people time and again in their disobedience to his word, and it was written that 'they went whoring after strange gods' (Exodus 34:15 AV), and the first infringement of this law is in chapter 32, the story of the Golden Calf.

The Lord alone is to have first place in the hearts and lives of his people. That was so vital, so imperative that the warning of verse 5 is given. Idol worship and the fruit of that in the lives of God's people brought misery upon the whole nation, as is outlined in the book of Judges. The converse is that God-loving and God-serving people bring joy and contentment to their lives from the God they worship and serve. Someone has said 'that which a fallen man creates cannot help in the worship of the God who created him'. Beware of idols offered today, of money, self, pleasure, and so on, which all bring sorrow ultimately.

Jesus used these verses in defeating Satan in the wilderness, for he knew that to bow down to the evil one would mean service and slavery to him. And that is true for us too, so, dear friends, 'keep yourselves from idols' (1 John 5:21).

SEPTEMBER 3

THE LAW OF BLASPHEMY

Exodus 20:7; Proverbs 18:6-10

How this commandment hits home with the language of people today! The second half of the verse shows it is no small matter to use the Lord's name 'in vain', for he will judge those who do.

It is impossible for even those redeemed by the blood of Jesus to fulfil the law of God, but praise him, it is the Holy Spirit who fulfils the Law in us, as was shown in the studies in Romans. So do not feel overwhelmed by the 'do's' and 'don'ts' of the Word of God, for while they show our weakness and sinfulness, as believers we can call on God's Spirit to do for us what we cannot do in our own strength. This command is important because a name expresses the character of a person, therefore we cannot belittle God and get away with it, for there is to be a day of reckoning.

Blasphemy is not the only way in which the Lord's name is used wrongly. See Matthew 7:21, where even a believer, in a subtle way, can say 'Lord' in a context that is invalid. To call him that, but fail to obey his word, is as big a sin as outright blasphemy. His Name is the only one by which men may be saved (Acts 4:12), and whoever calls on him in repentance and faith finds his wonderful salvation (Romans 10:13).

How pure is your speech? What are you doing with his Name? How do you react to those who use God's name in jest or as a swear-word? Lord, set a guard on our lips that we do not sin against you.

SEPTEMBER 4

WORSHIP AND WORK

Exodus 20:8-11; Mark 2:23-28

The law of the Sabbath is not to bring gloom, but gladness. God's will is that we work and worship, for honest work is part of worship, whereas praise and meditation form the highest work of which we are capable.

God rested on the seventh day after creation, and ordained it as a day of recreation after days of toil. To ignore this law produces physical breakdown, and to use the day wrongly brings no true rest of heart and spirit.

To read the Gospels is to find Jesus observing the Sabbath in the synagogue, and also doing miracles of healing (e.g. Matthew 12:9-13). When rebuked by the Pharisees and accused of being a Sabbath-breaker, Jesus replied, 'The Sabbath is made for man, not man for the Sabbath' (Mark 2:27). In God's wisdom and love he gave man this rest day, which the religious leaders promptly hedged around with rules and observances that turned a wonderful day of freedom into a day of gloom and negativism.

The early Christians changed the Jewish Sabbath, the seventh day, to the first day of the week to remember the resurrection of Jesus Christ, for he appeared to the disciples first on what is now Easter Sunday. He is truly Lord of the Sabbath, and we need to remember to use his day for his glory and in his will, to worship and praise him in joyous freedom, liberated from man-made regulations, for where the Spirit of the Lord is, there is freedom. Remember his day, to keep it holy, set apart for him.

SEPTEMBER 5

FAMILY MATTERS

Exodus 20:12; Ephesians 6:1-4

What a timely commandment this is, with the loosening of family ties so rampant in the world of today. To respect and enjoy family responsibility is in reality a blueprint for happiness. Obedience always brings harmony with the purposes of God and in relationships with others, for holiness and happiness are inseparable.

The first four commandments had to do with our relationship with God, and the final six with our relationship to our fellows. It is significant that the first of these concerns the home and family involvement. To honour means to have reverence, for in the home – the ideal home – the parents are God's representatives, the father being the head under the Lord. In such a home the child should see the parent exhibiting the character of God, as the one to be obeyed, as the one who loves and provides and guides. If that is true, then as the child grows it will be easy for him or her to respond to the claims of Christ, and live to love and obey him. How can those who have never been taught or trained in obedience in the home be expected in later years to understand what submission to Christ involves?

Honour means more than obey, for when obedience to parents ceases, honour never ceases. Therefore even to old age a parent should be respected by sons and daughters, and this generally is the case when father and mother have proved themselves worthy of this respect.

Paul, in Ephesians 6, stresses the promise of this commandment. In its immediate context it was given to a nation on the move, marching from one land to another. It is still true today, for love in the home brings the joy and blessing of the Lord upon each generation. May we each fulfil our obligation to obey this law.

SEPTEMBER 6

THE SANCTITY OF LIFE

Exodus 20:13; Psalm 125

The world says life is cheap; God says life is sacred, hence this law. There are basically two ways to kill, by murder (intentional) or by unpremeditated killing (accidental). All murder is of course killing, but not all killing is necessarily murder. Numbers 35:9-34 shows the difference, when the six cities of refuge were established into which a man, who had unintentionally taken the life of another, could find protection from the avenger. A premeditated killing (murder) gave the perpetrator no such protection.

This is not the place to discuss the right or wrong of serving in the armed forces, except to say that in O.T. times warfare – at the command of God to rid the land of idolatry and paganism – was the only right men had of taking the lives of others.

To kill another person does not only include physical death, as the Lord Jesus taught in Matthew 5:21,22. There is character assassination, mental and physical torture caused by someone of uncontrollable anger and all that accompanies such lack of self-control, which can annihilate the victim's self-esteem and ruin his entire life.

At the arrest of Jesus in Gethsemane, when Peter drew his sword to defend his Master, Jesus said, 'Put up your sword, for all who use the sword shall perish by the sword' (Matthew 26:52,53). He is the Prince of peace who urges his people to be at peace with one another (Mark 9:50; 1 Thessalonians 5:13).

It may be a certain fact that no committed Christian would ever be a murderer, because we side with God in knowing life as sacred; but let us be sure that we honour others in love – the love of Jesus – and will never cause them any form of harm or hurt.

SEPTEMBER 7

THE SANCTITY OF THE HOME

Exodus 20:14; Psalm 127

This commandment sets a flaming sword around the only relationship on earth which has the power to bring life into existence. God's first circle of society is the family, and all other relationships – social, racial, political – spring out of it. How essential for the wellbeing of all society it is that this, the source of all others, should be carefully guarded against every abuse. The law had no forgiveness for adultery, and both parties were to be put to death (Leviticus 20:10).

It is a sin against the individual, and in today's world the stigma still holds. The man or woman who falls into immoral habits commits inevitable spiritual suicide. The law says 'thou shalt not', but gives no reason, for none is necessary.

It is a sin against the family, as is seen all too well in the horrific rise of one-parent families and single mothers. This automatically makes adultery and immorality sins against society, for by them marriages and families are blighted. Above all it is a sin against God, the Creator of all people, the one who loves enough to give his only Son to redeem fallen mankind. Because he is holy he cannot look on sin, therefore those who continue on their downward path, unrepentant, reap the consequences (Revelation 21:8).

Adultery is the only ground for divorce (Matthew 19:3-9; Mark 10:2-12), because the precious link that constitutes marriage, the 'two made one flesh', is torn apart. The ultimate evil is seen in Paul's words in 1 Corinthians 6:15, 16, a sordid picture of what is going on all around in this so-called permissive society, bringing with it social tragedies unheard of previously. Read also John 8:1-11 and see the love of Jesus to a fallen woman, ending with the words, 'Go and sin no more'. In Christ there is forgiveness even for what was once unforgivable.

SEPTEMBER 8

STOP THIEF!

Exodus 20:15; Malachi 3:1, 2, 8-12

The first seven commandments, under the law of Moses, were punishable by death because they violated the most sacred relationships of life: with God, family, fellow man. The final three commandments deal with property, and the penalties are less severe, not because they are less important, but because a man's life does not consist in the abundance of his possessions (Luke 12:15). How human law turns things upside down. The crime for which the law inflicts punishment is not nearly as harmful as that which it cannot touch, for no human court ever convicts those who break the first three commandments.

There are many ways of stealing. Man is given the right of possession or theft would be impossible. Possession is by gift, inheritance, work or theft. The latter is forbidden here because it violates the right to proper possession, earned by service or work. In Ephesians 4:28 is advice to the ex-thief, a challenge to work and make restitution. Malachi 3 shows how we rob God himself by unfaithful stewardship, losing sight of the fact that all we possess has been given by him in love, therefore we must be faithful in what we do with his gifts – life, possessions, money, service. If every Christian at least tithed their income, the work of God's people at home or overseas would not be in need.

Beyond possessions, however, is our life, a precious gift from God himself, redeemed by the blood of Jesus, therefore we no longer belong to ourselves, but to him. Paul brings this truth home clearly in 1 Corinthians 6:19, 20, following on with yesterday's passage on immorality. 'The temple of the Holy Spirit' – you and I : do we rob God of his authority over us, or is our body truly the place of his habitation?

SEPTEMBER 9

SCANDAL

Exodus 21:16; Psalm 139:1-6

A man's reputation and character can be ruined by slander. It was the breaking of this law that led to the death of Jesus, when men falsely accused him, dragging his character into the mud. But God vindicated him by raising him from the dead, and the character and reputation of the Lord Jesus are pure and beyond dispute.

For those suffering from slander unjustly, there is a day when God will vindicate you, for the falsehood of others comes from the activity of Satan himself. What comfort there is in Matthew 5:11, 1 Peter 2:21-25, and Psalm 139!

The tongue is a dangerous weapon (James 3:5,6), and has to be kept constantly under control. This commandment is broken in so many ways, for example by invented lies (slander) to ruin a man's character; by giving false impressions to ruin his reputation; by innuendo or outright untruth. Silence on the part of someone who knows the truth, but is fearful of speaking out, makes him as guilty as the one who is spreading the lies. In an unguarded moment it is all too easy for any of us to be guilty, and how thankful we should be that others cannot read our hearts to see the wrong thoughts bottled up inside, the criticism towards others, and so much which, if spoken aloud, would be slanderous.

God knows our hearts, for he knows all about us, and what a comfort it is to know he understands, and what a challenge to know he alone has the answer: forgiveness when we acknowledge wrong, and the Holy Spirit to renew a right, loving spirit within us. Read Ephesians 4:30-32 on your knees, then before you speak about another person THINK and first ask: is it *T*rue, *H*elpful, *I*nspiring, *N*ecessary, *K*ind? and if the response in your heart is negative, then keep your mouth tight shut (Psalm 141:3)!

SEPTEMBER 10

A WRONG LOVE MADE RIGHT

Exodus 21:17; 1 John 2:15-17

It was this commandment that convicted proud Saul of Tarsus of his sinfulness (Romans 7:7, 8). The difference between this law and the others is that it can be broken and no other human being need know about it. However, a persistent, private violation of this commandment will be brought to light, as it will inevitably lead to action. Therefore it is important to know the control of the Holy Spirit over heart, mind, and emotions. Unsatisfied desires can poison every relationship of life.

To covet is to desire eagerly what belongs to others, to set one's heart on something that they possess. Eve coveted the vision of life Satan showed to her, and grasped the forbidden fruit. Her steps toward that were: she saw, desired, took, ate, gave (Genesis 3:6). James pursues this thought in 1:13-15, showing the similar steps taken between a thought and an action, and John in his letter reveals the areas of danger – the world, the flesh, the devil.

The command spells out the scope of covetousness – the things belonging to others. That is very heart-searching in this consumer age of 'keeping up with the Joneses'. God's answer is to delight ourselves in him, and he will give us the desires of our heart (Ps. 37:4). A right relationship with him brings the satisfaction of every desire, for they will be centred in doing his will. Jesus warned of this sin in Luke 12:15, and reminds us that life is more than things, which at best are only transient and fashions change so fast. Keep your eyes on the Lord Jesus, the one who alone can bring the joy and peace everyone seeks, and delivers from the sin of envy and the desire to possess, for Matthew 6:19-21, 33 shows the antidote to this wrong and evil spirit.

SEPTEMBER 11

THE NEW COMMANDMENT

John 13:34, 35; 15:9-17

It is often humorously said that the eleventh commandment is, 'Thou shalt not be found out'. Break all ten of God's laws, but never the eleventh!

Seriously, the new commandment was given by Jesus himself, and it is that we love one another. This is not just a happy idea, a good rule to follow, but a *commandment*. How do we feel about that, and how do we react to it, and put it into practice?

Jesus came not to destroy but to fulfil the Law. All the requirements of God's Law met in the life of the One whose every action had its motive in love: and as he learned obedience to his Father, so he commands us to do the same, and implants Holy Spirit love in our hearts to enable us to do so; for love is the fulfilment of the Law (Romans 13:10)

Therefore if a person loves God perfectly, he finds no room for other gods.

If he loves God supremely every false idol is cast out, and the name of God is hallowed.

If a person loves God supremely the Lord's day is his delight and he will know power to honour his parents.

If a person loves God supremely there will be no thought of murder, no thought of unchastity and impurity, no thought of theft.

If a person loves God supremely there will be no thought of false witness or scandal, no thought of desiring the possessions of others, of covetousness.

Love for the Father, commanded by the Son and made possible by the Holy Spirit, is our wonderful provision to fulfil God's Law by the means he provides fully and freely —love. Lay claim on that and fulfil his plan for your life, and enjoy his unclouded presence.

SEPTEMBER 12

LOVE COVERS ALL

Ephesians 1:3-10; Colossians 1:21-23

One day we will stand perfect and blameless before the living God, without spot or wrinkle. Holiness is Christ's life in us *now* to prepare us for that great day, and is not gradually improving oneself, but a replacement of 'self' by Christ.

The first fruit of the Spirit is love, and to love turns duty into privilege. Love goes the second mile, sweeps through every boundary of race and creed, pouring out precious ointment without regard to the cost. Love cares nothing for the critic, but continues to serve the lonely, bring hope to the despairing, comfort to the sorrowing. Love thinks of others, forgetting itself. Can we, and do we, really live and love like that? Jesus did and he said, 'As the Father sent me, so I send you.'

This is *the* miracle of the Christian faith, imparting the love of God through human channels to others. This is the very opposite of murder, adultery, theft, false witness, coveting. It is very clear that we desperately need a fresh baptism of love to counteract the spirit of the age as seen in these areas of life forbidden by God's holy Law.

Test your heart and your actions by the commandment to love, and assess your deepest thoughts to know if all you say, do, and think is motivated by the love of Jesus.

A Prayer:
Oh to be like thee, pure as thou art!
Stamp thine own image deep on my heart.

SEPTEMBER 13

THE BRIDE OF CHRIST

Ephesians 5:21-33

This letter of Paul's is devoted to wonderful truths regarding life in union with the Lord Jesus, and between 5:20 and 6:10 he inserts a page, it seems, on very ordinary things of life – husband and wife, parents and children, employers and employees. What a good thing he did so, for many people master the great truths of the faith, and fail to apply them where most needed. Paul wrote on the fullness of the Spirit in 5:15-20, and now asks his readers to consider the application of that at home and in marriage. To help us understand the ideal marriage Paul draws an analogy between the relationship of Christ to the Church with 'a marriage made in heaven'.

Christ is the Head of the Church, his bride (v. 23). He is the fountainhead of wisdom and knowledge, reason and activity, and his authority is exercised in supplying his people with all that is good, and protecting them from all harm and danger.

Christ loved the Church (vv. 25-27). Who can measure that love, as he *gave* himself for us? He did so to make us holy, cleansed, perfect, as his own bride.

Christ cherishes the Church (v. 29). He kindles our love, nurses our affections, softens our hearts, and takes away all hardness.

Such is the mystical relationship between the heavenly Bride and Bridegroom, the evidence of which should be seen in Christian marriage. Just as Eve was taken from the side of Adam to be his bride, so our spiritual life has its source in the wounded side of Jesus, close to his heart, and now he is *in us*, the hope of glory.

SEPTEMBER 14

ATTENTION ALL HUSBANDS!

Ephesians 5:25-33

'Love your wives' – that is the foundation of all marriages, and should of course be revealed first in courtship. True love is founded on spiritual reality, growing in mutual respect and attraction as the years go by. No marriage can be ideal without love as the abiding force.

True love is more than physical, for it expresses itself in a desire for intimacy. Lovers want to know each other, their doubts and fears, experiences and interests. One aspect of love is the desire to share, for to do so brings out new strength and virility. They find themselves drawn to God in a new way through their own love for each other.

No man or woman can learn too early to love as Christ loved, and as a couple live and love together that love deepens into comradeship, when the secrets and problems of life are shared, the events of the day, at home or in business, are discussed and then prayed over with the Lord.

1 Corinthians 13:4-6 is the goal, and every husband should pray over these verses regularly, and assess his behaviour in the light of them. The measure of his love for his wife is that of Christ for his Church, which was considered yesterday. Therefore as head of the home the man loves and cherishes his wife, and such wonderful affection will bring a deep response from the heart of the fortunate lady. In verse 28 is seen the reality of a man's love for a woman, and may that be true in our homes.

SEPTEMBER 15

THE HAPPY WOMAN

Ephesians 5:22-24

Paul writes far more to the husbands than to the wives, and if we have understood the two previous meditations it will not be hard to see why. The wife is told to submit, and perhaps that causes some hackles to rise! However, a woman with a husband such as Paul portrays will never find it hard to submit to him as head of the home, and her true love.

A man in the place of the head is not a petty tyrant, but the one who is responsible under God for all under his roof to live worthy of the family name, and above all, the name of our Father in heaven. The husband has no authority of the stamped foot, but of the Cross. He is not lord, but part of his wife's relationship to Christ is submission to her husband *because* they are both submitted to the will of God.

It is a submission of love to the husband, and a relationship in the Lord, for she is never called to obey her husband where to do so involves disobedience to God. That clash of loyalties will never arise when both are committed to Christ and can take all the cares and problems to him in prayer. The two have become one in Christ, for the marriage relationship is a true eternal triangle, man and wife at the bottom angles, and Christ at the top. So long as they both look to him there is joy and harmony, for they know he is Lord and Head of their home. If they look only to each other and neglect the headship of Christ, trouble is in store.

I quote a salutary word I read recently: Marriage needs to be understood before divorce is discussed. Oh that all would heed that advice and build their home life on Christ the Rock!

SEPTEMBER 16

EARLY LESSONS

Ephesians 6:1-4

There are two things here to which the child must give attention, and one for the father to think about. Consider first the general situation in which children are growing up today. Bring to mind your city, town or village, and what do you see happening among the young? How little there is in secular life, in their schools and among their companions that can ever bring children to hear and know about the Lord Jesus. How few go to Sunday school unless they are from Christian homes, and they learn nothing of Christ, by and large, at school assemblies. The welfare state has taken on itself much of the responsibility of parents with disastrous results.

Paul urged the children to obey their parents 'in the Lord', as he addressed Christian families. Each child needs to come to personal faith in Jesus, but they are set already apart, sanctified, to God through their parents. Read 1 Corinthians 7:14 and see how important it is for Christians to pray for the conversion of their children, and to live so that the little ones see Jesus in them. If that is the case, the second point Paul emphasizes will come true, for they will love and respect their elders.

To fathers (why just them?) Paul says, 'don't nag'. Justice, tenderness, strength and truth are so easy for a child to understand, and if father, as head of the home, demonstrates these in his attitude and in the way he raises his children that is a happy home (v. 4), and the young folk have the privilege of a godly, dedicated role-model in their own father.

THE IMPORTANCE OF A CHILD

Matthew 18:1-6

Can a child know salvation at an early age? Yes, for many Christians can testify to real faith in Christ when only four or five. They will grow in maturity as they grow in understanding as the years go by, but the seed is received at whatever age the Lord reveals himself.

To win a child for Christ one must have a child's heart (vv. 3, 4). Humility is the hallmark, for that is the childlike attitude which says, 'I know that I don't know, but I want to know.' The Lord also points out how fertile is the heart of a child to receive the seed of the Gospel. Therefore to ridicule a child's questions and desire to know the things of God is a fearful sin, as Jesus says in burning words in verses 5 and 6.

A child is automatically waiting for instruction. Children learn so much in the first seven years of life, and they should be learning also the precious truths about God and Jesus, so that the Holy Spirit may work in their tender hearts.

There is no guile in children, and they often have amazing insight and perception. The older person sharing the simplicity of a child will receive and understand the needs of that little one, as Jesus said, with the wonderful proviso, 'Whoever receives one such child in my name *receives me*'. What a commendation for child evangelism and Sunday School teaching! It is therefore understandable that Jesus should condemn so strongly those who have no time for little ones, and no concern to see them trust him. Never despise a child, never offend, but receive them with love and childlike faith so that they will never be intimidated, but will see Jesus plainly revealed through you.

SEPTEMBER 18

WITNESS IN THE BUSINESS WORLD

Ephesians 6:5-9; Colossians 3:22-4:1

Paul has a word for every stratum of society, and what he says still applies today. In his time, of course, there was slavery, and while he did not speak against it, he gave guidelines by which slaves should live once they knew Jesus as Lord.

Paul tells them to obey their masters from the *heart*, not as clock-watchers. At all times they were to fear (reverence) the Lord and serve him at their work, knowing that they too will receive their reward the same as every other believer, for there is no class distinction or favouritism with God. How does this apply to the 'employee' today? Surely the spiritual conditions are just the same though status is different. An office worker might feel like a slave at times, but unlike those in Paul's day, who received no wages, they are paid, and perhaps need to be reminded of what John the Baptist said to the soldiers, 'Be content with your wages' (Luke 3: 14b)! The behaviour of one Christian in an office, a hospital ward, in any area of work, can have a much deeper effect on the other workers than may be thought.

Employers who are Christians are to be fair in all their dealings, knowing that the Lord Jesus is their Master and ultimately they will give account to him of all they have done in this life. 'You know that', he writes, so live in the light of that knowledge.

A Prayer: Heavenly Father, in all my relationships, at home and in the world, may my words and behaviour reflect the presence of the Lord Jesus, and I pray his Spirit will guide me in every decision I have to make.

SEPTEMBER 19

A FORGOTTEN WORD

Matthew 4:17; Acts 2:36-42

As we have studied the Law of God in the Ten Commandments, it is very possible the Holy Spirit has convicted us of areas of disobedience. It is now time to look at other aspects of Christian living in the light of Exodus 20 and our response to God's voice individually.

How often is there a sermon on repentance? It is too often the missing strand in the glorious truth of the Gospel, yet it was the first message of Jesus, as it had been of John the Baptist (Matthew 3:1-3). The first disciples were to proclaim it (Mark 6:12), and the risen Lord stressed the need (Luke 24:47), as did Peter in his first sermon (Acts 2:38).

Men see no need to turn to Christ unless they know their sinfulness and the necessity to repent. This is not sorrow or remorse, but something much deeper. It concerns intellect for it means a change of *mind*; it concerns the *will* for the word means to 'turn', and that implies a choice, to do or not to do, and choice is the will in action.

To repent is to turn from one direction to face the opposite. The blind man in John 9:25 said once he was blind, now he could see. That complete reversal is what happens as we, blind to our sin and selfishness, have the light of the Gospel brought to us, and we see the shame of our lives in contrast to the purity of Jesus. As we cast ourselves before him, acknowledging our sinfulness and seeking his living forgiveness and cleansing, so we turn direction, and that is repentance.

The clarion call today is still 'repent, and then believe the Gospel', but it also needs to be a daily exercise as the believer maintains a right relationship with the Saviour. Keep short accounts with God.

SEPTEMBER 20

THE TWO SONS

Matthew 21:28-32

Just prior to the War we went to Westminster Chapel to hear Dr Martyn Lloyd-Jones preach his first sermon as minister there, and he spoke on this parable. It has stayed in my heart and mind ever since, for one so rarely is brought face to face with the need to repent. To trust, yes; to believe, yes; to have faith, yes. But to *repent*?

The context is a debate between Jesus and the everpresent religious leaders over the source of his authority. Then he related the parable. There was the seemingly docile son who said 'I'll go' in response to his father's request, but never moved. The other boy refused outright to go, then repented and went. What happened? Briefly, he experienced a change of heart that led to a change of mind, that finally led to a change of direction. He did a mental and physical right-about-turn, and did the will of his father. He was not sorry for his flat refusal, but repented of his attitude of heart and response to his father's request.

The key word is 'afterward', which means he thought through the whole situation and summed up its possible outcome, which was disobedience and disregard of his fathers authority.

This was the message Jesus rammed home to the priests. They were not prepared to see any sin or shortcoming in their lives, whereas those despised by the self-righteous were seeking the light and life Jesus came to bring to all who repent. The Lord forgive us for criticizing the mote in our brother's eye when a plank fills our own!

THE ONE SON

Luke 15:11-24

In the well-known story entitled The Prodigal Son, the word 'repent' does not occur, yet that is the underlying message.

The young man leaving home with his share of the inheritance thinks the world is his oyster, but alas, the bubble soon bursts and he finds himself destitute and friendless. That scene is enacted daily all around us, as the plight of homeless young people, penniless, often drug-dependent, are constantly brought to our attention. The younger son has a lesson to teach all those in his situation, for when he, in his starving condition, really looks at himself, sitting there among the pigs, we read 'he came to himself'.

That is repentance: to see oneself as God sees – the rottenness, selfishness, desperate spiritual need and bankruptcy. The young man jerked himself back to reality and said, 'I will go to my father and confess my sin.' He did not realize that he could never assess his true situation in the crowd. He had to get alone, into depths of despair, before he saw just what he was, and all that his father could provide.

The wonderful part of the story is that the father met him with open heart and arms, and listened to the words of confession and repentance before reinstating him as one of the family.

Think of these things in relation to your own standing before God, and also as a means of sharing God's love with friends who may still be in the far country of loneliness, need, and sin.

THE ELDER BROTHER

Luke 15:25-32

The parables of Luke 15 were told to a mixed crowd, including the Pharisees, who always were spying on the Lord's movements and words. The story of the Elder Brother is all about a cold and envious heart, unresponsive to love of family and love for family, and was designed to speak to the stony-hearted clerics.

While the younger son was far from home, the elder one stayed on the farm, yet he was in heart far further from the father than the tearaway. So on this particular day, as the farmer returned home he heard music and dancing, and on hearing the reason he was filled with anger and jealousy. The father, rejoicing in his young son's return, tried to persuade the older son to join in the rejoicing, but was met by sullenness. Then came a recital of all his good living and obedience, and keen resentment that they did not seem to be acknowledged. He could not share the love of the father's heart because hate and envy against his brother filled his own. Did he really come into harmony with his father and brother, or did he bear a hard and critical spirit all his life?

This is no old tale, for it is because of similar grievous and unconfessed bitternesses that families are divided, homes are broken, Church fellowship torn asunder. It is time to search our own hearts and pray the words of Psalm 139:23, 24, 'Search me, O God, and know my heart! Try me and know my thoughts! And see if there is any wicked way in me, and lead me in the way everlasting.'

SEPTEMBER 23

A MAN WITH A GRIEVANCE

Luke 15:25-32

Sadly there are many people nursing grievances. They may be against their own family, against church fellowship, against the preacher, or even against the Lord himself. Some incident can spark off a situation that grows out of all proportion, a mountain out of a molehill. That happened in Luke 15, where the story of the younger brother provoked the grievances in the older brother's heart, and basically it all started with self-pity. This is a soul-destroying condition, for it presses a person down so much by his own introspection that he can never look up to get things in the right perspective.

This man's first reaction to his brother's homecoming is anger. Self-pity destroys happiness, and he became out of sympathy with what was a joyous occasion. Instead of joining in he held himself aloof, touchy, awkward. Alas, some Christians can be like that when they hold a grievance, and are too full of self-pity and false pride to see their wrong.

This state destroys oneness, and father and son were faced with a break in fellowship and understanding. The returned prodigal son was no longer 'my brother' but 'your son'. There are believers who pull out of vital fellowship because of some grievance, and are now isolated, useless, unhappy, and causing unhappiness.

Finally the selfishness of the older son comes out in his outburst to his father: 'I.... me... my' (v. 29). His vision was restricted to himself, and he had no love left for anyone.

Before a close look is given to the father's reaction, there are many pointed lessons to learn from this elder brother. We do not need to be Pharisees to see that we can fall into the same trap as this man, and take offence at whatever may come to challenge our right to ourselves.

A FATHER FULL OF GRACE

Luke 15:31, 32

In marked contrast to the aggrieved and aggressive son is the gentle and gracious father. See three ways in which he responded in order to bring the young man back into fellowship and love.

The father first reminded him of his abiding presence, 'Son, you are always with me'. The son was part of the family, but not within it in spirit. He had a chip on his shoulder which probably arrived there the day his brother went off with his half of the inheritance. So long as a Christian harbours a grudge he fails to remember he is still part of God's family. In order to restore fellowship horizontally and vertically an apology is desperately needed, a humbling of spirit, and true repentance, which means such a change of behaviour that such behaviour will not happen again, by the help of the Holy Spirit within.

There was the father's abundant provision, 'all that is mine is yours'. If you feel depressed and feel the pangs of self-pity, read Paul's letter to the Colossians, and meditate on such verses as 2:9, 10, and see afresh the abundance of the provisions the Lord has for you as you lay claim to them in faith.

The older brother had to see the father's achieved purpose, and share from his heart in the return of the young spendthrift. The end result of self-pity is to alienate us from the eternal purpose of God, and to render us ineffective in his great task of seeking and saving those who are lost, so that we can share in his rejoicing in their salvation.

Pray that the Lord will keep you always in tune with him in his particular purpose in your own redemption, to be a disciple and witness.

LOST!

Luke 15:3-24

Jesus is challenging his critics because they accused him of keeping bad company. So he gave them a study in values. He spoke of a sheep, a coin, and a man, all of whom were lost. A farmer needs sheep to make money, and a coin may be worth more than a sheep, but a man is of infinite worth.

A sheep knows it is lost but can never find its way back. Maybe this sheep was the only one to find the gap in the hedge, and it went through. Now it was without the shepherd and the fold, and in great danger, but it had to be found. The shepherd sought it as though it were his only possession. While it was in the mountains the other 99 simply had to look after themselves.

The coin was insensitive to its lostness, maybe feeling that it was not its fault it fell off the chain that held the other nine. But the woman was desperate to find that one coin, which could have been part of her dowry. The remaining nine gave her no comfort, so her search was urgent and the outcome a great cause of rejoicing.

The man was deliberately lost because his heart was set on the far country. The father is not consoled by the one son at home. So long as the prodigal is far from home the father's heart is breaking. How concerned are we with lost humanity? Some people are lost involuntarily like the sheep, some unconsciously like the coin, some deliberately like the son. Yet God loves them all and yearns for their return. Are we one with him in his quest, and as diligent in seeking the lost as the shepherd, the woman, and the father?

A Prayer: Lord crucified, give me a heart like yours, to show Calvary love to those who are still far from you, and are walking the broad road that leads to destruction.

INNER CLEANSING

Matthew 15:18-20

In these verses the Lord is explaining what he had been saying to the Scribes and Pharisees as given from Matthew 15:1, words which had baffled his disciples. They might seem strange to us too, but they represent an important aspect of our acceptance of the lordship of Christ.

'Out of the heart', the inner man – that is the true person and his response. Here life, as most people know it, is depicted, and a terrible list of evil is given, things that start in the mind and then become part of behaviour. Compare the list Paul gives in Galatians 5:19, the outflow of the unregenerate life, so no wonder the verdict is that they who do such things shall not inherit the kingdom of God.

What is the answer? 'He who believes in me . . . out of his inmost being shall flow rivers of living water' (John 7:38). This is life as God can make it, an internal spring-clean resulting in overflowing life. Christ offers:

Forgiveness	inner cleansing from all defilement.
Flow	a clean and pure fountain of living water, the Holy Spirit
Fullness	'Springing up', unending and eternal, without measure or ending.
Fruitfulness	the overflow which is the fruit of the Spirit as given in Galatians 5:22

Base your prayer for today on these four thoughts, and go out to live as one cleansed, forgiven, Spirit-filled, and fruitful.

SEPTEMBER 27

THE CHURCH AND DISCIPLINE

Matthew 18:15-18

The very word 'discipline' is disliked and avoided in these days, because it sounds repressive, denying people the right to be and act as they wish, no matter the consequences of their actions. In the Christian context, it is important to remember that while God is love, and a God of mercy, he is also a God of justice who cannot tolerate sin in any shape or form. With him there are no grey areas.

In Matthew 18 the Church in action is seen, in these verses concerning a case of discipline. One member has sinned against another, but discussion has led nowhere. A few other believers are consulted, but the effect is the same. The only resort is to take the matter before the church in prayer. The outcome is that the offending member is removed, for his life displayed nothing of the inner life of the Spirit. Does such action take place in our fellowship when there is a bitter conflict between two members? Or is the poison allowed to flow and fester through the whole congregation? Satan is always there to stir things up and make matters worse.

See how Jesus interprets the action taken in removing the offending person. Verse 18 is a hard one to understand, but it shows that the removal of this man is registered in Heaven, but on the glorious day when the backslider is restored, then the result is again observed in Heaven. What an encouragement this is to all involved in helping and counselling people with deep hurts and disappointments, knowing that the Lord understands, he has made provision for those showing repentance to return, and the angels in Heaven will rejoice!

SEPTEMBER 28

TRUE DISCIPLESHIP

Matthew 16:24-26

It is important to understand that there is nothing we can do or be or give that would either gain favour with God or bring blessing to others. The ability of Christ in us is the power to make us what he wants us to be, and it is only through the principle of the Cross that we experience his power.

Because we can never experience Calvary, yet as Christ went to the Cross in order to obtain eternal salvation for all who believe, so we must die to self and everything except the will of God in order to experience his presence and power. This means that true happiness and fulfilment come from dying to every self-interest and areas of pride. The two fundamental principles of life are sacrifice or selfishness. For the believer the first should dominate his life, and the second be driven out. To deny oneself is to turn one's back on all self-interest and self-pleasing, and take up an attitude of death to the sinful past, and follow Jesus to the place of sacrifice which brings joy and peace.

This is not an easy life, but neither was the way of the Cross for Jesus. He asks us to do nothing that he has not already experienced himself. Discipline and self-denial are words unknown to this generation but they are still expected to be part of our response to the call of Christ to true discipleship.

SEPTEMBER 29

THE POSSESSION OF NEW LIFE

Romans 6:1-11

Was Paul reading Matthew 16:24-26 as he penned Romans 6? This chapter makes very clear how to lay claim to the fruit of death to self, and the awfulness of the alternative: bondage to Satan. This is not an easy aspect of Christian living, nor is it often taught, but it is essential to understand Romans 6 to know the secret of victory over sin. The experience of a crucified life does not rest on some thrill or feeling, but on facts which faith reckons. The *fact* is that at the moment of receiving Christ as Saviour we are saved and receive the Holy Spirit, and at that moment we *were* crucified with Christ.

As we acknowledge and count on these facts, God makes them real in experience. However, we must be willing for all the implications of such a life. Get alone with the Lord, and in a simple, personal way yield yourself utterly to him so that you can put the government of your life on his shoulders, and all your future service will be through his power alone. Make Romans 12:1, 2 your daily prayer of commitment, and let the sacrifice of Calvary be the measure of your willingness, that in all things Jesus may receive the glory. To fail to lay hold on these principles and make them personal may result in a 'saved soul, but a wasted life', of which I was warned in my early Christian life by the man who led me to Christ. The awfulness of this thought brought me to make the initial full commitment of my whole life to Jesus, and to the beginning of a lifetime of service in his name.

A LESSON ON FAITH
Matthew 15:21-28

How the Lord travelled! In this incident he is on the northerly coast near Tyre and Sidon, seeking solitude, but once again faced with desperate need. A Greek woman begged him to help her demon-possessed daughter. Who was she? From Mark 7:24-30 it is clear that, so far as the Jews were concerned, she was an outcast, outside the covenant of Israel, a worshipper of pagan gods.

Her approach to Jesus brought from him an answer of denial (v. 23), for he was silent. She had appealed to him as the Son of David, and as she had no claim on him in that capacity, he waited in silence. Sometimes this is his response to our prayers when we approach God on the wrong basis, for only the name of Jesus, his cross and atonement, give us the right of access.

How like us are the disciples! They spoke a word of discouragement to the woman, as well as pride, as they said to Jesus, 'Do something, for she cries after us!' To them she was only a nuisance. How cold and off-putting we can be when people do not want *our* chatter, but to meet Jesus.

The Lord spoke, but what a word of disillusionment! Children versus dogs – how could she stand the rebuke? Only her desperation kept her at Jesus' feet as she pleaded for even a little crumb of his grace such as was thrown to puppies by children at the meal table.

His heart was touched by her worship, her pleas, her sincerity, and her need. Jesus uttered words of deliverance, 'Great is your faith!' and her daughter was healed. What a joy this incident must have been to the Lord after the battles in the earlier verses of this chapter! May we rejoice his heart as we pray in faith, on the merit of his shed blood and in the assurance that he hears and answers prayer.

OCTOBER 1

TRAINING MEN FOR MISSION

Matthew 10:1-16

A most important aspect of living for Christ is to be a witness to his saving grace, a soul-winner. It is therefore essential to discover how the Lord himself set about the task of world evangelism, for he said he had come to seek and to save those who are lost (Luke 19:10).

Learn first the message he preached, given first in Mark 1:14, 15, that the kingdom of God is at hand, men must therefore repent and believe the Gospel. Breaking through all class barriers he put all men in one category, and exposed sin and the fact of punishment for the unrepentant (Luke 5:32). The only remedy he offered was the new birth (John 3); and when Jesus preached, his supreme authority was instantly recognized (Mark 1:22).

There must be no watering down of the message of salvation to fit either the age in which we live or the types of people to whom we speak. It is timeless and universal.

Learn about the men and women Christ called to this task. The calibre of his chosen ones was so essential he spent most of his three years of ministry in teaching them. John 1:29-51 tells of the call of the first five disciples, a little band that was to become a great multitude whom no man can number. Later Jesus called twelve, then the seventy who were sent out to preach. These were men of humble origin, mostly uneducated, but with hearts burning to know the truth, weary of the dead formalism of their faith, and therefore receptive to the challenge of Christ's message.

Learn about their mission. At first they were only to go among the Jewish people, for they were not yet ready to be sent worldwide. Yet they were obedient to the Lord in so far as they were capable of fulfilling the task he set them to do.

OCTOBER 2

THE LORD'S DIAGNOSIS
Matthew 9:9-13

Yesterday the call of five men in John 1 was referred to. Here is the call of Matthew the tax-collector, whose response to Jesus was immediate. In spite of his business he must have been a man with a hungry heart, and he knew Jesus to be a unique teacher so he gladly followed him. What is more, he arranged for many folk to come and dine in his home to meet Jesus and hear his message. The unkind reception the Lord received from the Pharisees prompted him to reply very pointedly, yet stating his mission with equal clarity (v. 13). It is important for us to see him at work, for not only can we understand how we can help others, but also how he has dealt with us. In his approach to the individual note his omniscience in John 2:23-25. He knew all men individually, and he knew them all generally by nature – he knew what is in them. Because of who he is, as John 1:3 shows, he knows each person intimately (John 1:42-48).

Jesus also knows everyone spiritually, for he is sensitive to what goes in the innermost recesses of our personalities. So with this intimate and detailed knowledge Jesus was able to meet every need, as he went to work to seek and to save those who are lost. He knew the truth about human personality, and from those days until now he has confronted all sorts and conditions of men, knowing each one and their needs, and dealing with them according to his infinite knowledge. And that, praise him, includes you and me.

Remember he is not just a teacher among others, but the Word made flesh, who knows and understands every incidental fact about every person he has created, and the very nature of all of us. May we all sing the doxology of Romans 11:33-36 with full and grateful hearts, for he has not left us desolate in our sin, but has loved us with a love everlasting.

OCTOBER 3

PEOPLE DIFFER

Matthew 4:23-25

Amid all the varying temperaments and differing situations affecting all people, the Lord saw a common denominator, therefore all are treated alike by him.

Everyone is spiritual in essence. Jesus never neglected the mind or the body in dealing with people. He was always challenging men's minds with questions about himself and his ministry. He often met spiritual need by way of bodily healing. But the keynote of his approach was spiritual. Because men are wrong there they are wrong everywhere, therefore his first word was 'repent'. That is a spiritual challenge that needs mental and physical response, as we have seen in previous studies.

Everyone sins in experience, for sin can be defined as missing the mark. To fail at the centre, the core of one's being, is to fail everywhere and become totally lost, as seen in Matthew 9:36.

Everyone can be saved by grace. Never did Jesus face a hopeless case. When no one else believed in the recoverability of a soul, he did, as in the case of the man at Bethesda (John 5:2-9). In this respect he treated all alike, and his approach was the same, yet see the variety of ways in which he dealt with individuals.

Nicodemus was reached through shock tactics (John 3).

The woman of Samaria (John 4) was confronted by her sin and need, resulting in her sense of guilt.

The rich young ruler (Matthew 19:16-22) was challenged regarding his commitment, and failed.

You can complete this list as you study the Gospel records, and think about the way the Lord came to you which led you to trust in him.

OCTOBER 4

FISHERS OF MEN

Mark 1:14-20

We fail in our witness because we lack the knowledge that Jesus had, as he looked into the hearts and motives, the hopes and aspirations of the people with whom he was dealing. To redeem this lack the Holy Spirit is given, and the measure in which we are living in true fellowship with him will be the measure of our understanding of others and our ability to help them.

The Lord's dealing with Simon Peter illustrates this, for he saw beyond the rugged exterior of a fisherman. Only a few words are recorded, but each is essential (v. 17). 'Follow me', he said, 'and I will make you. . .' A transformation was about to take place in Simon's life, and his response was immediately to forsake his trade and livelihood and join the ranks of the as yet unknown Teacher.

Jesus took Simon Peter from the Lake to use his skill in catching men. It is interesting that Jesus used that terminology, because the initial work of evangelism is like casting a net into water, and watching the Holy Spirit work among the hearts of people whom the preacher is waiting to 'catch'. Three years later the Lord gave Peter another commission, to feed his sheep. Those following Jesus were no longer like fish swimming in water, but were now gathered into the great Shepherd's fold, and the need was for the under-shepherds to teach them, and train them also in their turn to become fishers of men.

We are in that line of succession, and Jesus says to us, 'Follow me, and I will make you', for we can never equip ourselves. An old chorus says:

> I heard the call, Come Follow,
> That was all ...

Will you not follow if you hear his call?

OCTOBER 5

CHRISTIAN LIVING
1 John 1:5-2:6

There are some basic principles that are greatly in need of emphasis, even though they are not popular. It is very hard for present-day believers to realize that, as followers of Jesus, they have to be prepared to swim against the tide of modern life and worldly judgement. We now consider some areas of revelation that may be unknown or ignored by many of us. Unless these facts are faced the Christian is useless as a fisher of men.

The whole life of the believer should be an act of repentance. To rule that out of personal and church life is disaster in spiritual warfare. Repentance is not real unless it produces a holy life. It must get into every relationship – home, church, ethics, business (Colossians 3:5-8). For sin to be forgiven it must be forsaken. Unfortunately we learn to live with it, and it is hard to let go of something with which we have become familiar.

There is no salvation without discipleship (Luke 14:27), for Jesus is not only Saviour but Lord. He is so often called 'our Lord and Saviour' (e.g. 2 Peter 3:18; Philippians 2:11). He is Lord first, as he has been since before the foundation of the world, and Saviour to those who believe. The way of the Cross is hard. Paul was ready to lay down his life for his converts (2 Corinthians 12:15). The Lord wants those who are ready to give their *all* in his service, for he seeks worshippers before workers.

It is impossible by prayer to justify disobedience, nor can we cover up disobedience by becoming a missionary. A spiritual malady can never be cured by more activity, but by a new infilling of the dynamic power of the Holy Spirit. He alone can live in us the kind of life God desires.

Pray over these principles, and ask the Lord to show where you might be falling short – then do something about it.

NO BED OF ROSES
1 Corinthians 2:1-16

Christians today have the same needs as the early disciples, for the challenge of preaching Christ to needy people is the same, as is the opposition or indifference that is encountered when the message of love and salvation is given to them. The Lord promised power when the Holy Spirit was poured out on his followers (Acts 1:8). See now this mighty power in every area of human personality, without which witness is totally ineffective.

1. Intellectual power. We are called to witness to Christ, but do we fully understand the implications of the cross and his glorious resurrection? It is obvious that a witness must *know* what he has seen and heard, therefore those who testify to Christ's power and saving grace must have a deep understanding both experientially and intellectually. Jesus therefore gave the promise of Holy Spirit enlightenment in John 14:26; 16:12-15. Spiritual illumination of the mind is needed to change cold facts into a living experience (vv. 3-5).

2. Spiritual power. Read 1 Corinthians 3:1-3 and see the three strata of life to which Paul refers. The unsaved man he calls 'natural', the saved but immature he calls 'of the flesh, carnal', the mature believer is the spiritual man. Those who witness to Christ simply must demonstrate that a life *can* be lived which is not mastered by fleshly desires, that it is possible to keep the body in subjection, and have the mind of Christ. This is not something one can do by self-effort. A spiritual power is needed to lift us above the pull of self and sin, and give victory over the territory of our own lives. This is the work of the Holy Spirit, as Paul testifies.

Ask the Lord to search your heart regarding your submission to his overwhelming love and ability to meet your every need.

OCTOBER 7

HEARTS SET ON FIRE

Acts 4:8-20

To continue yesterday's thoughts we see:

3. Willpower. The disciples were going out as sheep among wolves. They loved their Lord truly, but when the storm broke upon him, they fled. After his resurrection they were again commissioned to be his witnesses, and so expected battle and conflict, but were they any more prepared? They urgently needed a new willpower to keep them strong in the fight, and of course the mighty power of the Spirit of God endued them with all they needed at Pentecost. We have only to look again at Peter before and after that great day to get the impact of the total change in his life (vv. 18-20).

4. Functioning power for service. What was the disciples' mandate? They were sent to proclaim the Kingdom of God, and to declare that he had vindicated the Kingship of Jesus by raising him from the dead. They were to bring men into this kingdom by the submission of their wills to the will of God, by repentance and faith. But there was to be no armed struggle, no coercion, no gimmicks, just the glorious truths about Jesus.

No human government would extend its territory by telling a story! When people *heard* the story, however, and obeyed the commands and submitted to Jesus as Lord, then they would be disciplined, trained and taught. There has never been any fanfare in the spread of the Gospel throughout the world, only the going forth by men and women inspired and empowered by the mighty Holy Spirit, because their hearts had been set on fire.

Is that how the Church functions today? Or is it bogged down by so many extraneous concerns that the command to 'preach the Gospel' is forgotten, and the power of the Gospel discredited?

OCTOBER 8

A TRUE DISCIPLE

Mark 8:34-9:1

Let us recap what the Spirit is teaching us:

Without intellectual power there is no clarity or reality in our message, for it will be only the recital of a formula.

Without spiritual power there is no victory in our witness and service, for it will be dry and sterile, lacking in love and conviction.

Without willpower there is no loyalty to Jesus, because the pressure of outside forces is so great – the pull of the world (without), the flesh (within), and the devil, the author of all conflict. How easily we fall to one or other of these pressures, or maybe to all of them at some time or another! No wonder the Lord had to stress the teaching of the verses for study.

Without functioning power there is no ability, no urge to fulfil the commission delivered to his people by the risen Lord in Matthew 28.

It is possible many of us may have fallen by the wayside because of a worn-out commitment to Jesus which has not been a daily renewal of love. Because of this he becomes distant and we have no joy in our lives, which we looked upon as the hallmark of our walk with him. We urgently need to return to the place where Jesus is all-in-all, so real and vital in our lives that we cannot but speak of what we have seen and heard (Acts 4:20). In that way the life of our fellowship will see the rekindling of the flame of his love and passion within them, and once again be living lives as true disciples to give joy to the heart of the Lord Jesus.

OCTOBER 9

NO LONE WOLVES
Acts 2:41-47; Ephesians 4:1-7

Learn now how Peter and his fellow disciples put into practice the Lord's teaching on evangelism. The early Church was being established, so try to picture yourself as one of the 3000 who had just been saved. Fellowship with others is an essential part of Christian living, for to be a Christian is to be part of the body of Christ. So every newborn believer here was encouraged to join with all the others, and they worked, prayed and shared together. Here are the branches sharing the life of the Vine.

To reject such oneness is to reject Christ, for God's purpose is not the salvation of scattered individuals, each doing their own 'thing', but the creation of a new community, the eccelesia, 'called-out ones'. This is very true in remote parts of the world, where tribespeople who find salvation in Christ immediately desire above all to learn more, gather together, and then build a special meeting-place, a 'church'.

It is impossible to be in the army without being attached to a unit. There is strength in unity, and Christians working in lonely places are the ones above all who crave and value the prayer support of their distant friends. Remember our battle in life is a spiritual one, and we need support and to be supportive, therefore our unity is threefold:

1. To worship, not to receive only, but to offer ourselves to God.

2. To help each other, Christ is not a private possession but a commonwealth. We share our experience of him, and this is part of what Paul was stressing in 1 Corinthians 12.

3. To serve together, not as individual units, but a team. The great truth to remember is that we are all one in Christ: every barrier of prejudice and self-esteem is swept away as we share his life the one with the other.

OCTOBER 10

PULLING TOGETHER

Philippians 2:1-11

Such fellowship is not automatic, as Paul points out in Ephesians 4:3, and note the word 'eager'. Does that express your desire to promote harmony and Holy Spirit love in your fellowship? Otherwise we can be disruptive and do the enemy's work in tearing apart the body of Christ.

What are the qualities that bind a team together, without which there is neither order nor cohesion?

1. Loyalty. We share the same life of Jesus, therefore our first loyalty is to him, then to each other. How the tongue can be used to destroy and cause havoc among a fellowship! No wonder Paul, Peter, James and the Lord himself stressed the danger of speech. Let us all take heed, and in the bonds of love maintain unity and loyalty by the Spirit's power.

2. Responsibility. There are some in our fellowships who are just passengers, but those with hearts aflame for Jesus are active, responsible, prompt, reliable, efficient in every detail of work committed to them.

3. Co-operation, a vital necessity of any team. There must be willingness to work in harmony, of abandoning pet ideas for the good and growth of the fellowship. It is possible you may be wrong and the others right! Even if you don't agree, there must be love and charity (v. 3). That is the secret of Christlikeness, as Paul goes on to reveal in this chapter to the Philippians.

Add your own marks of fellowship to this brief list, and lay them before the Lord to check your own right to a place in the Lord's team as a fully co-operative, loyal and responsible member. Read carefully Romans 15:5, 13.

OCTOBER 11

EVIDENCES OF NEW LIFE

Acts 2:40-47

There are three important facts of church life seen in these verses, and the first is *fellowship* (v. 42). The new believers 'devoted' themselves to teaching, prayer, and communion with each other and the Lord Jesus. Oh that that were true of our fellowships today! If it is not how we live, what is the reason?

The second fact is in verse 43, that *fear* came upon everyone, meaning awe. What was happening in their city to so many people? All the new wonders and signs they were seeing – what did it all mean? Alas that our neighbours see so little to cause them to be awestruck, and to marvel at the power of the Lord in our midst.

In verse 47 these early Christians found *favour* with the people. To picture their living style, their communal sharing and love for each other should make us wonder what we are missing, for it all demonstrated qualities that caused the outsider to desire with all their hearts this new Way. The Lord answered the prayer, devotion and witness of his people by adding to their number *day by day* those whom he was saving. Oh Lord, do it again!

THE NAME OF JESUS

Acts 3:1-20

This is the first miracle Peter and John performed in the name of Jesus. It is a well-known story and demonstrates Holy Spirit power overcoming the paralysis of sin. As the lame man leaps for joy so a sensation sweeps through the crowd (vv. 9, 10). When someone has been truly delivered from the paralysis of sin and begins to rejoice in the Lord, people will talk. The people seemed unable to take their eyes off the man they knew to be lame from birth and was now walking and leaping, so they followed after Peter and John to see what would happen next. What a responsibility rests on those of us who profess to have been transformed by the power of the living Lord Jesus!

The people's attitude demanded an explanation, and Peter preached the second sermon recorded in Acts. What, they were asking, has happened to this lame man? Peter's answer is in verse 13, 'the God of our fathers has glorified his Son Jesus. . . and his name, by faith in his name, has made this man strong' (vv. 16, 6). But how can Jesus glorified explain the miracle?

In John 7:38,39 Jesus spoke of the living water, the power of the Holy Spirit, and that Spirit was flowing through Peter and John, and their faith in the all-powerful name of the Lord Jesus had given power to heal and to save.

No doubt the crowd continued to stand and stare, so Peter gave his challenging appeal in verse 19: repent, be converted (turned), know the forgiveness of your sins, and you too will experience the refreshing streams of life from Jesus himself. That is still the message to meet the needs in our lives, and through us to others. Pray for your own daily witness, and for the message to ring out clear and plain from the pulpits of our land.

OCTOBER 13

THE POWER OF THE GOSPEL

Acts 3:17-26

In the last glimpse we take of Peter boldly proclaiming the Gospel, remember that people out of touch with God will always be amazed – and sadly, sceptical – at the miracle of new life in Christ, and will seek an explanation on human levels. In this chapter Peter gave the explanation in verses 13-16, and then launched into his appeal in verses 17-26.

He immediately diverted attention from himself by preaching Christ, and showing the need of the people to repent and believe. At the conclusion of his message he showed the purpose of the Gospel (v. 26): God – Jesus – you. In verse 19 the people were exhorted to 'turn again', to reject sin and turn to Christ for forgiveness and salvation. In verse 26 God's special blessing is to 'turn away' everyone from their sin. Think over the implication of these two statements.

Dr Chalmers, a great Scottish preacher of a former era, spoke of 'the expulsive power of a new affection', and that is what God promises. In the spring the new life rising in a tree, causing new leaves to grow, at the same time casts off any remaining dead foliage. The new life in Christ, with new hopes, desires, ambitions, under the control of the Holy Spirit, fills our hearts with a burst of heavenly joy and freedom, and we experience release from the old power and sinfulness in which we had previously been bound. Only the Lord can give us that release in response to our willingness and obedience. What folly it would be to want to continue under the downward drag of sin when he is waiting to 'turn us away' from its power!

WHY PARABLES?

Matthew 13:10-17

If we are vocal in our testimony it is often necessary to illustrate spiritual truths by using everyday events. Dr Wm. Sangster spoke of 'the art of sermon illustration', and the Lord Jesus demonstrated this in the use of parables of which there are 38 given in the four Gospels.

Why parables? the disciples asked. We need to read very carefully the Lord's answer in verses 11-13. His teaching had taken a new turn, and in speaking to the crowds he used parables. The disciples' question stressed the word 'them', and in his reply Jesus differentiated between the disciples (you) and the uncommitted crowd. In this chapter Jesus gave eight parables, four of which were addressed to the disciples (from v. 36), which showed that they were still in need of instruction as well as the people.

The disciples were given insight into the secrets of the Kingdom because of something they possessed – faith in God through the Lord Jesus. The crowd lacked this, so they were not as yet entrusted with the secrets of the Kingdom (v. 11). How full of awe the disciples must have been as they realized in a new way the privileges of their relationship with the Lord Jesus, King of the Kingdom.

It would seem the emphasis of verses 12-15 is not that only a privileged few were admitted into a close fellowship with Jesus, but rather that without acknowledging who he was, the rest of mankind would never be eligible to be part of his Kingdom. Therefore in love and mercy and grace Jesus spoke great truths to them in parables to enable them to understand and enter into the blessing which the disciples already experienced (v. 16). Faith opens the eyes that ignorance and unbelief would keep closed.

OCTOBER 15

SOWER, SOIL AND SEED

Matthew 13:1-9, 18-23

The Lord called this the parable of the sower (v. 15), but nothing is actually said about him, though verse 37 identifies him as the Lord himself. The emphasis in this parable is on the seed, the soil, and the sequence. In verses 3-8 the chief lesson appears to be learned from the nature of the soil, whereas verses 18-23 is concerned with the seed. If we read only the first part of the story we might say harvest depends on the nature of the four kinds of soil, but the explanation of Jesus emphasizes the quality of the seed that is cast into the soil: *he* who hears (vv. 19, 20, etc.).

Connecting this parable with that in verses 24-30, the seed is the people of God sown into the varying soils of the generation in which they live, for he himself is the sower. In Luke 8:4-15 the emphasis is on the reception of the seed of the word of God into the soil of the hearer's heart, which is probably the more widely taught interpretation.

See the seed sown by the path, those to whom the message is meaningless, and so Satan retains his grip on that life. The seed sown on rocky ground is the person easily stirred emotionally, but never making a deep or real commitment to the Lord. The seed among thorns represents the man or woman who again is moved by the Gospel, listens intently, but on counting the cost of discipleship finds it too great. The love of the world and its ways numbs the conscience, and chokes the growth of the truth in that person's life. How often that is seen in people today, as well as in every age.

The seed on the good soil is that which takes root and reproduces. May the Lord see this happening in our own lives, as we pray for those who seem to reject the Gospel for the varying reasons outlined in this parable.

GOD'S SPOTLIGHT ON WORLD EVENTS

Matthew 13:24-30, 36-43

What is God doing in the world today? Perhaps people have been asking that question since the beginning of time, and this parable is the answer. It gives the lie to the suggestion that his great redemptive purpose has failed, but rather that the ultimate triumph is sure.

The Lord's activity is the sowing of the good seed, 'the sons of the kingdom' (v. 38), and it is being sown in *his* field, the world (Psalm 24:1). Yet the world scene is chaos and disorder, and into that the Lord scatters his people to bring peace, order and reason – the harmony of lives in tune with himself. To look into the future, read Revelation 7:9-11 to see the glorious fulfilment of the sowing of the good seed.

The enemy also is at work, the evil one (v. 39). The only object of this work of malice is to ruin the harvest. The field does not belong to the enemy, and Satan is a squatter in this world which by creation belongs to God.

As the Lord works through men, so does Satan; the former are regenerate, the latter are not. And the enemy carefully sows weeds that resemble the good seed as they grow together. The tares represent reformation and not regeneration; church rather than Christ; programme in place of power; pressures instead of prayer; the world in place of the Word. And how successful are Satan's tactics.

'Let them grow together', said the Lord, for only he, who knows the secrets of men's hearts, can clearly distinguish the wheat from the weeds. All present and future events are safely in his almighty and all-powerful hands, and the day is coming when evil will be finally vanquished and those possessing the life of Christ will be with him in his 'barn' forever.

OCTOBER 17

SPIRITUAL BATTLES
Matthew 13:31-33

There is a similarity in these two parables which complete the four the Lord spoke to the crowd, revealing the outward progress of the Kingdom of God throughout this present age.

Many interpret the parable of the mustard seed as the phenomenal growth of the church, giving shelter to all (the birds). I feel, however, that one must compare Scripture with Scripture to obtain a correct interpretation, especially of some more difficult passages. Therefore the thought of a seed of mustard producing a great tree is unnatural, whereas birds are omens of evil. In the previous parables the 'seed' was sown in soil with various results, and one was that the birds swooped down to devour it. The lesson here, in my judgement, is not that there is failure and defeat imminent, the point is that three-fourths of the seed was unproductive of real, Holy Spirit growth. The Kingdom of God will be plagued by counterfeit, and that is so very true.

The woman making bread adds the yeast to the flour, and again this is often regarded as the purifying and permeating power of church growth. Look at the meaning of leaven in 1 Corinthians 5:6-8, which goes back to the Passover when all leaven had to be destroyed (Exodus 12:8; 13:3). There is the leaven of malice, evil, hypocrisy, impurity (see 1 Corinthians 5:8) which can destroy a life, and also the work of God through his body the church.

Notice again that the woman took three measures of meal, to which the yeast was added. This speaks of the remaining one-fourth of the seed sown, those who in obedience to 1 Corinthians 5:7 are cleansed from the old leaven and free from it, now that Christ has died and delivered us. Rejoice in this as you read 2 Corinthians 5:17: the old nature has gone, the new is within, so let Christ be magnified in you.

GOD'S TREASURE
Matthew 13:44; 1 Peter 1:13-21

The four parables told to the crowd speak of the Church of Jesus Christ between his first and second coming. There is the age-long conflict with evil, and it seems a story of little success. The parables were spoken to those who were not in the Kingdom, who would judge by what they *saw*, a dark story to give them grounds for saying Christianity is a failure.

There is, however, another side to the picture which Jesus revealed to the disciples (v. 36f), the sure and certain triumph of his purposes. He is working in the world today, and in this first parable he likens the Kingdom to hidden treasure, found and bought. To continue the analogy of the previous parables, the field is the world, and the 'man' is the Lord himself. What, then, is the treasure?

The purpose of creation in the heart of God was a people who would love, honour, worship and obey him. We know man (Adam) failed and sin ruled, and God's purpose was thwarted. So the treasure is his ultimate restoration of the wonderful things he intended for the human race.

The man found the treasure: the Lord saw men as sheep without a shepherd finally brought to pasture and still waters. He saw salvation replacing the ruin of sin, and rebellion changed to harmony. Then the man hid the treasure – the story of the O.T. and in fact of all those whose hearts are still blinded by sin.

Finally the man bought the field and the treasure. What a picture this is of John 3:16! Jesus gave up everything, including his life, to redeem mankind, and we read here he did it with joy (Hebrews 12:2). He did not pay either God or Satan for the field and the treasure, but on his own behalf to rescue what was precious to him. Yes, you and I mean that much to him; may his sacrifice be reciprocated by the devotion of our lives.

THE PREPARING OF THE CHURCH
Matthew 13:45, 46; 1 Peter 1:3-9

I do not accept the interpretation of the parable which regards the Saviour as the pearl and the sinner as the merchant who buys it. That is contrary to the facts of experience and to all the teaching of Scripture.

A pearl is one jewel not mentioned in the O.T. apart from Job 28:18, so the Jews put no value on a pearl, though it was sought after by the Gentiles. It therefore became known in the East as a thing of beauty, purity, and great worth. The merchant is seeking the finest pearls for others to buy, and he finds one worthy only for a king to wear.

During this age there is to be brought out and presented to God the most glorious jewel that will flash upon him through all eternity, for the Church of the Lord Jesus is the pearl, the secret hidden from all previous ages, but now revealed to his followers (Colossians 1:26-27) – Christ *in* you, the hope of glory.

In this parable Jesus is seen discovering the pearl, going away and selling all in order to purchase it. He went away from heaven to earth in order to do so, for the pearl has been seen by him through all eternity. Read with awe and wonder Ephesians 1:3,4. For love of it and desire for it, he surrendered everything he had, that he might purchase it and take it back with him to his home in glory. Held in contempt by the Jews, it is to Jesus *the* pearl of great price, his Church which he purchased with his own precious blood.

So the parable speaks of the building of the Church, the value of it, and the ultimate destination of those redeemed by his life, when they are gathered with Jesus in the presence of the Father, presented pure and faultless, in his eyes *the* pearl of great price. May the beauty of Jesus be seen in us as we are prepared by him for that great day.

OCTOBER 20

ENTRUSTED WITH A MESSAGE

Matthew 13:47-50; 2 Corinthians 5:11-21

Speaking to the crowd Jesus showed them the joys of Heaven to give them heart-hunger to know God (v. 43). In this parable, spoken to his disciples, Jesus showed the reality and horror of lostness to spur them to sacrifice for the salvation of the unsaved.

The Church (Kingdom) is likened to a dragnet that is cast into the ocean, covering a huge area and made to catch an immense amount of fish. That operation demands the correct amount of tackle and the dedicated, trained and disciplined crew. How carefully the Lord trained first the twelve, then the seventy, and all who have followed him in obedience and love, as we have seen in previous meditations. Are you today among the crew manning the net cast out by your fellowship to win those in your neighbourhood for Christ?

When the fishing is done the net is dragged ashore, and the tedious task of separating good and bad fish begins. When the net is in the water the fishermen cannot see what is in the catch, but everything is brought ashore.

In evangelism the Church is to make the Gospel known far and wide, and it is not the task of the fellowship to decide who is truly saved and who is lost. While men can separate good fish from bad, the task of separating the evil from the righteous is given to angels. That severance is final, and the evil are cast out eternally from God's presence.

Does this thought not spur us on to witness to those around? Have we understood all this (v. 51)? Mission, at home or overseas, is not a branch of church life. It is the total life and reason for the Church, and a fellowship that is not fully involved in mission is failing in its reason to exist.

IN UNDERSTANDING BE MEN
Matthew 13:51, 52; 1 Corinthians 1:18-31

When Jesus asked the question in verse 51 he was asking whether his disciples had fully grasped the implications of his teaching, and he asks us now the same question. This is not intellectual understanding, but that of the heart. Have you understood the teaching of the seven parables? The enemy seeks to destroy the seed of the Gospel; the visible Church has had abnormal growth and taken within itself that which is evil. Have you understood that Christ gave all he had to purchase out of the world his Church, to shine as his jewel through all eternity? Also that we are partners in the great enterprise of fishing for men – is that understood?

The disciples said, 'Yes, Lord'. May the Holy Spirit enlighten our minds so that we can say the same, for the Lord follows his teaching by putting responsibility on his people.

They are to be as the scribes, a strange thought, for though trained in the understanding of the Law, they surrounded God's word with rules and traditions that made religion a grievous burden. Jesus demands of his disciples true recognition of the Word of God in its purity and power.

They are to be like the overseer of a household; the word 'householder' conveys the meaning of authority, for he has charge of his master's treasures. For the Christian the great treasure is the knowledge of God through the Lord Jesus as revealed in his Word. The truth of the Gospel is committed to us, his followers, so we must be students of Scripture, able to extract the truths that are old but never age, and have application to the times in which we live. We are to apply eternal truths to every area of life, and every circle of society we touch.

Have you understood? Now act with the power and blessing of the Holy Spirit to make you a true witness of the grace of God.

OCTOBER 22

DON'T CAVE IN!
Luke 18:1-8

Jesus had been speaking of the signs of his return in chapter 17, of Godless living and injustice, and then used this parable as a challenge to pray and not lose heart. 'To lose heart' is to faint, or to cave in, to give up in despair. So we meet the persistent widow who came to the judge, not seeking vengeance but justice, and she came again and again with no result.

The judge is an evil man in the sight of God and at his own admission. He flouted God's laws as well as those of men, but because the woman 'bothered him' (v. 5) he did what she requested. He had no concern for the rightness or wrongness of her case, but yielded to her demands in order to get rid of her – she was wearing him out!

Jesus is not saying here that we should keep coming to God until he gives us what we want. Contrast, not similarity, is the key, for all the judge is, God is not; all that God is, the judge was not. There are things God cannot do, and these are to be unrighteous, or fail in mercy, or stop loving.

That is the contrast in character, but that was also true of action, for the judge acted after unwarranted delay to avoid personal bother, while the Lord vindicates his people speedily, who cry to him day and night. There is no need to keep on pleading as if he were unwilling. Our attitude in life and prayer should be trust, dependence, content with his will, and the ability to live above turmoil through his power and grace.

Is that your attitude toward God as you pray, or do you struggle to get your own way? The Lord is looking for our faith in his faithfulness (v. 8). Those who through adversity still believe in his power to save and deliver are the ones who will never cave in!

THE MEANING OF LIFE

Luke 12:15-21

Many people heard Jesus tell this parable (v. 1), and we need to hear it today to heed its warning and understand its meaning.

The farmer had a problem of too much harvest, so he planned to replace the old barns with new and larger ones, then relax and enjoy life. That is, until his daydream was shattered when God broke in with a condemnatory word, 'Fool!' The man's folly lay not in the fact that he was rich, but because he failed to see it was God who had given the increase in his harvest.

The farmer's whole attitude was based on a false sense of ownership. Note the personal pronouns in verses 17-19. His horizon stretched no further than what his own hands could do. That is the outlook of the vast majority of people today in this 'me first' generation. To have wealth only stimulates the desire to acquire yet more, and so many base the whole meaning of their lives on what they have in the bank, and how best they can increase it.

The lesson the farmer had to learn is that nothing is ours unless it is first recognized as coming from the Lord himself (see 2 Corinthians 9:9, 10). The answer to daily problems rests in understanding that all things are mine if first they are his, and all I have belongs to me if I can say I am only a steward – they are mine, therefore his. If every Christian recognized their responsibility in stewardship there would be no lack of supplies for the Lord's work worldwide. May he make each one of us alive to our responsibility, so that we show him we know the meaning of life is expressing his Lordship in every area of living, including his control of our purse and bank balance.

THE PROBLEM OF AFFLUENCE

Luke 12:15-21

The farmer not only had his idea of sovereignty all wrong, thinking he owned all he saw because he had achieved it through his own labours, but also he was ignorant of the source of satisfaction. He did not deny he had a soul, but lost it in bodily appetite: he confused his soul with his body, and thought his inmost being would be satisfied with wealth and ease. This is the attitude of so many today, who often pay dearly before they learn that affluence cannot ward off pain, or trouble, or domestic problems . . . or death. God calls such a person a fool. So many men and women who have been public idols on stage, screen, or in glamorous careers have ended the victims of drug abuse and other sad situations, often in penury because of their extravagant way of life, which gave them no source of satisfaction.

Further, this man had a false sense of security. He anticipated 'many years' of relaxation with his wealth. God said, 'This night'. Life is not freehold but leasehold, and the lease runs on just as long as God decrees. In the midst of life God breaks in to say 'NOW is your soul required of you.' Life is intended for stewardship, not ownership, and we are called to be faithful to him and obedient to his will so long as he gives us life.

A Prayer: Father, never let me be led astray by the ways of the unbelieving world so that I fail to recognize that the true meaning of life is only found in my daily walk with you, following the way the Master went, for in him is fullness of life. Thank you for that knowledge.

OCTOBER 25

READY AND WAITING
Matthew 25:1-13

Jesus is talking about events prior to his return in power and glory, and the emphasis of the parable is in the warning of verse 13; this has to be borne in mind in the study of the story. The issue is a personal preparedness, with the onus resting on each individual, without help from anyone else.

The ten maidens were all alike in that they had lamps, they waited, they slept, they were there to meet the bridegroom. Five had no oil, so when the great moment arrived, they were not fully ready or prepared for the event.

We know that the bridegroom is the Lord Jesus, the event his coming in glory, the lamp is Christian profession, and the oil is the Holy Spirit. The wise had prepared themselves with a flask of oil, but the foolish had none, and when the shout went up, 'He is here!' they realized their unpreparedness and that there was no time to make amends.

The five wise went in to the feast and the door was shut, leaving the others outside. One cannot strain the meaning of such a parable but truths are obvious, for we all know there are those who profess faith in Christ, but who are very ignorant of what Christian living is all about. These maidens said their lamps were going out, and this can be said of lukewarm, uncommitted Christians whose faith is little more than skin-deep. The Holy Spirit is not evident in their lives, and that can be true of so many of us. We are slack in our devotional life; we try to walk with the world and its ways, and are not committed to the will and purposes of the Lord. Is that your state? Are you conscious of the light going out and the flame of devotion barely flickering?

Be warned before it is too late, and set yourself to seek the Lord afresh, to know the filling of the Holy Spirit, for you do not know the day or the hour when the Lord may come.

FULFIL YOUR POTENTIAL

Matthew 25:14-30

The Lord continues his teaching on preparedness for his return, as well as for living consistently for him each day.

The man going on a journey entrusts his property to three of his servants, the gifts being of differing value. After he went away two of the men traded with their share, and each doubled its value. The third man buried his talent in the ground.

When the master returned he called the three men to account for their stewardship, and the first two told of their investments and received high commendation from their lord.

The third man had a different story to tell. He had a totally different concept of their master from the other men, accusing him of being hard and despotic. The master was naturally angry and took away the one talent the man returned to him, giving it to one of the other servants.

The lesson here is not merely opportunity but commitment. Two men were utterly committed to their master and his welfare, and were diligent in showing their gratitude and understanding of his will.

The third man, the 'one talent man', possibly begrudged the fact he had received less, and acted as he did in a totally irresponsible way. The master no doubt knew he was incapable of handling more, so with his knowledge did not demand more of his servant than he could manage. He was not blamed for having only one talent, but for his misuse of it, on a false assessment of his master's character.

What about the 'talents' the Lord has given to us? Do we use his gifts to glorify him, or do we squander what he commits to us and count his gracious provisions as things we can disregard? Take warning from the one-talent man.

OCTOBER 27

TO FORGIVE IS TO OBEY

Matthew 18:23-35

This parable follows Peter's question in verse 21 about forgiveness, when he learned that there is no limit to the need for forgiving. There is no pat on the back for doing that which is commanded of us.

The king orders a servant to come before him who owed him an immense sum of money, and as he could not pay, his family was to be sold into slavery. When the man fell at his master's feet and pleaded patience and time for him to repay the debt, the king forgave him and set him free. What a glorious picture of our great redemption in the Lord Jesus, who has set us free from the immense debt of sin and the horrors of death!

The forgiven servant left the king's presence and found a colleague who owed him a paltry sum, and demanded instant repayment on threat of imprisonment. News of this was taken to the king, who was of course extremely angry with the man whom he himself had forgiven so much.

What is the lesson in this? It is given in the last few words of the chapter: 'if you do not forgive your brother *from the heart*.' How can one who has been forgiven so much by Jesus himself ever hold a grudge in his heart against someone else? Yet people do. Such action is sin compounded, and unless forgiveness is sought, the Lord will show his grief and displeasure. The answer is a quick reconciliation *from the heart*, and then the joy of the Lord will flood that humbled yet obedient life.

OCTOBER 28

THE HEAT OF THE DAY

Matthew 19:25-20:16

It is essential to put a parable within its context, and here we find a connection between 19:30 and 20:16. Peter claimed that he had made a great renunciation, 'we have left all and followed you: what then shall *we* have?' Peter so often pushed himself into the picture, but the Lord graciously assured him of a great reward (v. 29).

Then Jesus related the parable of the labourers in the vineyard to make sure Peter understood that the basis for service is not reward but motive, and in any event reward is for faithfulness.

The setting is the market place where the unemployed gather to find work. The householder went out to hire labourers for his vineyard, for it was his property but he needed workers. He went out early, then at intervals until the eleventh hour. Take notice of the word 'early' (20:1); how often has the Lord spoken to us, maybe soon after conversion but we have refused to listen. Shame on us! Yet how glad we should be for the eleventh hour.

The master agreed a wage, and when the day's work was finished he paid them, and they all received the same money. It is easy to understand the grumbling of those who worked all day, but the man who went to work at the eleventh hour did not have a chance earlier. Once he was called he went, and both he and all the others were equally faithful to the opportunity given to them.

Where do we stand? Are we working in the heat of the day, or have we only been called in later years of life? God is faithful, and if we prove faithful too, his reward is just and sure.

THE CHOICE SERVANT

Matthew 20:1-16

To continue yesterday's thought, look at the master's reply to the complaining workers: 'I am doing you no wrong; did you not agree with me. . ? Am I not allowed to do what I choose with what belongs to me?'

The only question is: has he the right that he claims to have? In 22:14 is the phrase 'many are called, but few are chosen', and that last word means 'choice'. Everyone called into his service is tested on their faithfulness to the opportunity given to them, and so become 'choice' or otherwise. Reward is not according to term of service; the man who preaches before thousands is no more 'choice' and receives no more than a mother faithful in her home and the training of her children.

Jesus says to all who might quibble, 'Friend, I do you no wrong; did you not agree with me... ?' At the moment of conversion, on the day of complete surrender to the Lordship of Christ, we agreed with his terms. The Cross is not only a place of forgiveness but of challenge to the denial of ourselves (19:29).

If you toil in the heat of the day, do you complain? If you come later into his service, do you grumble? If you expected an easy road, a 'health, wealth and happiness' package, but are experiencing a hard road, disappointment and loneliness, do not blame your Lord, for if you surrendered your life to him, to be obedient to him any time, anyhow, anywhere, then you are like the disgruntled labourers. The Lord is doing you no wrong, for he may do what he chooses with what, and who, belongs to him.

Kneel before him in a new commitment that says 'anywhere he leads me, I will follow on', and you will be among his choice servants.

LOYALTY
Luke 20:19-26

A very important aspect of living for Jesus is outlined in this incident in his life. It was a further challenge to his authority by the powers of the day. This incident is not just a matter of finance, but goes much deeper, embracing all life's responsibilities toward God and men.

Two bitterly opposed sects unite to destroy Jesus. The Pharisees would only agree with paying tribute under protest, affirming the people of God had no right to pay taxes to a pagan government. The Sadducees had no problems and were willing to conform. They were at daggers drawn, but joined forces to crush another hated by both. Rome had the power of life and death, so they must find some reason for Jesus to be condemned by the ruling authority.

On being asked the question Jesus realized if he said Yes he was no Messiah, and the crowds would quickly fall away. If he said No, then he would be a rebel, so either way the Jews had him – or so they thought.

How serenely Jesus goes through the cobwebs! He asked for a coin, and one was passed to him. Picture him quietly turning it over in his hand, and then asking, 'Whose image is this?'

'Caesar's', they were forced to say. Very well, render to him what is his due, for his armies protect you, you enjoy state privileges, and you are his subjects and must take your responsibilities as such. There is to be no cheating on taxation! Note how the religious leaders twisted this interview in 23:2; but also read Matthew 17:24-27. However, Jesus had more to say: 'give to God what belongs to him'. This is the highest loyalty, for though we all have secular responsibilities, if they clash with the word and will of God, then he must come first, as the disciples later said with great boldness in Acts 4:19, 20.

OCTOBER 31

IMAGES

Luke 20:25; Hebrews 1:1-4

Not only coins bear images of a sovereign, but so do we. In Genesis 1:27 it is said man (Adam) was created in the image of God, to have the capacity to know God, and the character to be like him. Through sin the character has gone, but the image remains, for we all have the capacity to love, think, discern between right and wrong, and to know God. The image on a coin is stamped upon it, and the threefold personality of man – body, soul, spirit – reflects the image of God.

This image was soiled, marred, and all that was Godlike in mankind has been lowered and become unrecognizable. Yet the Lord is still sovereign and demands that we give to him the things that belong to him. But humanity refuses to bow the knee to the Sovereign Lord, and therefore they know no rest or peace or purpose in life.

That is the bad news; but the good news is that the image can be restored. If man is made in the image of God, then God can become like men, and the incarnation of Jesus and his wonderful redemption hinges on that fact. He is the express image of God, yet in every point he was made like us, and he did this – taking the great leap of Philippians 2:6-8 – in order to restore in us the image marred by Adam's sin. At the new birth that likeness to God begins to be restored in us. Our thought patterns change, our life style should change, our loyalty is different as we begin to understand what it means to give to God that which is his. The ultimate restoration of that image in us will be when we see him in Heaven. In the meantime base your prayer and praise on 2 Corinthians 3:17, 18.

THE GLORY OF CHRIST

NOVEMBER 1

THE PROMISED DELIVERER

Isaiah 7:1-17

In the final section of these meditations we see Jesus in humility, and also in power and glory. Ignoring the calendar, the first days concentrate on his coming to Bethlehem in meekness, and the final section on his majesty now in Heaven. In between are studies from the Sermon on the Mount, when Jesus taught how his followers should live between his first and second coming.

Today's meditation is on Isaiah's first prophecy concerning the coming Messiah, and how explicit it is as it outlines the virgin birth of Jesus.

The historical background is in 2 Kings 16 and 17, and is a sorry story of the desperate state of Judah under the weak King Ahaz. He was fighting against enemies whom God had raised up, but the King would not listen to Isaiah, and so continued the fruitless battle although the enemies would be finally overcome sixty-five years hence (v. 8b). When Isaiah pleaded with Ahaz to seek the Lord, the King refused (v. 12), either through false piety or fear. Then came the amazing word in verse 14 which seems so out of context. Ahaz would not ask for a sign, so God gives one – a coming deliverer, not born of human power nor stained with human sin, fit to have the throne of his father David (see Genesis 49:10). However wilful God's people may be, he acts in love to fulfil his great purposes, as we shall see in tomorrow's reading.

A Prayer: Loving Father, may I never fail to obey you by my fear or wilfulness. It is possible at times to think I know best, but how wrong and sinful that is, and my heart's desire is to trust you fully and to do those things you purpose for me in your great heart of love.

NOVEMBER 2

GOD WITH US

Isaiah 7:14; John 14:1-17

The name given to this child of a 'young woman', a virgin, is Emmanuel, God with us. Think of those three words, for we are not only taken to the heights of Heaven – God – but right down to earth – with us. Here is the covenant made with David, and it is a promise that cannot be broken (Genesis 49:10).

God, the incarnate, almighty Creator came to inhabit this little world. God, before whom devils fear and fly, is *with* us. In Jesus we see the character of the Father (John 14:9), and so we find that:

God with us is the strength of every Christian.
God with us is the comfort of the suffering.
God with us is protection for the afflicted.
God with us is the hope of the dying.

What more do we need? That was the answer of God through Isaiah to a fearful and defeated people, and it is the answer for us today. Whatever problems or pain any one of us may have right now, the message rings as clear and plain as the Bethlehem bells – God with us! The mystery of the truth is now made plain, for Christ now lives *in* us, the hope of glory (Colossians 1:27).

The one question we need to ask ourselves, after we have had time to read and assimilate this staggering truth, is that we know God is with us, and is more than willing to supply our every need, and here are we in our need, sometimes trying to do for ourselves that which only God can do in us and for us. So the question is, are we with God?

NOVEMBER 3

THE PRINCE OF PEACE

Isaiah 9:1-7

The context of this section is the same as that of chapter 7, and in verses 1-5 is a message of hope in a hopeless situation historically, which leads to the revelation of God's mighty deliverance of all people at all times.

The contrast in verse 6 is striking, for the first half speaks of a child, and a son, and then is followed by divine titles of majesty, glory, power and government. Here indeed is meekness and majesty revealed in stark reality.

A child is born, yes, a human baby born of a woman, Mary. A son is given – the divine Son of God, *given* to the world to be Lord and Saviour as John 3:16 reveals. God's power is stirred into action to redeem those he created and on whom his love is set, to deliver them from opposition by the enemy, Satan himself. Therefore God's Son is **Wonderful Counsellor:** to save the world by dying for it is the miracle of miracles, conceived in the counsel of Heaven (1 Peter 1:20).

Mighty God: Jesus is not a man, a teacher, an example, but he is almighty, divine, and he is God.

Everlasting Father: though he died on the Cross for our sins, he rose again, and is undying, eternal, and one in the Godhead.

Prince of Peace: that title goes to the heart of his life and his life's work. He brought peace into restless, unhappy lives by the blood of his Cross; the peace of the knowledge of sins forgiven, and submission to the will of God.

Therefore is the government, the control, of your life placed on his almighty shoulders, for him to bear the burden of your needs and concerns as you obey gladly the words of 1 Peter 5:7?

THE MESSAGE OF CHRISTMAS
Luke 2:10, 11

Now we come to the fulfilment of Isaiah's prophecy, as we think of the first coming of Jesus to earth at the time we call 'Christmas'.

The first announcement of a very special baby's birth is the angels' message of Good News – the Gospel. Jesus Christ the Lord is the only Saviour from sin, yet here is the record of his humble birth, causing some questions to spring to mind:

To whom did he come? 'To you' – not only to all mankind, but to you and me, for salvation is personal.

How did he come? 'Is born' – here is the mystery first given to Isaiah, 'a child is born' (humanity), ' a son is given' (divinity). That is a truth that defies human explanation, but is the glorious fact of who Jesus is, and of his supernatural conception and birth.

When did he come? 'This day' – God's timing is accurate, for in Galatians 4:4 Paul says that 'when the time had fully come, God sent forth his Son, born of a woman'. And that day had arrived.

Where did he come? 'In the city of David' – to fulfil the prophecy of Micah 5:2. Jesus was born a Jew, but belongs to all people everywhere.

Why did he come? 'A Saviour' – the sole purpose of his coming from Heaven to earth was his journey from Bethlehem to the Cross and on to resurrection and glory.

Who did come? 'Christ the Lord' – the anointed one, the promised Messiah.

From whence did he come? The Lord laid aside the robes of deity to put on the rags of humanity in order that we might be clothed with the garments of his righteousness. We all know sin's reality; we can all know the Lord's forgiveness and cleansing.

NOVEMBER 5

DIVINE CERTAINTY
Luke 2:8-14

As the great day of God's Son's entry into the world arrived it was greeted with a choir and fanfare from the heavenly host. What a contrast we see! Heaven open and angels singing because a baby had been born in dire poverty in a stable of a country inn. No wonder the nearby shepherds were astounded and filled with fear, for the glory of Heaven must have almost blinded them as it struck them dumb.

This anthem of welcome was not only a welcome to the baby, but to a new humanity over which he was to be head, Christ the Lord. A further phalanx of the heavenly host joined the angel to proclaim the message of Christ's mission, for though it has not yet been fulfilled, nothing is so certain as its ultimate victory.

Peace on earth: certainly not visible yet among men and nations. To how many people will it be 'unhappy Christmas' because of personal stress, pain, misery, sin in all its consequences? Yet Jesus brings peace to troubled hearts when he is invited to enter in and calm the storm (John 14:27; Philippians 4:7).

The condition of peace is 'among men in whom he is well pleased'. This became operative in Christ's baptism when God made his great pronouncement (3:21, 22). From that time on Jesus brought peace to those who followed him, for it was a new beginning in history, a new race generated among mankind.

The source of peace is the knowledge that Jesus has come and therefore we give glory to God in the highest. Take Jesus away, and we have nothing, the world has no means of redemption, Satan rules and so does death.

Praise God for the certainty of the angels' message, and may their song be in our hearts too.

NOVEMBER 6

LOVE IN ACTION

2 Corinthians 8:1-9

Here is a message on Christian compassion and mission, and reveals the purpose of Christ's coming in our response to his claims on us.

Consider first the pre-eminence of Christ in verse 9. He was rich, writes Paul, and as I think of that I know he was not speaking of the Lord's social situation, yet he is rich in possessions, for the whole universe is his (Colossians 1:16, 17).

He is rich in honour, for at his birth the heavens burst open as the heavenly hosts came to welcome his coming to earth. Now in glory the angels and all the redeemed praise, worship, and honour him. May our voices down here blend with those above in heartfelt worship!

He is rich in love, for he *is* love. We can never even imagine the love of Father, Son and Holy Spirit, yet he prayed in John 17:26 that the same quality of love may be found in his disciples. How we fail in this aspect, but may our hearts respond once again to the deep, deep love of Jesus. Never forget that 'the highest place that heaven affords is his by sovereign right'. That is also his rightful place in our redeemed, blood-bought lives for *always*.

NOVEMBER 7

FROM HEAVEN HE CAME

2 Corinthians 8:9; Philippians 2:5-11

From majesty to meekness Jesus came, from the riches of Heaven to poverty, for he voluntarily became poor. We cannot picture this immense step without reading the Philippians passage on our knees. Can finite human minds picture the stripping off of all his glory as he prepared for the journey to earth, to the womb of a girl, and birth in a stable?

Think of his strength as he bears the government of the universe on his shoulders (Isaiah 9:6), and then see his helplessness as he is carried in his mother's arms. Think of his upbringing as a carpenter in a humble home, and content to be there for thirty years. Think too, how he, who created the universe, one day asked a woman for a drink of water; how he who had lived in the courts of Heaven, said that on earth he had nowhere to lay his head (Matthew 8:20). To think that he was taken, spat upon, stripped, led to a cross to bleed and die, and finally his dead body was laid in a borrowed tomb. 'From heaven he came, helpless babe', because he who was rich became poor.

WHY? For our sakes – for you and me as individuals, that we might become rich. All the wealth of Heaven is ours in Christ, all the rich promises of his Word, all the riches of his power (Acts 1:8). But first he had to empty himself so that as he shared our poverty, so we may share all the riches of his glory (Romans 9:23), of his grace and inheritance (Ephesians 1:7, 8).

Think on these things on your knees with grateful hearts, for this wondrous gift of love and life that came down from Heaven on Christmas day.

GRACE ABOUNDING
2 Corinthians 8:1-15

Read this passage again to see the reason why Paul wrote verse 9. It is that God's people might understand the grace of his giving in order to regulate their own giving. Jesus is the object of our worship because of his giving of himself, first through incarnation and then through his death at Calvary, endowing us with all the wealth the Holy Spirit can pour into the containers of our lives. It is only we who limit the flow, for like the streams of living water Jesus promised, his grace is limitless.

Such was the witness of the Macedonian Church, where the grace of God had been shown in their giving. Paul's language is extravagant in verses 2-5. The churches were plunged into trouble and great poverty, yet they gave far beyond what they could afford, for they could afford nothing. They gave far beyond prudence, without waiting to be asked, and they begged Paul to receive their gift. Just think of that! Why did they do it? Because they had yielded themselves totally to Christ, and at that moment they knew they were 'under new ownership'. Each individual Christian has to come to that place where he knows, because the grace of the Lord Jesus is so great, that he no longer owns himself, and never again will he say that he owns money or any material thing. All he has is Christ's also. The Lord's wonderful grace constrained him to become poor for us that we might become rich in him, and all we have and are should henceforth flow out in giving to others in the measure of the Spirit's inflow in our lives.

A Prayer: Lord Jesus, all I have and all I am – without argument, debate or question – is yours now and for ever. Thank you for the gift of your life for me and in me which gives me the privilege of sharing your riches of grace and glory.

NOVEMBER 9

LOVE CAME DOWN

John 14:9; Hebrews 2:5-18

Here is the purpose of Christ's coming, to reveal the Father. The way he came is incredible, to the manger in Bethlehem, not a king's palace. Yet the incarnation is central to all God's dealings with us, for without Christ's coming there would be no Gospel. The O.T. anticipated it, as we have seen, and all history looks back to it. How tragic it is that today the Lord Jesus is being elbowed out to make room for Santa Claus, therefore how necessary it is for Christians to share the real meaning of Christmas. It is so important to understand God's purpose for the incarnation, and in this verse Jesus shows that one aim was to reveal the Father.

To do this he was in conflict with all that was contrary to the purposes of God in human life. Men have always felt they can go it alone as masters of their fate, and still feel no need of God: he is extraneous to their thinking. The coming of Jesus to Bethlehem brought a new concept of what God was like and what was his purpose, and this is expressed so simply here: 'He who has seen ME'.

Philip had asked the question, and perhaps expected some display of majestic glory such as was seen on Mount Sinai. But Jesus replied, 'you have seen me – my humanity, my humility, as well as my majesty and holiness, my love and my giving. You *have* seen the Father in me.'

I have seen the face of Jesus,
Tell me not of aught beside;
I have seen the face of Jesus,
And my soul is satisfied.

BORN TO BE KING
John 18:33-38

A strange passage for a Christmas meditation, but the scenes around the Cross throw new light on the meaning of the incarnation.

Pilate asked the question in verse 33, either in great bewilderment or with a sneer, as he saw the exhausted figure before him. Many times the people had wanted to make Jesus king, and he avoided them because he was not claiming an earthly kingdom. Now Pilate was challenging him, and he said that he was (v. 37b). At this hour of betrayal and accusation, which brought upon Jesus derision rather than honour, he openly claimed his Kingship. He made it clear his Kingdom was not of this world; he was not in contention for Caesar's throne, as the Jews tried to persuade Pilate to believe (19:12). No, Christ's Kingdom was not sustained by force, but by truth, for it was spiritual and not material.

To this day, by and large, the Gospel is shrugged aside as unattractive and irrelevant. Jesus is as misunderstood now as he was when he stood before Pilate; holy living is almost unknown, while to be spiritually-minded is to be scorned. Things do not change.

Jesus said plainly that he was born to be King, 'for this I was born . . . to bear witness to the truth.' He has always been Lord and King of all, but now he was setting up a new Kingdom through the power of truth (14:6). His subjects are those who believe in his message of truth and abide by the laws of his Kingdom as given in Matthew 5, 6, 7, for example. So in the fullness of time he was incarnate and born, and thereafter he has been establishing his Kingdom in the hearts of men and women who turn to him in faith, seek his truth, obey his voice, and love him with all their hearts.

NOVEMBER 11

THE KING AND THE KINGDOM

Matthew 5:1, 2; Psalm 24:1-10

The message of the Sermon on the Mount covers Christian living between the first and second coming of the Lord Jesus. It teaches life in the Kingdom for those who are committed servants of the King.

The superficiality of most church life, as well as the lives of so many professing Christians, is so completely out of line with the teaching of Christ that it is essential to know just what he said to those who were close to him.

It was to the disciples that Jesus addressed these words as verses 1-2 clearly state. The people must have gathered around to listen, for their reactions at the conclusion are given in 7:28, 29. What a privilege to be in the Master's class and sit at his feet, and be taught by him! Well, we can as we study prayerfully and carefully the three chapters containing his teaching.

Jesus had said (4:17) the Kingdom is at hand, because he, the King, was present to proclaim his authority. In Luke 10:11 he said the Kingdom is near, or within, you. He exists in every true Christian and indicates the reign of God, for wherever Christ is enthroned as King, *there* is the Kingdom. Therefore it is important to take the teaching of the King very seriously, and seek the Holy Spirit's power to live out in us what he reveals to us.

A Prayer: Dear Lord, as I approach these chapters of your Word, may I be teachable, ready to learn new truths and to throw aside wrong ideas. I desire with all my heart to be worthy of your love and of your concern that I should be one in your Kingdom, and may your Spirit give me the strength to be obedient to all you show to me.

THE KEY TO THE KINGDOM

Matthew 5:3; Isaiah 61:1-3

There are seven Beatitudes, and Jesus did not place them in their order by accident. This first one is the key to all the others, showing there must be an emptying which prepares for a filling. Conviction must precede conversion. Christianity is not a 'do-it-yourself' faith, but a recognition of utter inner corruption and the inability to save oneself. That is what it means to be poor in spirit.

To be spiritually poor is true of everyone, for we all are lacking in love, truth, right living, and are guilty before God as those needing redemption.

To be poor in spirit is the outcome of that truth when the Holy Spirit reveals our spiritual poverty. We are nothing and have nothing by which we can improve our standing before God *until* we confess our desperate need and trust Jesus as our Saviour. When that transaction takes place we experience the fact that we are now 'poor in spirit', utterly dependent upon the fullness of the Spirit, because we know there is no good thing in us apart from Jesus.

The consequence is admittance to the Kingdom – now, instantly, present tense. So understanding of, and obedience to, this first beatitude is the key to the Kingdom, and to the Lord's teaching that follows. May we all know that blessing because we know him in reality.

A Prayer:
    Make this poor self grow less and less,
    Be Thou my life and aim.
    O make me daily through Thy grace
    More meet to bear Thy name   Charles Wesley.

NOVEMBER 13

MAJESTIC MEEKNESS

Matthew 5:4, 5; Colossians 3:1-10

Shallow living is the result of sin and its consequences which, for our sakes, resulted in the life and death of the Saviour. While the joy of the Lord is our strength (Nehemiah 8:10), the Beatitudes are teaching about the deep things of the human heart and experience, and of *sin*, for what it is and what it does, should cause us to grieve.

How do we regard our own failures, our bad temper, unkindness, jealousy, criticism, and all the rest? Do we mourn over our sinfulness, or just shrug our shoulders and say, 'Well, it's a natural reaction'? That's the problem, because if we are part of the body of Christ, the 'natural' is changed to the spiritual because his Spirit now indwells us.

To mourn is to see sin as a desperate experience, because of what it did to Jesus, who 'became sin' on our behalf. Immediately we confess that to him, then he comforts, cleanses, heals, and blesses. Again I say, keep short accounts with God.

The next Beatitude follows in obvious sequence, for the person who understands the meaning of sin in his own life, and the grief and suffering it brought to the Lord Jesus, will in future walk with care and humility. That is meekness; not weakness, but something much stronger, because meekness does not assert itself but reflects the mind of Christ. The fruit of such a life is in the future, such *shall* inherit, when we see the Lord, and his reward is with him. Therefore let us pray that his 'mind' may live in us from day to day, so that we can reveal the true meekness that is seen to perfection in the King of kings.

NOVEMBER 14

LIFE ON A HIGHER PLANE

Matthew 5:6; Romans 5:1-11

The Beatitudes have to be seen from God's point of view rather than ours. We do not associate happiness with poverty of spirit, mourning, meekness, hunger and thirst. But these are essential from Heaven's viewpoint, because sin is such a deadly curse. It is not only the cause of war and killing in the world, but of all human misdeeds and the misery they bring, right down to the evil within our own hearts.

So having looked within and seen such failure, this verse brings one of the great statements of the Gospel for all who are unhappy about their spiritual state and long for a life on a higher plane.

Do we really hunger after righteousness? To do so results in happiness, but we are not to crave only for that which is the pursuit of the world. To be in tune with God, to desire only what he desires, to be like Jesus in thought, word, and deed – that is true happiness because it is impossible for human nature to achieve that, only the new life of the Spirit within the believer.

To be righteous is not only to be cleansed from sin and justified before God, but to be sanctified, set apart for him and filled with his Spirit. It is to be free from the power *of* sin, and the desire *to* sin, then to live and please God. It is when we get off the fence of a half-hearted commitment to Christ and yield ourselves utterly to him that we will experience the joy and peace he promises and longs to give. It is the 99% commitment we so often offer to God that must grieve him, because he gave his all in the giving of his Son, therefore he has a right to our ALL.

NOVEMBER 15

OH TO BE LIKE HIM!

Matthew 5:7, 8; Psalm 103:1-5

What do we know about mercy? It is not only to endure wrong, but to bless those who hurt us. It is not only a longing to *be right*, but to *do good*. Every step of the 'Beatitude ladder' is connected, and one rung cannot be disconnected, for Jesus was speaking of progress, for the whole ladder rests on the grace of God and of his Son. There are merciful people around – a few – but only the Holy Spirit can enable a person to be right with God and therefore do good to others.

The Beatitudes are not the way of salvation, but the outcome and evidence of a saved life. Mercy is one of the characteristics of God (Psalm 103:8), and if we fully understand his mercy toward us, who are so sinful, then we can extend the mercy and grace that flows from his Spirit to others, and so enjoy a continual stream of his power.

The words of verse 8 challenge us to say 'is this possible?' But remember it is the next step of the ladder, and if you reread verses 3-7 you will see the sequence. To take verse 8 by itself would bring despair, but in its setting it brings hope. Read 2 Corinthians 7:1 and 1 John 3:1-3. To have a pure heart is to know the life of Jesus within, and to do those things that please him. In this we will 'see', or understand God, and be unafraid to come into his presence, for it is there that we find fullness of joy (Psalm 16:11).

Pray that the Lord will make these truths plain to you, and lead you into deeper fellowship with himself, and therefore a radiant witness of His love and grace to your friends.

NOVEMBER 16

THE PEACE OF GOD

Matthew 5:9; Colossians 3:12-17

As each Beatitude is like a rung in a ladder, it also represents a feature in the character of God's ideal man, the kind of person he expects you and me to be if we claim to be in his Kingdom and obeying the King. Here is the last feature, the top rung.

A peacemaker is more than someone who patches up quarrels, though that is very commendable and necessary. It is a person's relationship to God, outlined in verses 3-8, that makes an abiding impact upon his relationship with others. It is impossible to adjust human relationships without first adjusting our relationship with God himself.

A peacemaker does not want peace at any price, for you cannot bring to others what you do not possess yourself. The peacemaker is only such because, by the grace of God, he is at peace within himself. He is meek, he is merciful and pure, and then peaceable. Unless he has peace in his own heart he cannot bring it to others, and he cannot know peace of heart unless he is in tune with the Lord Jesus, the Prince of peace, who imparted that quality to his followers prior to his death: 'My peace I *give* to you' (John 14:27).

The peacemaker knows the peace of God in his heart because he has made peace with God by way of the Cross (Romans 5:1), and that peace rules and regulates his life (Colossians 3:15). Such a person is owned by God and recognized by men. May that be the mark on our lives daily, that in this modern life where there is so much clamour, discord, distrust and turmoil, we may be sharers of that peace which passes all understanding.

NOVEMBER 17

FOR JESUS' SAKE

Matthew 5:10-12; 2 Timothy 3:10-17

These three verses could be called the eighth Beatitude, though in verse 11 the words are spoken to 'you', not 'they'. They are addressed to believers who have ascended the ladder, so to speak – and then what do they find? Persecution.

This was very true of the early Church, and has been true recently in Russia, and at the time of writing, in China, persecution for righteousness' sake, not for crime or treason. The writers of the epistles all spoke of the suffering to be confronted by those who named the name of Christ. To be a believer is no immunization from physical pain and discomfort, nor from fierce and often death-dealing persecution.

Why? you may ask. Because there is an enemy, Satan himself, who hounded the Lord to Calvary, and continues to wreak havoc on his followers, so do not be surprised at what may happen (1 Peter 4:12).

The world heartily dislikes being shown up and pours scorn on those who live righteously. Many workers suffer misery because they insist on the truth, and will not lie to please their bosses. This all lies behind verse 10.

There is, however, a deeper reason for persecution, and that is when it is for the Lord's sake. The early believers counted it joy to suffer for Jesus (Acts 5:41). Do we react like that to scorn and ridicule? They were certainly in line for the blessing of verse 12, for though the promise is in the future, when we get to Heaven, in the present we follow the crucified One, and we must never forget that, nor must we ever try to escape the Cross in our own lives.

NOVEMBER 18

SALT AND LIGHT

Matthew 5:13-16; 2 Corinthians 4:1-6

In a previous study we thought about salt in the Gospels. That metaphor is often linked with light, so the two must be considered together, as Jesus did.

Salt is needed for savour and preservation, and speaks of the sort of people we should be, bringing freshness and purity into a world full of corruption. Light has the power to banish darkness, and we are entrusted with the light of the knowledge of the glory of God in the face of Jesus.

Darkness is a frightening thing, and John 3:19 graphically describes its power, broken only when light comes. There is great darkness in the world today, with men turning ever further from God, the ascendency of the powers of darkness through the occult and Satan worship, that it is no wonder men's hearts fail for fear.

The Lord Jesus is the light of the world, and it is he who says, '*you* are the light of the world,' placed here as his representatives. And we are all he has to continue this light-bearing. Think of that sobering thought. No wonder he said the light must not be hidden but displayed in all its power and brilliance.

The wise of this world are in the dark and baffled by the way things are going on all fronts, and only the believer knows that the only way out of darkness is the provision of light. May we each one rise to our responsibility to fulfil the purpose of Jesus in shedding his true light in this needy world, and we can only do this as we walk in the light with him (Ephesians 5:7-14).

NOVEMBER 19

THE LAW AND THE GOSPEL

Matthew 5:17-20

These verses introduce the teaching that follows in the rest of Christ's sermon. They give the attitude first of himself, and then of his followers, towards the Old Testament. This can only be looked at briefly in today's meditation.

The Law of God is unchangeable (v. 18), meaning his moral law, the Ten Commandments. The ceremonial law ended when Jesus died and the veil of the Temple was rent in two, for he had now obtained eternal redemption by his blood and sacrifice (Hebrews 9:12). We are, however, expected to live in the light of the Law, as previous studies have shown.

The love of God is unfathomable (v. 17). Man is judged and condemned by the Law, because he can never by 'doing' gain salvation from sin. Here is the answer of love – Jesus came to fulfil the Law on our behalf, and Galatians 4:4 says he was 'made under the law', therefore he, the Son of God, was obliged to fulfil it. He obeyed all God commanded in the Law, so that no one could accuse him of sin (John 8:46). On the Cross he endured the full penalty of sin on our behalf, and if we acknowledge that fact and claim him as our Lord and Saviour, we are forgiven. What wondrous love!

The life of the Christian is unmistakable (v. 20). A new life in Christ demands new behaviour towards others, a totally new conception of what Christian living is all about, and only the Holy Spirit can achieve that in us. Let us seek his fullness to meet every challenge that comes to us day by day.

LAW AND LIBERTY

Matthew 5:20-22; 2 Corinthians 5:11-21

The pivotal point of chapters 5, 6, 7 is 5:20. Prior to that the Lord had been describing the marks of a genuine Christian, and from then on his teaching is to show how the believer's righteousness is to be seen in the world as a sign of personal redemption, and the hope of salvation for everyone, for no one is without hope if they come to know Christ as their Lord.

In chapter 5 Jesus shows the Christian's responsibility to the true nature of the Law as distinct from the slant given to it by the Pharisees. In chapter 6 he shows the true nature of fellowship with God as compared with what was practised by the Pharisees. In chapter 7 he defines true righteousness again in contrast to the Pharisees.

So in the passage above is the first of six challenging statements in verses 21, 27, 31, 33, 38, 39. The very words of verse 21 show how words had been added to Exodus 21:12, so Jesus said, 'You have heard' rather than 'you have read'. Then came his words of divine authority, 'But I say to you'. Because he is God, he originally gave the Law, and now he came to fulfil it, and to enable his people to do the same.

In these verses the final word on murder is not on our personal opinion or on the word of a court of law, but on the word of the Son of God: I say to you. Therefore in these studies we must heed every word he says to us, and act upon them rightly.

NOVEMBER 21

THERE IS NO TIME FOR DELAY

Matthew 5:21-26

In this chapter Jesus applies some principles regarding the subjects with which he is dealing. It is the spirit and not the letter of the Law that matters. The Pharisees had concentrated on the latter and had lost the spirit, so they reasoned that if they had not murdered anyone, or committed adultery, they were perfect. So Jesus makes it clear that what matters is not whether I have shot someone, but do I hate him? Further, do I hate someone *without a cause* (v. 22 AV)? Do I dare call someone 'worthless fool' (Raca)? This is the spirit that can ultimately lead to murder.

From abuse Jesus progresses to anger, specifically against a *brother.* How many broken relationships there are in families, among friends, in church fellowships, that are never put right because of pride, and the refusal to bow the neck in confession of wrong to the other person. Forget your acts of service, leave your devotions, and even if you think you are the innocent party, get right with your friend *quickly* (v. 25). You only have NOW, today, in which to put things right, for you do not know when the Lord might call you to himself. Be reconciled, make friends, restore love and fellowship, defeat the enemy, and rejoice the heart of the Lord. Do it quickly!

NOVEMBER 22

THE SINFULNESS OF SIN

Matthew 5:27-30

Are people getting better morally? Has education and environment – the pet themes of pundits earlier this century – had the desired effect on people's behaviour? Definitely not, because morality and behaviour are not shaped by environment but by the recognition of the sinfulness of sin.

Jesus is the only Saviour from the power and guilt of sin, but he offered no easy believism, but always told his would-be followers to sit down and count the cost of discipleship, because self-denial is required on the part of those whose desire is to follow Jesus with complete devotion into a life of purity and holiness.

So in the passage for today Jesus hits hard at a way of life that is now so over-publicized, its wrong is being totally ignored. Jesus reveals the awful sin of adultery. The strength of this sin (v. 28) is that it is so subtle, because without committing an overt act one can fantasize in one's heart, and be just as guilty before God. How we need to take 2 Corinthians 10:5 seriously, and confess sins of thought and mind to the Lord for his cleansing.

The cure for impure thoughts is drastic (vv. 29, 30). Only Jesus can deliver us totally, for we have to be so strict with ourselves that it is as if the eye and the hand, the offending members of our body, have to be removed in order for us to know victory. This is the outcome of self-denial and self-crucifixion, as we read also in Colossians 3:5-7. If you are tempted to sin, read these verses in prayer, confession and obedience.

CHRIST, HEAD OF THE HOME
Matthew 5:31, 32; 19:3-9

Another ageless but very modern problem is focused by Jesus, and how much we need to understand his view on divorce. The subject is first mentioned in Deuteronomy 24:1-4. Adultery was not the problem, because that had been punished by death of the offenders. Moral uncleanness was the only ground for divorce, and these verses show the Mosaic Law sought to teach people they could not walk in and out of marriage frivolously or at will.

In Matthew 19:3 the ever-attendant Pharisees asked if divorce could be procured *without cause*, to which the Lord answered a resounding No, because of the sanctity of marriage, the one-flesh union of husband and wife, which only unfaithfulness through adultery could sever (5:32). Deliberately to divorce one partner in order to marry another – unless for adultery – is in itself adultery, and so breaks God's Law and the teaching of Christ.

The divorce law is being made easier and easier, but no human law can destroy a blood relationship, therefore Jesus declares that there is only one basis for divorce —unfaithfulness, for the 'one flesh' of marriage is then broken beyond repair.

Paul brings to notice a query posed by young believers regarding the position of a Christian with an unsaved partner. Should they separate or divorce? they ask. See Paul's reply in 1 Corinthians 7:10-16: no, they stay together, for the unsaved partner and the children have a strong possibility of knowing Christ through the witness of the Christian parent. The teaching of Scripture is the sanctity of marriage, and Christian couples need more than ever to show the love, loyalty, and joy of a home in which the Saviour dwells in full control.

NOVEMBER 24

AVAILABILITY

Matthew 5:33-42

In previous meditations on the Ten Commandments we thought about the holiness of the Lord's name, and the sin of false witness. In these verses Jesus teaches that his followers must have even greater control over their tongues. This does not concern the taking of an oath in a court of law, but to speaking the truth without exaggeration or fear. A Christian's word should be his bond, and he should be known for his loyalty, honesty, and trustworthiness at all times and in all places.

In the Lord's 'Law for Christian living' he comes to the heart-searching test in verses 38-42. The words of verse 38 from Exodus 21:24, were originally to restrain revenge, to order punishment to fit the crime. What does Jesus teach? Remember he is speaking to his disciples and not to the world. An unregenerate person could not live under the laws of Christ's Kingdom, for only those who acknowledge his kingship have the power within them to obey his precepts. He is dealing here with relationships between believers, in family and church fellowship, and not about pacifism or state relationships.

First (v. 39) there must be no retaliation to insult or abuse, no hitting back, for those things cannot affect a 'dead' person, who has reckoned himself to be crucified with Christ. There is to be no claim to 'rights', even though that brings on the suffering of injustice (v.40). There must be concern for the needs of others to the extent of going beyond the demand made upon one, either in physical effort or sharing in a spirit of Christian love and oneness (vv. 41, 42).

Think of all these principles in the light of Calvary, and then assess your own willingness to put them into practice.

NOVEMBER 25

BOUNDLESS LOVE

Matthew 5:43-48

This is the climax of the first section of Christ's teaching on life in the Kingdom. The Beatitudes revealed the kind of person a believer should be, and that he is salt and light in the world. But there are obligations, and as children of the King we are expected to live on a higher plane than those outside his Kingdom. So the Lord taught how we can obey his word by the power of the Holy Spirit and live a life of holiness and righteousness (v.20).

In this final paragraph Jesus challenges the Christian's attitude to himself. In verses 38-42 the negative attitude is shown in that he offers the other cheek, goes the extra mile, gives to those in need, showing that he has died to all self-interest, and to please his Master is his consuming passion.

Positively, he loves his enemies and is therefore perfect as his Father in Heaven. Impossible! you may well say. True, apart from the Cross and the grace of God. How we need to apply this teaching in today's world, and to our witness to Christ.

God's love is universal (v. 45b), and he certainly didn't redeem us because we are more lovable than others. He loves us *in spite* of ourselves, and his love has no selfish interests. We are to love others with his love flooding through our hearts. We are never called to *like* people, but to love them with the love of God shed abroad in our hearts by the Holy Spirit – in short, the love of 1 Corinthians 13. Make this your goal and your earnest prayer.

NOVEMBER 26

OUR WORSHIP AND DAILY WALK

Matthew 6:1-4

Having taught the principles of his Kingdom, the Lord now instructs his people how to live them out vertically (vv. 1-18) and horizontally (vv. 19-34). To become a Christian is not to find every problem in life is solved, but to find one's path is beset by snares and pitfalls, and Jesus gives both warning and a way of deliverance.

The verses above commence a very challenging section regarding our worship and its relationship to daily living, our walk with God. So the first word is 'beware', take heed, and Jesus pinpoints three aspects of a life of worship: giving (v. 3), prayer (v. 5), fasting (v. 16). These are fundamental in a life of worship: how I give, how I pray, how I exercise self-restraint in putting to death the desire of the flesh-life.

The righteousness (piety) of a Christian is not to be flaunted before the world, for that is not the way to witness to Christ. To act like that is the very opposite of the promise of Jesus in 5:16, as the light of his love shines through. Hypocritical piety is anathema, and those who act in that way receive their earthly reward – maybe!

The Lord looks within to see the motive behind our devotions, and our aim should be to honour him in all we do. So what is the motive in your giving – to further his kingdom in obedience to his word in your heart, or to allow some praise to come your way too? Honour the Lord, and he will honour you *in secret.*

NOVEMBER 27

THE SECRET PLACE

Matthew 6:5-15

It is shocking to realize that sin can be in our hearts in the most holy moments, when we give our tithes and offerings, when we pray and fast. Be warned, says the Lord, and be honest, forthright, with no trace of hypocrisy. No doubt you know times when Satan flashes evil thoughts into your mind, even when you are praying, for sin is an attitude of heart, and self intrudes into our worship.

To pray is to commune with our Father in Heaven, therefore there should be no false spirituality in giving the impression we are great 'pray-ers', or false piety in mouthing words that do not come from the heart. 'Empty phrases', said the Lord, that rise no higher than the ceiling.

Go into your room and meet the Lord in quietness, avoiding distraction as much as possible. Know that your Father is there with you in the secret place, and that he already knows your needs (v. 8). Take time to get your heart in tune with him, to hear his voice, to know his plan for you today, and unite with him in the fulfilling of it. Always remember he is no man's debtor (v. 6b).

There is nothing more objectionable than pious hypocrisy, and it is so easy to detect. On the other hand, there is nothing more precious than to meet with our Father and pour out the needs of our hearts, and hear his loving words to calm our minds. Read afresh the Lord's pattern of prayer and use the words to express your own deepest needs.

NOVEMBER 28

THE DISCIPLINE OF DENIAL

Matthew 6:16-18

It is easy to see how the Lord gave the pattern prayer at this point in his sermon, because it shows what is pleasing to the Father, compared with the mouthings of verses 5 and 7. As we have studied the prayer in detail already, we pass on to the next section of fasting, self-denial and discipline.

Fasting, abstinence from food in order to pray and meet with God, is the primary meaning, but from my observation it is very rarely practised in modern life. Are we too busy, too diary-bound, too much involved with our own affairs to be able to take time of this quality to get alone with God? The Pharisees found time, and advertised what they were doing by their dismal faces!

To fast is to seek the Lord in such a single-minded way that we willingly deny ourselves legitimate needs – food, sleep, the society of family and friends – for a period of time. Where are our priorities? How much does it cost to be a Christian, in giving, praying and fasting? Where is truly sacrificial living to be found?

The trouble with so many Christians is that they have little conception of the meaning of denial of 'self', of which much has been written in these meditations. It is rarely preached, because it is not an exciting subject, not one likely to draw the crowds, and that is just what happened when the Lord began to speak about the way of the Cross, and the people began to drift away. May the Lord not find us in that category, nor wanting in showing our love for him and devotion to him, for he promises his reward in his own time and way.

THE HEART'S TREASURE

Matthew 6:19-24

Treasure on earth means what it says, that which people can accumulate by work or other means, which they hoard and call their own. What madness to be content with things that can be stolen or rot away! Yet multitudes of people are doing just that, and they find no lasting satisfaction in what they possess, and finally have to leave it all behind.

Treasure in Heaven is all that the Christian finds in the Lord Jesus, when that person lives not for time but for eternity. Yet the Lord teaches emphatically that each one must make the step from worldliness to holy living, for the *heart* is possessed by the treasure (see Colossians 2:3). The seat of the emotions, the area of deepest feelings, must be under the control of the Saviour, and his very life installed in our deepest recesses, for he is our treasure and he alone is worthy of our total dedication.

In verses 22,23 Jesus speaks of the *mind* which can only be 'full of light' when the heart is centred in loving Jesus. What we think, the things we dream about as being the most desirable, all must be under his control, or the light of his presence dims. In verse 24 Jesus speaks of the *will*, the place of decision. Each individual attaches allegiance either to God, or to Satan in the form of worldly gain and fading treasure.

What a challenge this section presents! Treasure on earth or in Heaven? Inner light through the revelation of Jesus as Lord, or the darkness of sin and disobedience? A lifetime of service to Christ or a life wasted in selfish pleasure? Where is your heart's treasure?

NOVEMBER 30

WHY WORRY?

Matthew 6:25-34

In the second section of this chapter we are taught in verses 19-34 how, as Christians, we should live out the life of worship, outlined in verses 1-18. Because we face daily contact with the world which runs contrary to the principles of Christianity, Jesus taught the danger of a positive love for worldliness (vv. 19-21), and of divided loyalty, for if Jesus is not Lord of our lives, then the light within is hampered from shining by sin and lack of commitment.

So Jesus says, 'Therefore ... do not be anxious'. The children of the King have no need to worry, but those who have no relationship with Jesus have every reason to be desperately anxious about their souls and their eternal destiny, as well as their daily living.

We are to take no thought, to have no anxious care – which is not being rash or reckless – in our way of living, but understanding 1 Peter 5:7: 'Cast all your anxieties on him, for he cares about you.' Peter was no doubt recalling this passage of the Lord's great sermon, and he himself demonstrated this release from corroding worry in his prison experience (Acts 12).

It is said that if we worry we do not trust, but if we trust we do not worry, and there is a lot of truth in that, for worry and faith cannot live side by side, when we think of 'worry' as the sort of anxious care which paralyses us. That is the meaning of the word in this context, because of course it is normal to have concern for others, and be anxious on their behalf.

A Prayer: Dear Lord, save me from worrying over things which are under your control, but to be lovingly concerned for those who need my help and prayer support.

DECEMBER 1

FREE TO LIVE
Matthew 6:25-34; Philippians 4:4-7

Jesus made a threefold appeal regarding anxious thought, and we will look at each briefly:

Do not be anxious about food – what you put *in*. The slaves in Roman times were housed, fed, and clothed by their masters, so did not need to worry on that account. As slaves of Jesus Christ no more do we. Life is more than food (note that!), and as God created our bodies, so he will supply its needs. Worry is needless, senseless, and useless.

Do not be anxious about clothing – what we put *on* (vv. 25, 31). Remember true beauty is from within, the life and light of Jesus shining out. Look at the flowers, says Jesus – more glorious than Solomon. Look at the worldlings: this is their life, their quest, and see their anxiety. Look at your Heavenly Father, because he knows your every need, and he will provide. Do you believe that?

Do not be anxious about tomorrow, because of what we must put *first*. The heart of this section is verse 33, and the person who obeys this command will experience the faithfulness of the King. The promise of this verse is so all-embracing, there is no need to doubt the ability of the one who spoke to fulfil his promise, so learn to trust him as perhaps you never have done in your life. Paul understood what Jesus was saying, for he adds his word in Philippians 4:6, that we are to have no anxiety about anything, but in prayer . . . let your requests be made known to God, and then his peace will stand guard over your heart to forbid the entry of anxiety and care.

Why worry about an unknown future when we follow the one who holds the future in his hands? Release from anxiety brings freedom to live in the joy of the presence of the living Lord Jesus, and faith in his eternal faithfulness to his Word and his people.

DECEMBER 2

HOW REAL IS YOUR FAITH?

Matthew 6:33, 34; 2 Peter 1:3-11

Never add tomorrow's burdens to today's, for each moment has enough of its own. Don't sap today's strength by worrying over tomorrow, because tomorrow's grace will be there to meet its need. New every morning is God's mercy (Lamentations 3:22-24), and we need to count on that and praise him for that knowledge.

In yesterday's meditation we saw the comfort of Christ's words and now we face their challenge. Worry that drives people distracted is not primarily a mental state but a spiritual one, and can only be treated on that plane. Jesus warns that to worry over the future is not only futile, but is crippling to the present.

The source of worry is in verse 30, 'you of little faith', because all forms of despair and anxiety are caused when there is lack of faith due to taking one's eyes off the Lord, the source of all comfort, strength, and supply. No doubt we all experience that at times, but remember that little faith fails to lay hold on the promises of God, for we get taken up so much with the problem at hand and try to work out our own solution to it that we forget the Lord is waiting for us to confess our need to him.

Refresh yourself constantly in his Word and in his presence; memorize his gracious promises (i.e. Matthew 11:28-30); let him speak to your heart. Peter exhorts us all to do just that in the verses above, and it is such an encouragement to soak oneself in his testimony and teaching in that passage. Worry is silenced when we fully understand verse 31b and obey verse 33. No wonder Jesus said, 'THEREFORE don't be anxious.' Rest your heart in his faithfulness.

DECEMBER 3

THINK BEFORE YOU SPEAK
Matthew 7:1-6

Life is a journey leading to a final judgement; it is a proving ground, and one day we will stand before Christ to account for our stewardship of his gift of life. This passage does not teach that a Christian should have no opinions, but defines the word 'judge'. We are not to criticize others or stand in judgement over their words or actions, because the Lord one day will judge us for our conduct. We are not to expect higher standards from others than we put on ourselves. That is a very common human criticism which Christians must shun, for one day God will judge them on their unloving and ungracious attitudes.

We are not to judge, because we are incapable of doing so. Our own sins and failures put us in no position to cast judgement on the behaviour of others. How often we try to help others by pointing out their shortcomings, but the Lord says clearly it is impossible to do so if you are blinded by sin in your own life. So often the fault of another is but a 'speck' compared with the 'beam' of criticism which is a glaring sin we are committing. The vivid imagery the Lord used showed the folly as well as the wrong we commit when we are judgemental and critical of others, seeking to put them right when our own lives also need a lot of sorting out. Therefore verse 6 makes it plain when and to whom we present truth, in a spirit of love, with the guidance of the Holy Spirit who alone can save us from making grievous errors by our lack of discernment or unthinking behaviour.

A Prayer: Dear Lord, it can be so easy to put people right in our own views when we ourselves are so wrong in our attitudes, and unable to understand situations aright. Please forgive me for the times I have blundered in trying to help others, or spoken a word to someone who was not prepared by your Spirit to receive it.

DECEMBER 4

SEEKING AND FINDING

Matthew 7:7-11; Philippians 3:7-14

It would be difficult to find a more comforting promise in the Bible than verse 7, repeated more emphatically in verse 8. God never promises to change circumstances, remove difficulties, or ease trials and pain. He does promise that we need never fear or be anxious, because in this passage is the secret of peace: ask, and you shall . . .

Following on the Lord's condemnation of criticizing others without looking at our own spiritual needs, he now supplies his gracious answer to our deepest requirements. First, however, we must realize our own emptiness and inadequacy, and then when we see it we ask, seek, knock in persistency until we know we are in a right relationship with Jesus. If we *really* want his blessing we must persist, and never rest content with a second-class commitment. This is what Paul was writing about in the verses above, that his one aim in life was to go on and on in his quest to know the Lord Jesus in the deepest possible way that a human being can. Can we follow him in determination to 'know the Lord' in that way too?

We must realize God is our Father, and be confident always in his love and care, and also that he has good gifts for us, the Holy Spirit (Luke 11:13). So when we ask, seek and knock we are desiring all that God has for us, not just our own desires and wants which might be right out of line with the will of God. The needs of life are given us if they are according to his purpose, and we must always remember that when we come into his presence in prayer.

DECEMBER 5

THE GOLDEN RULE

Matthew 7:12

A thread of judgement runs through this chapter in the Lord's concern that his people should not be censorious, critical, and ungracious, followed by his revelation to supply needed grace to walk aright with him if we but ask. So in verse 12 he says, 'Therefore', because if we admit the condemnation of verses 1-6 we are still in no state to witness to others. Only the empowering of the Holy Spirit can change our attitude to other people and enable us to love them.

This thought has been considered before, but it needs to be emphasized again that we are told to love other people, even our enemies, but nowhere are we told that we must like them. It is only the love of Jesus in our own hearts that can give us the power to love the unlovely and unlovable. We are to show that love by understanding others are like us, and so we are to respond to them in a way that will not hurt.

This is an unchanging rule, and in our witness to friends we need to think out the implications carefully. We don't like gossip, so don't gossip about others. We don't like sharp-tongued, critical people, so don't be like that with others. And so we could go on. However, when we take all the meanness in our own character and lay it at the Cross, we look up into the face of Jesus and see his holiness and power, and gladly surrender our sin and weakness to his gracious indwelling, as he fulfils verse 11. For what hurts us will hurt others, what helps us will help them too. His power alone will give the love, patience and discernment we need to make us acceptable to the people to whom we seek to witness to the power of the Lord Jesus.

DECEMBER 6

THE FINAL CHALLENGE
Matthew 7:13-27

Having spoken about Christian living in all its aspects, the Lord now says, 'What about it? what is your verdict?' In verses 13, 14 is the test of direction, for the way into life is through a narrow gate, where the repentant sinner leaves the load of sin behind together with all worldly hopes and ambitions, and he begins to walk alongside the crucified Son of God. The alternative is the crowded way that leads to destruction. Which road are you travelling?

The test of fruit (vv. 15-20) is the evidence shown in our lives, of which John 15:1-7 is the teaching. Do you pass the test of true Holy Spirit fruitfulness and the life more abundant which Jesus promised? The test of obedience in verses 21-23 shows that it is actions and not words that count. Many speak his name, but know nothing of doing the will of God from the heart. Do you pass this test of complete submission to the joy of obeying the good and perfect will of God? The test of stability (vv. 24-27) shows what happens to our lives when the storms crash around us, as they inevitably do.

In these brief sketches we read that all heard, but only some obeyed, and the outcome was the same floods of final judgement. What is the difference in the two structures? It is all a matter of foundation, and it is plainly stated that there is only one on which a life can be firmly rooted, and Paul writes, 'no other foundation can any one lay than that which is laid, which is Jesus Christ' (1 Corinthians 3:11). That is as categorical in its meaning as the words of Jesus, I AM *the* Way, *the* Truth, *the* Life. Take heed you remember this when confronted by other faiths, cults and sects, for unless the house of one's life is built upon that Rock it will collapse when the storms of life and death come upon it. Do you pass that test also?

DECEMBER 7

TREASURES OF WISDOM

Matthew 7:28, 29; Colossians 2:1-7

While the Lord was primarily teaching his disciples (5:1, 2), the people were also crowding around to listen, and we might well say, 'Oh, to have been among them!' Their reaction is given in the verses for study, and the word that came to their mind was 'authority', but so very different from that of the Jewish teachers.

To find the source of that authority, read again the verses in Colossians, and note Paul's well-chosen words: love, riches, understanding, mystery, treasures of wisdom and knowledge.

Paul is writing to people who have not met him personally (v. 1), so that includes us, and he writes for our encouragement, and once again to beg believers to be united in the bonds of love in the Lord Jesus. This will ensure our obedience to all he has to say in verses 2b, 3, where we are told of the mystery of God, the Gospel (1:27), revealed to us by Jesus, the fountain of wisdom and knowledge, and he alone can open our own understanding of the mind and purposes of God.

The only way to avoid being drawn into false teaching and cults is to stand firm on the Word of God, get your roots deep down into the truth, and build on the One who is the only true foundation (vv. 4-8). This is a wonderful summary of Christ's teaching in the Sermon on the Mount, and as we understand and obey his words, we should be overflowing in thanksgiving for all he has done for us, unworthy as we are.

A Prayer: Praise God from whom all blessings flow!

DECEMBER 8

PERFECT LOVE
1 John 4:13-21

John is known as the Apostle of Love, for he wrote so much about this aspect of Christian life. How glad we are that he did for it should be our life's response to the Lord's teaching we have just studied. In this passage love is shown as the antidote to fear (v. 18). The entrance of love into our hearts means the exit of fear. This is obvious for one cannot love and fear someone at the same time. However, it is only *perfect* love that does this; imperfect love still lodges with fear.

There is the dominion of fear, and so many people live under this cloud. Suspicion, mistrust, fear of exposure or exploitation, fear of death – so much in and around to paralyse people with fear. There is also the fear of God, because of the torture of guilt. Those out of step with him have reason to fear, for they trample on his Son and scorn the Cross and all John talks about in verses 13-17.

There is the deliverance of love – perfect love. This is found only in Christ and supremely at the Cross. He does not love because we are worthy, but because we are sinners who need the salvation he alone can give (Romans 5:8).

Of our own we cannot love God. We all break the first commandment, and are therefore under the condemnation of sin. It is when it dawns on us that 'God loves even ME' that he fills our hearts with his love (vv. 16,19). Our love for him is evidenced by our lives, so how often are you in his presence in prayer and worship? Do you obey him and keep his commandments with a joyful, loving, fearless heart?

There is also the display of love, because it casts out fear and enables us to love from the heart (v. 20), and gives us confidence as we know one day we will meet God (v. 17).

Is all this true of you, that his perfect love replacing your poor, human affection, is that which overcomes all fear?

DECEMBER 9

LIFE'S GREATEST QUEST

Philippians 3:1-17

As you read this passage, what words stand out from the page to attract your attention? For me, they are found in verse 10, only five words, 'that I may know him'. Paul spoke of all that became loss to him when he gained the knowledge of Christ, and now reveals his greatest quest in these words: 'that I' – the rebel – 'may know' – a channel of revelation – 'him' – the great Redeemer.

'Me, a rebel?' do you say. Yes, for man, made in the likeness of God, dependent upon him for everything, made a moral choice of independence, deliberately disobeying God's word. Instead of the almighty Creator being the centre of life, man thought of himself as a sun around which everything must revolve. In that way God's dominion ended where man's began, and that is rebellion copied from Satan, as Isaiah 14:13 shows.

So our hearts are basically enthroned by 'myself', and we, created to worship our Creator, sit on our self-created throne, and imagine each is the centre of our personal universe.

That is the essence of sin, and because it is so universal, it is taken as a natural part of life. Because of this vile sin, sins multiply, and the rebel can do nothing about it, and only when he has restored his stolen throne to God are his works acceptable. It was to bring this to pass that Jesus came to save and deliver, to reverse the bent trait in our nature, and plant within us a new principle, a new nature, that will produce the desire to bring glory to God and the knowledge of his love to others.

DECEMBER 10

GROW IN KNOWLEDGE AND LOVE
Philippians 3:10; 2 Peter 3:14-18

If you recognize yourself as a rebel – either in the past or the present – see now the channel of revelation, 'may know'. How views of God destroy the Gospel, which means nothing to anyone until we sense the burden of guilt, the obligation to love God with every power we possess, and then catch a vision of him adequate to transform our lives from rebels to sons and daughters.

How may I know him? We have to have a clear concept of God in Christ. The nearer we approach him the clearer he becomes. For generations we have taken Almighty God so much for granted that he has never been revealed to this generation, and therefore he is pronounced to be 'dead', and he just doesn't count any more. There is no sense of his might and majesty, his holiness and power. Therefore people are never disturbed by the mention of his name. To 'know him' is meaningless, sin is rampant, and the Church is completely ineffective.

The answer to the problem of revelation is only found in the Lord Jesus, HIM, who reveals himself even to the rebel heart, not by reason but by faith. Faith is the means of knowledge; love is the test of experience. God refuses to be analysed by reason or logic, but is known in personal experience when he is trusted.

Think afresh of all that you have been learning of the character of Jesus, the self-sufficient, unchanging, omniscient, holy, loving, sovereign Lord. May your prayer be that you may know HIM, not a little mental image you have made in your thoughts, but the almighty Redeemer of Scripture. 'Your God is too small', wrote J.B. Phillips, and that is tragically true for so many in the world today, for often he is no bigger than their own estimation of themselves, for 'self' is their idol.

DECEMBER 11

LIVING IN THE LIGHT OF HIS RETURN
Philippians 3:7-21

The return of the Lord Jesus is mentioned in twenty-three of the twenty-seven books of the N.T. – search for the remaining four! The Second Advent is the 'blessed hope' of the believer, and verses 20, 21 show Paul's yearning to see Jesus face to face. It was the flaming passion of evangelism in the early Church, the burning motive for a holy life (2 Peter 3:11-12a). This is a neglected subject now, rarely taught, and is therefore the incentive lacking in encouraging Christians to live in the light of his return.

Paul brings two aspects of living in this way; in verse 20 he reminds us we are citizens of Heaven *already*. Here on earth we are part of a colony of Heaven, it is only our temporary residence, because we do not belong here – we are an outpost of God's Empire. Therefore Paul says, we wait with intense eagerness and hope for the coming of the King.

Because of this there should be a striking contrast in behaviour and outlook in comparison with unbelievers. Paul knew about the pressures such living would bring to the infant Church in Philippi, and so he exhorts them to understand the great and glorious hope before them. Read how he did this in verse 17, pointing back to verses 10-16. In 1:6 he spoke of the power for holy living: God's grace he alone will bring to completion, in spite of constant attack on our lives from within and without. I say again, it is he who will complete the work, for what grace began, grace will perfect.

The reward of holy living (vv. 20, 21) is the glorious transformation we will all experience when we see Jesus. Until then there is no room for idols in our heart, slackness in our service, division in our fellowships, or sin in our lives. Live in the light of his return, eagerly awaiting the appearing of our Lord and Saviour, Jesus Christ.

DECEMBER 12

GOD'S TIMETABLE

2 Peter 3:1-18

This chapter has to follow yesterday's study, for it gives the reason why the Lord's coming has not already happened, for God plans a merciful delay. Looking on the state of the world today, one can see it collapsing, resources dwindling, every commodity controlled for the exploitation of wealth, and nations against nations. Surely the coming of the Lord draws near, for the reign of the Prince of Peace alone can restore sanity. Look at this problem from God's viewpoint:

His divine attitude is that he is not slack concerning his promise (e.g. Acts 1:11), because he is not willing that any should perish. Scoffers deride the idea of God's intervention, pointing to past history (v. 4). But he has not forgotten, and is waiting until the moment when the death of his Son is vindicated, and his redeemed are in his Kingdom.

His divine activity is toward us, in his forbearing toward men in his longing for their salvation. He withholds his arm of judgement in order to embrace repentant sinners. Peter describes earth's future, already in God's timetable, but delayed by his love.

His divine appeal is that all should come to repentance. How unconcerned people are with the offer of salvation by God, whose 'wish' (willingness) is their future life (v. 9). Having once turned to him, as we await his return – or our departure to Heaven – we are exhorted to live and please him in all things. Think prayerfully on verses 11-14.

A GOLDEN AGE?

1 Thessalonians 5:1-11

Having seen the implications of living in the light of Christ's return, we now turn to his teaching on that event. The world for centuries has been seeking Utopia, a Golden Age, which has been so illusive, because it can never come through education, legislation, culture or civilization, for men cannot solve the problem and outcome of sin and selfcentredness. Only God can bring in a golden age of peace, and one day he will. At one single stroke the return of the Lord Jesus from Heaven will accomplish that which all human effort has found impossible.

We must know from Scripture the basic facts that we must accept: Christ is coming to rule, and therefore we are optimistic about the future.

1. He will come for his Church (Acts 1:11). No language can be plainer, but up to the time of writing this study, he has not yet come. We are urged to expect this event as imminent (1 Thessalonians 4:16, 17), and receive comfort from the glorious prospect. Someone has humorously said, 'We don't look for the undertaker, but the Up-taker!'

2. He will cast down the great dictator, for as this age closes, a powerful personality arises, a super dictator. Can we see now the stage beginning to be set? I wonder. The Bible calls him the Beast (Revelation 13:4), and part of God's programme is his complete destruction (Revelation 19:11-21). What a day that will be, and what a comfort to know that the Lord Jesus is supreme in all the universe, and he alone can accomplish all he has promised to do (1 Thessalonians 5:9-11).

DECEMBER 14

THE GLORY OF THE LORD
Revelation 20:1-6

To continue yesterday's meditation:

3. God will crown his Son. The last view the world had of Jesus was as a malefactor on a cross, wearing a crown of thorns. But every eye shall see him again, crowned with glory and honour (Hebrews 2:9) when he comes to reign. For he is prophet, priest and king: as God's Spokesman he revealed the will and mind of his Father. As Priest he reconciled man to God. As King he will rule over all the earth (Psalm 2; Zechariah 14:9).

4. God will chain the devil. Behind all evil is Satan, and no one can dislodge him. No human governmental law can reach him, but when Jesus reigns he will be banished. As the Lord defeated him once in the wilderness, and again by his resurrection from the dead, ultimately when Jesus is King, Satan is doomed. Until that great day righteousness, truth and peace can never prevail with the devil at large.

5. God will clean up the world. All the environmental ideas ever thought up, however good and commendable, can never clean up the world. Think of the devastation caused by constant warfare worldwide, the death, misery, heartbreak, as well as the havoc brought to earth itself. Think of the pollution of earth and sky and sea. What will be the final outcome of it all? Does Revelation 6 have something to tell us about it? In God's gracious planning there is to be a new Heaven and a new earth (Revelation 21:1), where God's glory will be all in all.

Our prayer surely is 'Come, Lord Jesus' (Revelation 22:20), but until that day let us set our hearts on living to please him, so that whether he comes or calls us into his presence, we may not be ashamed or overawed by his glory.

DECEMBER 15

THE COURSE OF THIS AGE

Matthew 24:1-33

This chapter intertwines Christ's teaching regarding his second coming with the effects of the destruction of the Temple by the Romans in AD 70, a critical time for the Jewish nation. The question of the disciples in verse 3 followed the Lord's prediction of that particular event. No, he would not return at that time, but the disciples were not to concern themselves with God's timetable, but to get on with their life and witness *until* he shall come. And that is our instruction too.

Basically the Lord spoke of world events between AD 70 and his own return. This was not to satisfy the disciples' curiosity, or our own, but to deliver us all from doubt and perplexity. Therefore he gave no timetable, but signs, and the warning to be watchful, not idle or lazy.

There would be false Messiahs (vv. 4, 5), and how other faiths and cults clamour today for attention! There will be a world at war (vv. 6-8) with commotion in the political sphere and calamity in the physical realm.

The role of the Church would be suffering and Christians would be hated (vv. 9, 10). The Church would become corrupt by the pull of the world and false teaching, but those who endure to the end will be saved (vv. 11, 12). In all that turmoil there will be missionary enterprise (v. 15), evangelism and outreach to an unbelieving world. Finally people will be caught unawares through their indifference to and ignorance of the Word of God, and multitudes will be completely unprepared for the climax of all history.

No wonder the Lord said Watch! (v. 42), for in the period we call NOW, the hours and days we have, we must preach the Word, evangelize to a finish, and live for his praise.

DECEMBER 16

WATCH!

Matthew 24:36-25:13; Luke 14:15-24

Reading the parables in this section we see clearly that careless living will be very evident prior to the Lord's return. His coming will be sudden, as was the flood or the thief in the night. It will be unexpected, therefore his servants must be ready at all times for the return of their Master. Every believer should be prepared for his coming as the bride is for the bridegroom. Therefore how ready are we? In former years a framed picture would be seen on the wall of a room with just two words, often surrounded by paintings of flowers: PERHAPS TODAY!

To watch for his coming and to be ready involves witness to the world. The fact of Christ's return should spur us on to speak of his love and saving grace, as well as the judgement of unbelievers.

To be ready involves warfare with the enemy, for the challenge of meeting Christ should inspire in us a desire for holiness of life and war against sin, to be constantly under the control of the Holy Spirit, without whom we are defeated by the enemy before we join battle with him.

It involves worship in our daily walk with the Lord. To be really ready to meet him is only possible as each one of us lives at the foot of the Cross, applying the principles of Calvary to every area of life, for that alone is true worship.

The invitation from the Lord in Luke 14:17 is 'all things are ready... come!' Are we ready to meet him face to face? We are to be watchful of our behaviour, of our life before the world and before God, and to be careful above all that we never let the Lord down. Watch, be alert, for no one knows the day or hour when he will come, but oh joy, to see him!

DECEMBER 17

THE KING IS COMING

Zechariah 14:1-9

The prophecy of Zechariah is a wonderful book. It is very up-to-date and also goes far beyond the past and present into the future purposes of God. He and Haggai encouraged those rebuilding the Temple after many setbacks (Ezra 5:1), and their message was given at a time of great frustration. In chs. 1-6 Zechariah drew them from sighing for the good old days to the work at hand, with some glorious promises of God's faithfulness (2:5, 8; 4:6).

In chapters 7 and 8 he dealt with the dead formalism of their religion, then in the final chapters he proclaimed future glory. This is mainly addressed to the Jews, but as people of God through faith in Jesus we share these promises. In 9:9 the Lord is shown returning in triumph and victory. While Jesus fulfilled part of this prophecy on Palm Sunday, his victory is yet to come.

The promise of the recognition of Jesus as Messiah by the Jews is graphically portrayed in 12:10 and 13:1. At last they will see the risen Lord as the one pierced for them, with the way of the Cross open for their redemption – the fountain of cleansing and forgiveness that never ceases.

'On that day' is Zechariah's clarion call, fully explained in 14:4, when Jesus returns to earth triumphant. The King is coming (v. 9)! With one glorious Ruler over all the world, what transformations will take place, and verses 6, 7 transport us into Revelation 22:5: whether we are on earth or in Heaven itself, the presence of the King is all that matters.

A Prayer: Lord Jesus, may your presence be real and precious to me today, for though as yet unseen, I own you Lord of my life.

DECEMBER 18

I GO AND I WILL RETURN

John 13:31-14:6

We return once again to this amazing passage to dig further treasures from the Lord's words. Judas had left him and the disciples, and a release of tension is felt as Jesus said, 'NOW is the Son of man glorified.. .' He spoke of glory in the deepest gloom, about love amid fierce hate, and about joy in the hour of pain and sorrow. Now he had to be frank with his followers, as he spoke of departing from them, and Peter instantly took him up on that statement by asking 'Where . . . Why?' For Peter it was bad news; for Jesus it was good news as he calmed their fearful hearts, and then gave a glimpse of his programme.

Jesus was returning to his Father to prepare a place for his beloved followers. Imagine that! Like an innkeeper preparing rooms for his guests, so Jesus is preparing our future abode with him in Heaven. He had already secured that place for us at Calvary, and we laid claim to its reservation at the time of our conversion. Amazing grace that saved such unworthy ones as we are! And to crown it all, we are confident of a home in glory, prepared by Jesus, who will come again to take us there, either through the portals of death, or by his return in person.

Well can we say, 'Death, where is your sting, or grave your victory'!

DECEMBER 19

THE MIDNIGHT HOUR

Matthew 25:1-13

Time is running out, it is now the hour of midnight, the time of reckoning. At that time of night many people are drowsy (v. 5), and there are a lot of sleeping Christians. They are unaware of the opportunities God gives them, to the needs and plight of the unsaved, afraid to testify, asleep instead of praying, too drowsy to serve the Master.

People get chilly at midnight; coat collars are turned up and scarves put on. Sadly Christians can be like that, love has grown cold (24:12). At midnight there are plenty of lights in the streets, neon lights flashing in stores, all artificial. As we approach the midnight hour false teaching abounds, cults arise unchallenged, Satan worship is openly practised (24:11). Do not be surprised as the hands move slowly on toward midnight, for the Lord warned us of these things.

As the Bridegroom delays his coming there is opportunity for evangelism, for we are to work while it is still day (John 9:4, 5). There are multitudes still in the world who have never heard the name of Jesus. There are educated people in our homelands with no knowledge of the Gospel and salvation found only through faith in Jesus.

Those minutes before midnight are a time for examination (24:44). What about unconfessed sin, an unforgiving spirit, an undisciplined life, an unaccepted commission from God? What about the lack of devotion and submission to Jesus himself? Be ready, for we don't know the timetable, and suddenly that shout will go up, 'The Bridegroom comes!' May he find us ready and joyfully awaiting his call.

TRIED BY FIRE

1 Corinthians 3:9-15

The Church of Corinth was in its infancy, untaught and unstable, still bearing the carnal marks of a dissolute city in their lives. Paul reminds them of who they are and to whom they belong: God's field, his building (v. 9) and his temple (v. 16), whereas Paul and his companions were God's fellow workers in Corinth. It was Paul who laid the foundations of their faith in the Lord Jesus, as a skilled master builder. What a foundation he laid, for it was none other than the Lord Jesus. Now he says, take heed how you build on that foundation, for it will all be tested by fire on that day.

During this week more has gone into the building of your life and mine. Is there a new window of prayer, some gold of a testimony, the silver of a life radiant for Jesus, precious stones of victory? God grant that may be so, for they are all indestructible in fire. For some it may be the wood, hay and stubble of prayerlessness, feverish activity, defeat, and the fire destroys them all. Take heed how you build.

Solemn thoughts, but one hopes timely. Only the Holy Spirit can produce the gems as well as the fruit in our lives, so allow him to control every area of your life. As has been said before in this book, may we all be delivered from 'a saved soul, but a wasted life'.

DECEMBER 21

CHRIST'S JUDGEMENT SEAT

Romans 14:7-12

Paul speaks of a judgemental spirit, and reflects in these verses the Lord's teaching in Matthew 7:1, 2.

Every Christian lives to the Lord and not to himself, for if we are united to Christ, identified with him in death and resurrection, we are answerable to him, and only to him. Whatever we do must be regulated by his Lordship in our lives. Therefore we have no right or basis to judge others, seeing one day we will all stand before Christ to answer for *ourselves*. So who, we may ask, can ever think he has the right to set himself up as judge in the place of Christ?

How sad that our fellowships are so often torn apart by the judgemental attitudes of one against another. Shame on us, who knowing so much doctrine, the recipients of such grace and love bestowed on us by the Holy Spirit, that we fall so often into condemnatory words and actions. The Church becomes a battlefield, then a hospital for those spiritually battered, and a nursery for the immature and weak. What a travesty of the true body of Christ! 'I will build my Church', said Jesus (Matthew 16:18) and his followers are busy with self-destruction. What a need to turn the other cheek, to go the extra mile, that peace may reign, but how rarely that happens.

Why, why? Paul asks in verse 10. Perhaps it is because we forget that one day we must answer for all this before Christ himself. It is an awesome thought to *stand* before him to give 'account of ourselves' there. Yet we must remember also that he comes, and his reward is with him (Isaiah 40:10), for the judgement seat is also the place of rewards, like a glorious prize giving! May Holy Spirit love be poured out continually upon us and in us to enable us to live and please God, and not miss his award.

NO MORE!
Jeremiah 31:31-40

Prior to studies in the book of Revelation there is a wonderful subject to ponder with prayer and thanksgiving. Have you ever thought how often God said, 'No more'? (v.34). To consider our constant ups and downs, our failures and fallings, can make us groan in despair; but the day is coming when God finally says, 'No more!'

To some there is the haunting of past sins, and people can carry guilt to their grave. However hard it is to forget, God's promise in the above passage is music to the ears: 'Their sins and iniquities I will remember *no more.*' It is said of Bruce of Scotland, when he was fleeing for his life, his own bloodhounds were set on his trail, and he escaped them by diving into a river. Yes, there is a river for the cleansing of all sin, and if God remembers them no more, who are we to disobey him?

To some there is the handicap of an evil bias. Remember Jacob, the deceiving cheat, to whom God said, 'You are *no more* Jacob' (Genesis 32:28), and Peniel became a place of brokenness and the beginning of a new life.

To some it is the hindrance of SELF. Paul knew something of that as he opened his heart in Romans 7. 'I', my Self, gets in the way all the time, resulting in hurt feelings, ruffled pride, resentment, and a host of sinful thoughts. Paul found the answer and gives it to us in Galatians 2:20, 'It is *no more* I who live, but Christ who lives in me.' Deliverance came when he acknowledged he had been crucified with Christ, so he was 'dead' to sin, and now lived by faith in the Son of God, who was at last in his rightful place, enthroned in Paul's heart, and therefore his life was dedicated to serve the living Lord Jesus. May we all follow this path of living in present liberty and not in past failure.

DECEMBER 23

ALPHA AND OMEGA

Revelation 1:1-8

Here we are on holy ground as we look at the Lord Jesus as the First and the Last. *Consider his person* in this respect:

A. He is first in creation, the Lamb slain before the foundation of the world (ch. 5; 1 Peter 1:20), when he came to the depths of the Cross to be the Saviour of fallen men. He is first in rank (Colossians 1:15), unique and supreme, with a name that is above every name (Philippians 2:9-11).

He is first in resurrection, the first fruits from the dead (1 Corinthians 15:20-22). What a glorious army has followed Jesus through death into glory! The fact that he became man, dying as men die, is what makes the promise of resurrection life secure, for Jesus led the way.

B. He is God's last word to men. Hebrews 1:1-4 is very important, for Jesus is God's final and complete revelation to mankind, as Jesus himself said, 'He who has seen ME has seen the Father.' His last words on earth were 'It is finished!' (John 19:30), and the price of sin was paid, so God has no more to say, for the blood of the Cross is the entry into life in his Kingdom. He is last in the day of grace, for his return ends the day of opportunity for men to experience God's grace and salvation. He is last in judgement, for he is the Arbiter, the final verdict upon men is in his hands, and he cannot be ignored (Revelation 20:11-15).

A Prayer: Lord Jesus, may you be Lord of all in my life NOW, so that when I see you face to face I may not be ashamed.

DECEMBER 24

COME TO HIM
Revelation 21:1-14

Consider the work of the Lord Jesus as the First and Last, and it is seen that he is left out of people's lives at their peril (v. 6). His first plan for each person is his/her new birth (see Jeremiah 1:5; Psalm 139:13-18). Like Job, some people wish they had never been born, but the Lord knows his purpose for every life, and it is a great day when we find new life in Christ, and therefore want to know his plan for us (vv. 5b, 6).

His last dealing with us is in death, and while we view death rightly as the 'last enemy', God's view is very different as Psalm 116:15 shows. Death releases the final bonds that tie the body to earth and enables the believer to enter the presence of the Lord. All along life's way he has given the water of life to sustain and refresh (John 4:14).

His last command is in Revelation 22:12-14, 'Blessed are they who do his commandments' (14a, AV). Obedience is the proof of love, and the Lord emphasizes this right to the end.

His last appeal is in Revelation 22:17, a call to come to him, even at the moment of death, the entry into glory. That has been his appeal all through history, from the very moment when Adam sinned and the Lord sought for him in the garden: 'Where are you?' he asked. It was the call of God to his people through the pages of the O.T. (e.g. Isaiah 55:1-3), and above all the loving invitation of the Lord Jesus as in Matthew 11:28. Sadly he also had to say, 'You refuse to come to me that you may have life' (John 5:40), and he lamented over the rejection of his people (Matthew 23:37-39). He never forces his way into a human heart, but gives opportunity for people to choose. 'I am come that they may have life, and have it abundantly' (John 10:10) is his glorious offer. Therefore we cannot ignore or escape him, and the response from every heart should be 'Come, Lord Jesus'.

HE CAME – HE WILL COME!
1 Thessalonians 4:13-18

A Joyful Christmas to You!

Jesus has come, he has lived and died, he has risen and ascended to Heaven, and he will come again!

How will he return? Personally, with a glorified body in the air with his angels. His first coming was quiet and secret, made known at first to a group of shepherds, but his second coming will be visible to all, when every eye shall see him.

When will he return? Suddenly, at the midnight hour, at a time which will be totally unexpected: as a thief in the night, as Jesus himself said. His birth was predicted, though no one knew the date, and it is the same with his return.

Why will he return? To take his people to himself, to live and reign with him eternally. He came to Bethlehem in order to fulfil the promise of a Redeemer, Immanuel – God with us. At his return he reaps the rich harvest of that immense and glorious sacrifice at Calvary, in all those who have claimed the cleansing of his shed blood.

Those who are dead will be with Jesus (v. 14), and those who are alive will meet him in the air (v. 17). Like a magnet extracting iron from a mass of scrap and rubbish, so the Lord will gather his own to meet him. What mystery! Our finite minds can scarcely grasp these great truths, but they are there for us to read, believe, and be prepared one day to witness and to share in the glory.

The immense step from the Babe at Bethlehem to the living, reigning triumphant Lord Jesus, returning to earth for his own people – that is the glorious truth proclaimed throughout Scripture. As the bells ring out the joys of Christmas, may we also be alert for the final trumpet that will announce his return, when we shall always be with him.

DECEMBER 26

REVELATION!

Revelation 1:1-18

The closing book of God's Word is the revelation of Jesus Christ to his servant John, and the reading of it brings special blessing (v. 1). It is interesting that even as John wrote, he anticipated the return of the Lord to be very near. Now almost 2000 years have passed, only two days in God's diary (2 Peter 3:8) but so long for us on earth that we need a constant reminder of this great event, and a new understanding of this great book.

John wrote in a time of intense persecution, and was himself in exile on the island of Patmos, and reckoned to be about 90 years old at this time. He wrote of the appearing of the Lord Jesus (apocalypse) when every eye shall see him, and Luke echoes this in 21:27, when Jesus outlined the state of the world and the signs of his coming.

While 'in the Spirit' John was caught out of time and transported to be a spectator amid a series of judgements and glorious visions on that great Day of the Lord, foretold by the prophets. This was not a Sabbath day, but a prolonged look into the area of God's future dealings with the affairs of the world as history winds up to become the Kingdom of our God and his Christ. We go on tiptoe with bated breath to join John as he pens what he saw for our blessing and encouragement. May the wonder of all we see and hear bring us, perhaps in tears, but with great joy, to the feet of our glorious Saviour, as we see him crowned with glory and majesty.

DECEMBER 27

THE VISION

Revelation 1:8-19

John had an unexpected vision, heralded by a loud voice, and when he turned he saw the Son of man in the midst of seven golden candlesticks: the Church with the risen Lord in the midst. The vision of Jesus is overwhelming as John saw him clothed in a white robe indicating his perfect authority, with a golden girdle, his perfect love. His glistening head and hair reveal his perfect holiness; while his eyes, as flames of fire, show his perfect knowledge as they search the inner recesses of human hearts.

His feet, which on earth tramped the trails of Israel to preach redemption, are now as bronze, his perfect righteousness. How beautiful they are to those who love him, how terrible to those who will be crushed by them.

His voice was as many waters, that penetrates all ages, and one day the dead will hear it and obey his command, for his voice is perfect power. He holds the seven stars, or ministers, in his right hand. What a place to be, within his perfect control! To those who are true to him nothing can touch them; if unfaithful, none can deliver.

What a vision! How wonderful that John was entrusted with this overwhelming experience to share it with us in our day and age! As we think of the perfection of Jesus, may we never, never think less of him than he really is, the Alpha and Omega, the First and the Last.

DECEMBER 28

SURRENDER

Revelation 1:12-20

To continue John's vision, he also saw the two-edged sword in the mouth of the risen Lord, perfect truth that is poured forth from the Word of God. Finally, his face shone brighter than the sun, his perfect glory. This was shown to the disciples briefly on the Mount of Transfiguration, and to Saul of Tarsus on the Damascus road. Dare we pray, 'Lord, show me your glory'? This most wonderful, glorious and royal Person is revealed to us by John, and this is the God whom men ignore.

What then shall *we* do? What did John do? He fell at the Lord's feet as one dead, in unqualified surrender. If we really saw Jesus as John did, no doubt our response would be the same. Perhaps our worship would be more real, our singing less thoughtless and flippant, our times in his presence less erratic and more truly devotional, resulting in lives that would be willingly and unconditionally cast at his feet, dead to self, but alive to him.

To his servant John, Jesus gave an unlimited promise, 'Fear not, I AM.' He placed his *right hand* on John, the hand that holds the universe, his Church, and his people, in its grip. No need to fear, for Jesus is all in all, giver of life, conqueror of death, and with his promise of eternal security comes the new commission. To John it was to write, which he did so faithfully. Ask the Lord what he would have you do in the days he gives to you *here*, as you have now seen his glory *there*.

DECEMBER 29

REDEMPTION DRAWS NIGH

Revelation 5:1-14

This amazing chapter brings us right into the courts of Heaven, introduced in chapter 4. No ground is more holy than this, and we need to come on our knees, as it were, into the Holy of Holies, so different from the Bethlehem stable that has occupied our thoughts at this time on the calendar.

Here we see a Book, a scroll, that at first could not be opened, as no one was found worthy to do so. This speaks of redemption, for who is able to undertake that great task? Redemption not only concerns past sins, but present living and a future accomplishment. Jesus spoke of this when he said concerning his return, 'When these things (the signs of his coming) begin to take place, look up and raise your heads, because your redemption is drawing near' (Luke 21:28). Yes, the body too is redeemed (Romans 8:22,23).

We also see a Lamb, the Risen Lord, who alone can open the seals of the scroll. He was announced as 'the Lion of the tribe of Judah', the Redeemer King, promised throughout the O.T. who as the Lamb of God has overcome sin and death and hell. He is now seen standing, bearing the marks of Calvary, alive with all the power of Heaven's glory.

Words fail when seeking to verbalize what can only be unspoken in our heart, but the final verses express our praise in the song of rejoicing. This is a *new song* sung by the redeemed (v. 9), for while the angels worship the Lamb, they do not know him as Redeemer and Saviour. Praise him now in these glorious words, sharing them with all the inhabitants of Heaven.

DECEMBER 30

THE FINAL ACT

Revelation 21:1-8

What an amazing vision this was for John, and is to us also! A new Heaven, a new earth, all things new! It is hard to understand a new Heaven, which no doubt implies the whole universe rather than Glory. A new earth can be pictured as Eden restored, our sinful, devastated planet renewed by the touch of his hand.

We have already seen the things that are 'no more', but to think again on the glorious facts that there will be no sorrow, no partings, no cruelty, nothing that causes pain and heartbreak, is to know that God indeed makes all things new.

The words of verse 6 point to so many truths in God's Word. The work of redemption was completed at Calvary, but now the total restoration of the redeemed is finished (vv. 2, 3, 6a) – God's final act.

Who are the blessed ones? Those who conquer and overcome (v. 7), for Heaven is a special place for special people, those who remain faithful to Christ to the end. So rejoice that anyone *in Christ* is a new creation (2 Corinthians 5:17), for even now in our lives the old is replaced by the new, the work of the Holy Spirit.

Those refused admittance are listed in verses 8, 27; 22:15. Oh, to see men and women delivered from these sins and evils so that they may find joy in the presence of their Saviour!

In this place of wonder and glory we see God in the midst, comforting and dwelling among his redeemed, and Jesus the eternal light shining at the centre. Oh the joy on that day to see the face of Jesus, to feel the touch of his hand, to breathe the air of Heaven, and join in with the praises and worship of the multitudes whom no man can number from every tribe and nation! Worthy is the Lamb, blessed be his Name!

DECEMBER 31

COME!

Revelation 22:1-21

The pages of history open, as we have already seen, with God calling to fallen man to come to him, and then giving the promise of a coming Saviour (Genesis 3). All through the writings of the prophets is the call to return to the Lord, until Jesus came with his arms open wide: 'Come to ME, ALL . . .' And his outstretched arms on Calvary brought salvation to all who repent and believe.

At the folding up of time God extends the same invitation through the Holy Spirit and the Church, the Bride of Christ. That is our commission, to proclaim redemption in Christ right up to our dying breath, or as Amy Carmichael wrote, 'with swords drawn right to the gates of Heaven'. Our prayer is 'Come, Lord Jesus', but until that moment may he see us faithful, showing forth his light and perfection, and by his love shed in our hearts by the Holy Spirit enabling us to live in the glorious freedom given to his children. For he is coming soon, his promise is sure and the prospect is glorious. Hallelujah! Amen! Come, Lord Jesus!

EPILOGUE

On 14 March 1989 Alan Redpath had been unconscious for three days, and on that evening Canon Tom Walker, vicar of our church, came to pray. Taking Alan's limp hand, he prayed slowly and clearly, and ended his prayer saying, 'Hallelujah, Amen!' And a strong, firm voice from the bed echoed these words. They were the first words spoken in days, and the last words spoken on earth, for Alan entered the presence of his Lord thirty hours later. God loves a praising heart, prepared for the 'new song' in glory, which only the redeemed can sing. Blessed is his holy Name, for Jesus is worthy to receive our worship and praise now and for ever.

INDEX

MATTHEW

Christian Focus Publications publishes biblically-accurate books for adults and children. The books in the adult range are published in three imprints.

Christian Heritage contains classic writings from the past.

Christian Focus contains popular works including biographies, commentaries, doctrine, and Christian living.

Mentor focuses on books written at a level suitable for Bible College and seminary students, pastors, and others; the imprint includes commentaries, doctrinal studies, examination of current issues, and church history.

For a free catalogue of all our titles, please write to
Christian Focus Publications,
Geanies House, Fearn,
Ross-shire, IV20 1TW, Great Britain

For details of our titles visit us on our web site
http://www.christianfocus.com